Corridor of Elphinstone College, Mumbai.

Courtesy: University of Mumbai

# Beyond Degrees

# Beyond Degrees

## Finding Success in Higher Education

Edited by Ira Pande

HarperCollins *Publishers* India

India International Centre

First published in India in 2008 by
HarperCollins *Publishers* India

Building 10, Tower A, 4th Floor, DLF Cyber City, Phase II,
Gurugram Haryana – 122002, India
www.harpercollins.co.in



ISBN: 978-81-7223-758-5

10 9 8 7 6 5 4 3 2 1

Cover and photo essays designed by www.codesign.in



Printed and bound at
MicroPrints India, New New Delhi

# Contents

•

# Preface

Sixty years after Independence, the general condition of our universities is a cause for concern. While there are certainly half a dozen or so centres of excellence, excluding the IITs and IIMs, the standard in several universities has not reached the desired level. There are several reasons for this, including a rapid expansion as we now have almost three times the number of universities in existence at the time of Independence. Also, there is a lack of suitable, trained and motivated teachers. The Unesco International Commission on Education for the twenty-first century, of which I was a member, states that:

> It is primarily the universities that unite all the traditional functions associated with the advancement and transmission of knowledge: research, innovation, teaching and training and continuing education. To this we can add another function that has been growing in importance in recent years: international cooperation.

A fundamental weakness in our university system is that research has received little attention. Moreover, research papers published in our academic institutions seldom measure up to international standards. The challenge of improving the standards of our universities, and coping with the inevitable expansion in higher education for which there is a tremendous thirst throughout the country, raises a number of interlocking questions. These include matters relating to public and private finances, training and motivation of teachers, regular upgradation of teaching skills, strengthening research both in the natural and social sciences, affiliation and equivalence, and balancing equity with excellence. As we rush headlong into the future, these issues become increasingly urgent, and will need to be tackled effectively within the next five years if our university system is to cope with India's growing stature in the global community.

It was keeping this in mind that the Editorial Board decided that our double issue for Winter 2007–Spring 2008 should concentrate on our universities. The Editor has compiled a broad and interesting spectrum of articles on various aspects of university education by

By **Karan Singh**

a number of distinguished intellectuals and academicians. I have pleasure in commending this publication, not only to members of the IIC, many of whom will be deeply interested in higher education, but also to the broader academic and intellectual public in the country.

•

: Karan Singh

# Introduction

'Why not call this volume "India's Temples of Doom"?' suggested a wit when we started to put together this issue. This mood of cynicism ran so deep that we wondered if we would ever find someone who had a positive response to the topic. The challenge was to create a collection of essays on our universities that would be read with both pleasure and hope. The task was daunting but slowly, as others took up the challenge, we were able to put together a rich selection of writers and writings.

It is ironical that despite being among the issues most passionately debated in this country, our universities continue to decline rapidly. A possible reason for this is that in India, we all know what is wrong: from the most learned academics to the local paanwala, there is no dearth of advice-dispensers and doomsday prophets. Moreover, offering opinions on problems absolves most of us from any responsibility to tackle them. This often means that once we have identified the problem we feel it now it is up to the government or God to sort out the mess. So although we have all seen a steady decline in our universities over the years, most of us have done nothing apart from shaking our heads sorrowfully and making sure that our children can somehow escape abroad to earn their university degrees.

This is a cause for alarm, not just because of a steady brain-drain over the years but also because the future of our country hinges so critically on the quality of education and research we create now. We are all aware that the present boom in our economic life has been fuelled largely by the wise inputs made by visionaries of the last century in the country's centres of higher education. Our universities, medical institutions, IITs and IIMs are more valuable than all the oil in Arabia because those who created this country's higher educational system in the years after Independence, were prescient enough to see that knowledge gives a nation the kind of power that mere gold and oil cannot.

The time has come, therefore, to consider whether the models adopted more than a century ago are those that have withstood the test of time or whether the dark cloisters of our universities need to be lit up with a new kind of light. In these globalized times, running a university throws up challenges that cannot be ignored or wished away. Today, a world-class

By **Ira Pande**

university must be both at the frontiers of new knowledge and, at the same time, function as a guardian of tradition. In India, this tradition stretches as far back as Nalanda and the great Buddhist viharas. Time was when Chinese scholars travelled to India to study: today, our children travel to Singapore for higher education! So often, by not accepting change, we have allowed traditions to wither away and destroyed what had taken centuries to build. We cannot afford to make such costly mistakes any more. It is a huge responsibility to preserve our individual identity as a culture and civilization while simultaneously creating an atmosphere for new disciplines and modifying tradition intelligently.

In the essays you shall read here, we place before the reader a wide selection of opinions and prescriptions. Educationists, historians, economists and administrators have written, often passionately, of their concerns and offered solutions that must be heeded. What is more, several writers have shared their personal histories so that the pain at the present state of our universities reveals how widespread this concern is. Some may seem to have repeated what they have written elsewhere, but their opinions, in most cases, are important enough to bear repetition.

As always, we have divided the essays into broad groupings that follow certain themes. In addition, we have two fine photo essays that honour the earliest institutions and scholars of the country. No doubt there are some missing links but the blame for this must lie in some measure with those contributors who did not meet their promised deadlines. However, the flip side to this was the law of serendipity that brought us some last-minute articles by those who cared deeply for the problems the issue outlined. To all those contributors, whether individuals or publishers, who made this possible, we have deep respect. May their tribe increase!

•

: Ira Pande

# 1: The Blueprint

# Crucibles of Modernity*

Founded in 1857, the universities of Calcutta, Bombay and Madras had an influence on India's destiny as profound as the popular uprising that took place the same year. In a sense, they were the crucibles of modernity in India, for as André Béteille has written, these universities 'opened new horizons both intellectually and institutionally in a society that had stood still in a conservative and hierarchical mould for centuries'. They were 'among the first open and secular institutions in a society that was governed largely by the rules of kinship, caste and religion'. Thus 'the age-old restrictions of gender and caste did not disappear in the universities, but they came to be questioned there'.[1]

The universities were also a crucible of nationalism. It was there that young men and women learnt to question the logic of colonial

* Abridged and edited from 'Pluralism in the Indian University', first published in the *Economic and Political Weekly*, 17 February 2007.

By **Ramachandra Guha**

rule, to hold up, as a mirror to their rulers, the British ideals of liberty and justice haphazardly upheld at home and comprehensively denied in the colonies. Gandhi and Ambedkar had their early education under the auspices of the Bombay University, C. R. Das and Subhas Chandra Bose under the auspices of the Calcutta University, C. Rajagopalachari and C. Subramaniam under the auspices of the Madras University. Tens of thousands of more 'ordinary' freedom fighters were also educated – in all senses of the word – by their time in these universities or in other universities set up in the period of colonial rule such as those in Allahabad, Punjab, Benaras and Aligarh. These soldiers of non-violence, who defied their family and sacrificed their careers to fill the jails on Gandhi's call, came from all sections of society. They were high caste as well as low caste, men as well as women, Hindu and Sikh as well as Muslim and Christian.

It is not just that the Indian university trained those who led and manned the freedom struggle. It was also that they trained those who led and manned the creation of a modern, democratic, nation state. For no new nation was born in more difficult circumstances – against the backdrop of civil war and privation, with eight million refugees to be resettled and 500 princely states to be integrated. That a nation was forged out of these fragments, and that this was henceforth governed on the basis of a democratic Constitution, was no minor miracle. This miracle was the handiwork of a group of visionary leaders – with Nehru, Patel and Ambedkar pre-eminent among them – aided by thousands of now forgotten civil servants, lawyers, doctors, teachers, social workers and soldiers, a majority of them shaped and formed by the Indian university system.

That 'system' was, and is, based on constituent colleges. The nurturers of nationalism and the nation state were educated as much in these colleges as in the universities of which they were part. Places such as Presidency College, Calcutta; Presidency College, Madras; Elphinstone College, Bombay; St. Stephen's College, Delhi; Government College, Lahore; Patna College, Patna; and Maharaja's College, Mysore, have all contributed in ways large and small to the shaping of modern India.[2]

It behoves us to recognize (and salute) the role played by our universities and colleges in nurturing Indian nationalism and building Indian democracy. Yet, since we live in the present, we must also admit that the state of our universities (and colleges) is not what it could and might be.

• • •

I have long believed that while India is sometimes the most exasperating country in the world, it is at all times the most interesting. The reasons lie in the unparalleled diversity of this country. Which other land can match India in its mix of different castes, classes, languages, faiths, forms of dress, cuisines, musical styles, *et al*?

For the scholar or writer, at his desk or in his ivory tower, the diversity of human forms is perenially interesting. For the citizen living life on the ground, however, it can at times be deeply exasperating. When people of one habit or temperament – or ideology or social custom – are placed close to people of another, they tend sometimes to react with prejudice and suspicion. Often, this manifests itself in conflict and combat, whether intellectual or physical, individual or institutional. Still, it must be acknowledged that while life would be less discordant, it would also be less interesting if everyone around us spoke and thought and dressed and ate just as we did.

Fortunately, the men and women who built modern India did not follow Israel or Pakistan in fusing faith with State by granting special privileges to citizens of one religion. Nor did they follow Germany or the U.S. in making it mandatory for all citizens to speak one language. And they did not follow Soviet Russia and communist China in constructing a single-party state.

The linguistic division of India has worked very well – for India as a whole. There has been friction at the edges, conflicts about towns and villages on the border, and about riparian rights, but had these states not been created, I believe, the conflicts would have been much more serious. Consider the examples of Pakistan and Sri Lanka, the first of which broke up and the second of which is mired in an apparently unending civil war largely because one community sought to impose a single language on the nation.

• • •

: Ramachandra Guha

Diversity is a social condition; it is what India is. Pluralism is a political programme; it is a manifestation of what we wish India to be. At the level of the nation, the practice of pluralism poses one set of challenges; at the level of the city or state, yet another. What then, of the university? What are the varieties of pluralism that a university in India must seek to foster? In my view, these are principally of five kinds:

First, the university must foster pluralism in the student body. There must be students of all ages; from those in their late teens to those in their early 30s (or even beyond). One way to do this is to have, within a single campus, programmes running all the way from the BA or BSc right up to the PhD. There must be many women students; in the ideal situation, fifty per cent or more. Students from low caste and working-class backgrounds must be adequately represented; so also those from minority religions. Finally, a university is made more Indian if it can attract students from other states of the union.

Second, the university must foster pluralism in the teaching staff. Like its students, these must be both women and men, who come from different classes, castes and religious groupings. And – this is even more crucial here – from different parts of India. But unlike in the case of students, it is not enough that the teachers come from different social backgrounds. They must also have diverse intellectual credos. Some must prefer abstract theoretical work; others, research that is more applied in nature. Since scholars are also citizens, university teachers have political beliefs; but these, again, must be of varied kinds. A university where all the teachers were communists, or all of them Shiv Sainiks, would be a very boring place indeed.

Third, the university must offer a plurality of disciplines. It should have at least some, if not all, undergraduate colleges which offer degrees in the sciences as well as the humanities. There must be graduate programmes in the major disciplines: mathematics, economics, history, political science, physics, chemistry, biology, literature, etc. – but also professional schools offering degrees in law, medicine and business as well as, ideally, faculties of fine arts and music. At the same time, the university must have the flexibility and imagination to create new departments when scientific progress or social developments oblige it to do so.

Fourth, a university must foster a pluralism of approaches within a discipline. Its department of economics must have Friedmanites and Keynesians as well as Marxists. Its department of biology should have space for experimentalists who splice genes, for Darwinians who study speciation, and for fieldworkers who live with animals in the wild. A university department all of whose members were wedded to one particular theoretical or experimental approach would be a very dull place indeed.

As Max Weber pointed out, unlike political parties or religious seminaries, universities are 'not institutions for inculcation of absolute or ultimate moral values'. Put less politely, universities must not be allowed to become vehicles of indoctrination, promoting a particular political or religious point of view. They teach the student 'facts, their conditions, laws and inter-relations', serving in this manner to 'sharpen the student's capacity to understand the actual conditions of his own exertions...'. However, 'what ideals the [student] should serve "what gods must bow before" these they require him to deal with on his own responsibility, ultimately, in accordance with his own conscience'.

This pluralism of methodological and theoretical approaches must be promoted at various levels: that of the university as a whole, by each of its constituent departments, and by each individual teacher as well. A century ago, in words that seem strikingly contemporary, Max Weber deplored the tendency in some professors 'of educating their students into certain political beliefs and ultimate outlooks'. He was himself clear that the university teacher 'is under the sternest obligation to avoid proposing his own position in the struggle of ideals. He must make his chair into a forum where the understanding of ultimate standpoints – alien to and diverging from his own – is fostered, rather than into an arena where he propagates his own ideals'.[3]

Fifth, a university must encourage pluralism of funding sources. It must not rely only on State patronage, but raise money from fees, its alumni and private corporations. By diversifying its portfolio so to speak, the university reduces its dependence on a single source of patronage, while, also engaging with (and making itself relevant to) a wider swathe of society.

Stated in this straightforward manner these ends seem self-evident. Surely any self-respecting university will always be plural in all these ways? Not, perhaps, in India, where one cannot say with confidence that any of our universities have met these ideals wholly or consistently. However, at various points in history, one Indian university or another has been plural in one or other of these ways. As André Béteille has noted, it took 600 years for Oxford or Cambridge to admit women, whereas Calcutta and Bombay admitted them from their inception. They also provided avenues of upward mobility for the lower castes: in the traditional system an untouchable like B. R. Ambedkar would have been condemned to a life of illiteracy. Those from minority religions also got, and took, their chances – some of the best scholars and teachers in the history of Mumbai University have been Parsi and Muslim.[4]

Likewise, there have been splendid examples of Indian universities promoting diversity in the social background of its teachers, and of these teachers in turn promoting a diversity of intellectual approaches. Determined to make Calcutta University more than a home for Bengalis, Ashutosh Mukherjee appointed C. V. Raman and Sarvepalli Radhakrishnan to chairs when they were young and unrecognized. Raman and Radhakrishnan eventually moved on to other pastures, but a contemporary of theirs who stayed in Calcutta was the Malayali from Merton, Kuruvilla Zachariah, among whose students at Presidency College were many future leaders of free India.

Third, many Indian universities have been inclusive in a disciplinary sense. The pattern was set by the three founding universities, all with departments of science and social science, as well as a faculty of law and a school of medicine. Thus in the 1930s and 1940s, Bombay University was perhaps best known, on the research side, for its School of Economics and Sociology, while for the past half century that honour has consistently been held by the university department of chemical technology.

Fourth, the best university departments in India have promoted a variety of intellectual approaches. The long-time head of the sociology department in Bombay, G. S. Ghurye, was a bookish conservative; yet among the students he sent out into the world were the superb ethnographer M. N. Srinivas and the Marxist theoretician A. R. Desai. Srinivas, in turn, bestrode the Delhi University department of sociology like a colossus; in turn, he did not impose his methodological preferences on those he taught or guided. Srinivas had little interest in comparative sociology, or in the industrial working class, or in the Sanskritic tradition; yet three of his distinguished students were to make these subjects their own.

It is with the fifth kind of pluralism that the record is most disappointing. The Indian university has relied too heavily on subsidies and hand-outs from the State. Middle-class and even rich students pay the same fees as the poorer students; in effect, almost no fees. There has been little attempt to tap the generosity of alumni – even the most prosperous ones. Few universities cultivate active links with the private sector or with philanthropic foundations.

Pluralism is one important ideal of the Indian university; it is not, of course, the only one. A university must also have an institutional cohesiveness, which allows it to reproduce itself regardless of the particular individuals who lead or staff it. Again, a university must have a particular and recognizable character, which encourages its students, staff, faculty, and alumni to identify with it. It must also set standards of academic excellence consistent with those in the nation and the world, and continually strive to maintain them.

These ends might not always be mutually compatible. Thus, in one particular case or another, say, the recruitment of students from under-represented social groups or the appointment of a new dean, pluralism might conflict with institutional efficiency or efficiency in turn conflict with academic excellence. Compromises have to be made, judgment calls taken. It would be foolish not to recognize that a public university serves multiple ends, and that these may sometimes be in conflict. That said, the varieties of pluralism enumerated above are, I believe, among the most important ends an Indian university should strive to fulfil.

• • •

In the history of the Indian university, the forces favouring pluralism have had to contend with the opposing forces of parochialism. These are ever present, often powerful, and sometimes overwhelming.

One form of parochialism is identity politics. Particularly in staff appointments, the claims of caste or region or religion can play as significant a role as academic qualification or distinction. Often, the candidate with the best connections gets the job rather than the best candidate. And so 'the disputes that now dominate many if not most of our universities are not over the principles and methods of science and scholarship; they are over pay and promotion and the distribution of seats and posts among different castes, communities, and factions'.[5]

A second form of parochialism is ideological. When the NDA government was in power in New Delhi, there was much criticism of the role played by its human resource development minister for placing in important posts, intellectuals more amenable to his own political ideology. The criticism was just – it would have been more just still if it had acknowledged that in this respect he was merely following the lead of the Communist Party of India (Marxist), which, in both West Bengal and Kerala, has consistently interfered with university appointments. No critic of Marxism stands a chance of becoming vice chancellor of Calcutta University, for example.

A third form of parochialism is institutional. There is, in almost every Indian university, a marked tendency to employ one's own graduates to teaching positions. This in-breeding has infected even the best departments in the best universities. Thus, the history department in the Jawaharlal Nehru University and the sociology department in the Delhi University are largely staffed by those who have, at some stage or another, passed through the same portals as students.

Whether based on identity or ideology or institution, these varieties of parochialism have had a corrosive effect on university life. They have undermined the quality of teaching, narrowed the range of subjects taught, and polluted the general intellectual ambience. By now, they have collectively impacted millions of Indians, who have got a more limited education than they hoped for, or, indeed, deserved.

Provincialism apart, there are other hurdles to the fostering of a plural ethos in the Indian university. One is short-sighted public policy. In the colonial period, the best science in India was done in the universities by men such as C. V. Raman and Satyen Bose in Calcutta; Meghnad Saha and K. S. Krishnan in Allahabad; T. R. Seshadri in Delhi; and K. Venkataraman in Bombay. However, at Independence the decision was taken to set up a series of laboratories under the auspices of the Council for Scientific and Industrial Research (CSIR). It was made clear that these would be the favoured sites for research, and that the universities would focus mostly on teaching. The best talent drifted away to the CSIR laboratories, impoverishing the universities. On the other side, without the challenge and stimulation of students, laboratory science got steadily more bureaucratic, and did not deliver on its promises either.[6]

In any case, in the Indian context what C. P. Snow called the 'two cultures' – the humanistic and the scientific – always had an uneasy relationship. Almost from the beginnings of modern education, Indian men were brought up to believe that the 'arts' were inferior to the 'sciences'. Even in the universities where the two coexisted, science students or professors scarcely came into contact with their counterparts in the humanities. After Independence, apart from the CSIR the creation of the Indian Institute of Technology (IIT) also contributed to the further moving apart of the two cultures. Although the IITs had departments of humanities, their concerns were integrated in a desultory way into the curriculum. The precedent had been set, well before, by the Indian Institute of Science, whose original charter (influenced by its visionary founder, Jamsetji Tata) had room for a department of social science, which, however, remains to be activated a century after the institute's founding. And so the finest young minds in the sciences have been encouraged to cultivate an indifference (even contempt) to the social sciences and to history.

The plural ambitions of the Indian university have also been severely tested by a now rampant populism. I have in mind the widespread suspicion of what are termed 'elite' departments and 'elite' universities. There is continuous pressure towards the equalization of resources, so that the public pie is shared equally by institutions good and bad, old and new. Institutions that were intended to be small and select are urged to let in more and more students, regardless of whether they can maintain standards while doing so. Where institutions of excellence should serve as a benchmark towards which others can aspire, they are instead asked to come down to the level of the lowest. In this manner, policies conducted in the name of democracy and egalitarianism only serve to degrade the education system as a whole.[7]

These prejudices sometimes operate within a single university. Thus the Delhi School of Economics has long attracted widespread (and, for the most part, undeserved) opprobrium. Professors in other departments resented its international reputation, actually a product of intellectual excellence and an institutional culture of team-work, but in the eyes of its critics a consequence of western-oriented 'elitism'.[8] Successive vice chancellors sought to erode its autonomy and bring it on par with, or down to the level of, the other departments of the university. Teaching vacancies were unfilled, sometimes for years upon end. Proposals to reform syllabi were held up. The end result could have been foretold: the Delhi School no longer has an international reputation.

A final hurdle is constituted by the invisible hand of the market. Universities work best when they have an integrated campus, bringing together undergraduate colleges, postgraduate departments of the arts and sciences and professional schools, thus allowing the students and teachers of these different units to mingle with and learn from one another. Among the major universities of India, only Delhi remotely approximates this ideal. The reason for this is that a large chunk of territory was set aside for it when the new capital of British India was being planned. As the university expanded, the new colleges that sought affiliation had to be located elsewhere, but by then the campus itself had a sufficient density of institutions to have a character of its own. It was also close enough to the city to be connected to it. On the other hand, the universities of our other metros, Bombay, Calcutta, Madras and Bangalore, grew in a random fashion, so that their constituent units were far-flung and in no real contact. Since the price of real estate forbids the consolidation of these units, the undergraduate colleges remain isolated from one another and from the postgraduate departments; even the latter are often fragmented, spread unit by unit across the city. Some universities, for example Bangalore, then thought to construct a new campus in land available on the outskirts. The postgraduate departments were relocated here, with the undergraduate colleges staying where they were. This new campus has only served to further separate the university from the city whose name it carries and of which it is presumed to be an integral part.

Rising property prices have inhibited the growth of university pluralism in another respect; by making it very hard for Indians to study or teach in parts of India far from their own. In about 1940, a modest apartment could be rented in Mumbai at about twenty per cent of a professor's salary; by about 1970 this figure might have jumped to fifty per cent. Now it must be close to, or even in excess of, 100 per cent. What this means is that the pool of available teachers has steadily shrunk; it now contains only those who have homes in the city itself. The consequences of this for the quality of intellectual life in the university are depressingly obvious.

The market works in mysterious ways. On the one hand, it has discouraged the movement of students and teachers within India. On the other hand, it has encouraged their movement to distant parts of the globe. In the 1960s and 1970s, large numbers of Indian scientists studied and then found employment in the western universities. Now, they are increasingly joined by social scientists, historians, and literary scholars to meet the demands of the growing Indian diaspora and the new found fashions of 'postcolonial' studies. Once, names such as Ghosh, Mukherjee, Srinivasan and Reddy were quite common in the payroll of the universities of Mumbai and Pune; now, they are more likely to be found in the faculty web pages of the universities of Minnesota and Chicago.

The influence of parochialism and populism on our universities is, in part, a consequence of the clash or contradiction between two varieties of pluralism. For the survival of the republic of India, it was perhaps necessary to create linguistic states, so as to inhibit the dominance of one language group over the others. However, this enactment of a plural politics at the level of the nation as a whole has sometimes led to a denial of pluralism at lower levels. This is particularly true in the state sector, where one can manipulate recruitment in a manner that the private sector forbids. Since an overwhelming majority of our universities are managed by state governments, they are particularly prone to local or regional chauvinism.

Ideally, a university would not want to be parochial even at the level of the nation state. The best western universities seek to draw students and faculty from all over the world. Such was also the original intention of Rabindranath Tagore's university as is suggested by its name: 'Viswabharati'. That our universities become more international in their composition may be too much to hope for, but let us at least try and make them adequately Indian.

• • •

Writing in 1968, the sociologist Edward Shils singled out student unrest as a major threat to the proper functioning of universities in India. Shils observed that Indian students had been restive in the 1930s and 1940s as well, but that this had found a focus and a constructive outlet through the independence movement. In the 1960s, however, student protest was directionless; it was, in fact, a form of 'juvenile delinquency'. Indian student agitation, wrote Shils, was 'demoralising and degrading the academic profession which is already in a worse situation than one cares to see'. If unchecked, student unrest would disrupt more than the universities – 'if they go on, they will demoralize the Indian police services and render them incompetent to maintain public order or they will precipitate harsher repression resulting in many deaths which will in turn place very heavy strains on the Indian political system'.[9]

These predictions were not entirely falsified. A few years later, students across India found a focus in the JP movement, which did in fact 'precipitate harsher repression' as well as the heavy strain on the Indian political system known as the Emergency. Still, it would be unfair to blame the general deterioration of our institutions of higher education solely or even primarily on discontented students. Indian universities have been undermined from above rather than degraded from below, corrupted and corroded by the forces of parochialism and populism itemized in this essay.

This writer is not the first to comment on the dangers of parochialism in the university – nor, to be sure, will he be the last. In September 1962, a month before war broke out between India and China, a group of liberal intellectuals met in Bombay to discuss the prospects for 'a national university'. The convenor of the symposium, the mathematician A. B. Shah, pointed to the 'growing regionalization of the universities under the pressures of a developing multilingual society'. This 'process of regionalization', he continued, 'is accompanied by increasing fragmentation of the intellectual elite and a weakening of the university tradition, which was never very strong in India'. Shah felt that the solution lay in 'the creation of a few national universities that would keep the tradition of the university alive till experience makes men re-examine the wisdom of what they have done'. He identified likely five carriers of this noble ideal, the three 'premier universities' in Bombay, Calcutta and Madras, plus two new universities to be sited in the north and the south, respectively. These national universities, he felt, 'could ensure the continuity and development of all-India cultural life so essential in the context of regionalization'. They would 'provide the nation with a window to the world, and also a yardstick by which the work of the regional universities could be evaluated'.

In his contribution to the symposium, the economist B. R. Shenoy focused on the declining quality of university and college teachers. This, he felt, was due to three reasons: abysmally low salaries, which meant that alternative professions were more attractive; bureaucratic red-tape in matters of university administration, which meant that administrators were more important and more powerful than professors; and regionalism, which 'on the one hand, repels from the academic profession men from outside the region, and on the other, adds to the pressure for migration out of the profession'. Shenoy also called for the creation of national universities which would be 'wholly autonomous..., free from interference by the government or any political organization'.[10]

This writer is not the first to sing the praises of university pluralism either. In a talk broadcast over the Delhi station of All India Radio on 17 March 1940, Maurice Gwyer outlined what he saw as the future of the university he was then heading. He called, first of all, for 'the transference of all the constituent colleges of the [Delhi] University to a common site where they may stand together as a solid token of that sense of unity and purpose, which is perhaps the most vital element in university life; secondly, the extension of the science laboratories and an increase in our present facilities for the teaching of science; and thirdly, the improvement and development of the University Library'. Gwyer went on to say that while the other and older universities of India were strongly rooted in their respective towns and provinces, 'Delhi University should not be afraid to draw its strength from a whole subcontinent. It should be a symbol of what India herself, above and beyond all her creeds or castes, can offer to the world'.

Gwyer also spoke of the importance of the university reducing its reliance on the public exchequer. He hoped that 'the time will come when to endow a chair of learning at Delhi University will seem to rich men a way, not less noble than others, of perpetuating their memory'. He ended his talk in words that rang true then, and ring truer today:

> I am speaking tonight more especially to the citizens of Delhi. Delhi University will always, I hope, be their university as well

> as a university for all India; and I look forward to the time when they will feel a great pride in its fortunes and in its work. I hope it will be a civic centre in the truest sense, and that those of its sons who are educated within its walls will learn there how to combine a love of their city with a love of their country, to look beyond the immediate conflicts of community and party to the greater unity which lies behind them, and to remember that of all the civic virtues for which a university should stand, a love of truth, a sense of proportion and a spirit of tolerance are not the least.[11]

• • •

Our universities are in crisis, but few people – and none, apparently, in positions of high authority – seem to be aware of this. But perhaps I should amend that last statement. One person in high authority has in fact spoken on the subject of university education. This is the ex-President of India, A. P. J. Abdul Kalam, who recently asked for the creation of a 'new Nalanda'. Now this is a charming idea, but also a hopelessly romantic one. Surely India's needs would be better served by renewing our existing universities, by making them more plural, in all senses of the term.

Crafting an agenda for the renewal of our universities is the subject for another essay, to be written by another (and better qualified) scholar. Here, I might just suggest a few items for inclusion on that agenda. First, I think we need to think more seriously about university size. Our big cities each have far too few universities for their own – and public – good. The universities of Mumbai, Kolkata, Chennai, Delhi and Bangalore each have several hundred institutions affiliated to it, with a combined student population that runs into three lakhs and more. How can these institutions be effectively run, or standards maintained, by a single chain of authority headed by a solitary vice chancellor?

Second, within each university, big or small, all constituent units must not be treated alike. In particular, colleges and departments with a tradition of excellence in teaching and research should be accorded institutional autonomy, including the autonomy to raise their own funds. Each university must be encouraged to cultivate its own areas of distinction. Words such as 'distinction' and 'excellence' need to have their meanings restored. For, as we know only too well, in the realm of the academy, parochialism and populism work only to propel a race to the bottom. Why not instead work to ensure that some institutions of quality exist, and that those not yet there are encouraged to emulate them?

Third, to attract better teachers one needs more flexibility in recruitment policies. Now, most universities allow only full-time faculty, whose jobs are secure until superannuation, in exchange for which they must come to work every day and not take outside employment. However, a university in a city such as Mumbai or Kolkata can and must take advantage of the talent available in the public and corporate sector, in the media, and in voluntary organizations. If a scientist in an industrial lab, an editor in a newspaper, a senior lawyer in the high court, were all permitted to come one day a week to teach one course a year to young and keen students, there would, I think, be a profusion of volunteers. Likewise, with the increasing drift of the finest Indian scholars abroad, statutes and prejudices must be amended to allow some professors to teach for one term only, while spending the rest of the year where they like. The encouragement of adjunct and part-time faculty would, I think, greatly enrich the intellectual life of the university – and also help towards balancing its budget.

At the same time, with regard to full-time faculty our universities need to more seriously combat the pressures of parochialism. A policy of not appointing one's own graduates, at least at the lower levels, would aid a cross-fertilization of intellectual approaches and perspectives. A policy of setting apart a certain percentage of teaching jobs – say thirty per cent – for candidates from other states would make each university less parochial as well as more national.

By making one's teaching staff less parochial one can fashion a student body that is less parochial as well. One function that the best colleges and departments have historically served – and can be made to serve again – was to attract outstanding students from outside the state or region. In their heydays, the Delhi School of Economics, the department of history at the JNU, the school of fine arts at M. S. University in Baroda, and the department of philosophy at the University of Pune, all had a catchment area that included all of India.

This brings me, finally, to the question of funding. Today, almost all Indian universities are funded and controlled by the State. In the long-term, we need to have many more private universities, which might challenge the public universities to reform and redeem themselves, in the same manner, as say, Jet Airways has forced sharp and mostly beneficial changes on Indian Airlines. In the shorter term, colleges and universities in the state sector must more actively woo successful alumni and industrial houses for funds. The money, when and if it comes, can be tied to specific programmes and departments, but its ultimate use must be left to the discretion of the institution.

The ideals that I have outlined here are the product of an experience that is individual but I think not unrepresentative. My mind was shaped and quickened by the University of Delhi, which I was fortunate to know and experience towards the end of its glorious period. But what I owe my alma mater is merely what other and greater Indians have owed other universities. The national movement, and the building of a free and democratic India, were both nurtured and sustained by men and women whose minds were formed by the universities of India.

It is commonly argued that the impressive growth rates of recent years will be stalled by poor infrastructure: erratic power supply, potholed highways, inadequate public transport, and the like. My own view is that India's economic and social development depends as crucially on a renewal of its higher education system. As we enter our seventh decade of freedom, what we make of ourselves will depend, far more than we presently seem to realize, on what we make of our universities.

•

ENDNOTES:

[This essay is based on the inaugural address to the symposium on 'The Quest for Excellence: Great Universities and their Cities, Mumbai, Kolkata, Chennai', Department of History, Mumbai University, January 2007. I am grateful to Mariam Dossal for inviting me to speak to the symposium, and to André Béteille, Aditya Bhattacharjea, Niraja Gopal Jayal and Sunil Khilnani for helpful comments on an earlier draft. I remain solely responsible for the views (and prejudices) expressed here.]

1. André Béteille, 'Universities at the Crossroads', in *Current Science*, Volume 92, Number 4, 25 February 2007. Béteille is among the few scholars who have written on the history and social role of the Indian university. The essay cited above contains his latest and perhaps most considered views on the subject, but see also Chapters 6 and 7 of his *Antinomies of Society: Essays on Ideologies and Institutions*, Oxford University Press, New Delhi, 2000.
2. Cf the valuable collection of essays edited by Mushirul Hasan, *Knowledge, Power and Politics: Educational Institutions in India*, Roli Books, New Delhi, 1998.
3. 'The Academic Freedom of the Universities' (1902), in Edward Shils, editor and translator, *Max Weber on Universities: The Power of the State and the Dignity of the Academic Calling in Imperial Germany*, University of Chicago Press, Chicago, 1974. pp. 21–22.
4. Béteille, 'Universities at the Crossroads'.
5. Béteille, 'Universities at the Crossroads'.
6. Cf Shiv Visvanathan, *Organising for Science: The Making of an Industrial Research Laboratory*, Oxford University Press, New Delhi, 1985.
7. For valuable suggestions on to how to retain academic standards while at the same time being socially inclusive, see Béteille, 'Universities at the Crossroads'.
8. Cf Dharma Kumar and Dilip Mookerjee, editors, *D. School: Reflections on the Delhi School of Economics*, Oxford University Press, New Delhi, 1995.
9. Edward Shils, 'Students, Politics, and Universities in India' in Philip G. Altbach, editor, *Turmoil and Transition: Higher Education and Student Politics in India*, Basic Books, New York, 1968, pp. 2–3, 9.
10. A. B. Shah, editor, *A National University*, Popular Book Depot, Bombay 1964, pp. 5, 30–1,34–41.
11. 'The Future of Delhi University' in Maurice Gwyer, *Convocation and Other Addresses*. Cambridge Printing Works, Delhi, 1942, pp. 183–91.

Rajabai Tower under construction. The scaffolding holds the future clock tower.

Courtesy: University of Mumbai

# Knowledge into Power*

*Knowledge is the most powerful resource for nation building.*

Indian universities, in modern times, are faced with an enormous responsibility: that of building the nation through the enrichment of our higher educational system. This is as true of the disciplines of science, engineering, technology and life-science, as of the humanities – arts, commerce, management and languages.

India's prosperity as a nation is powered by its economic development, which is driven by the spirit of competition. Competitiveness, in turn, is fuelled by knowledge and knowledge

* Based on the Address by Dr. A.P.J. Abdul Kalam at the Vice Chancellors' Meet at Anna University, Chennai, on 28 November 2007.

By **A.P.J. Abdul Kalam**

by science, technology and innovation, which are then enhanced by investment-rich resources. As reservoirs of knowledge, universities are thus the prime knowledge-generation centres of the nation, because the transformation of any society has a close relationship with the quality of education and national development. This is why I feel it is imperative that universities should impart a value-based education to our students.

The primary purpose of education in a country such as India is to develop and enhance the potential of our human resources and progressively transform it into a knowledge society. Such a society will generate products and services that are rich in both explicit and tacit knowledge. In fact, the true capital of such a knowledge society lies in its knowledge workers. One feature of this society is that it will be highly networked to create a knowledge-intensive environment along with an enabling process to efficiently create, share, use and protect knowledge. Our educational system should, therefore, re-align itself at the earliest to meet the needs of these challenges and gear itself to participate in this process of social transformation. The networking of universities is the first step towards creating knowledge centres that can meet the demands of an age that was born out of the convergence of technologies. Therefore, it is only natural that human minds should also converge in the knowledge era.

• • •

The importance of research cannot be underestimated today when it has emerged as the driving force in the process of self-reliance in all cutting-edge technologies. In certain universities, research has been the main contributor and guiding force in realizing its core competence. Our road map for the next few decades will witness the conquest of many new frontiers in nano-science and engineering, space technology, advanced materials and composite technology, biotechnology in the fields of drugs and pharmaceuticals, among others. Scientific organizations such as ISRO (Indian Space Research Organization), DRDO (Defence Research and Development Organization), to name just a few, spend more than Rs.500 crores per year in sponsored research. However, equal emphasis is required in research in the areas of the arts and literature, humanities, political science, law, economics, commerce and management to promote the balanced growth of a society that seeks to preserve its civilizational heritage.

An appropriate networking of universities with these scientific organizations and other government departments is urgently required to spearhead important research programmes in these emerging areas. This synergy will provide the necessary inputs in achieving self-reliance in the years to come. With this objective in mind, the Department of Science and Technology (DST) and other departments have introduced novel schemes such as REACH (Relevance and Excellence in Achieving New Heights in Educational Institutes).

Indian industry is engaged in ways and means to achieve products of a better quality, a practice currently aided by the transfer of technology from other countries. However, there is no reason why Indian industry cannot be assisted in this endeavour by our own universities through indigenous research projects. Ideally, our universities should lead in the networking of multiple organizations and industries, and our vice chancellors should encourage opportunities that enable students and teachers to undertake advanced research. This will serve to build essential knowledge resources and develop core competences, and transform these universities into centres of excellence in specific areas.

• • •

With India's entry into the league of nations with trillion-dollar economies and the continuing ascent of its economic trajectory, concerns are being voiced about the rise of unemployment and illiteracy. To my mind, the issue of unemployment is not the major problem: the greater crisis is the matter of unemployability.

According to the India Labour Report, 2007, 53 per cent of employed youth suffer some degree of skill deprivation, while only eight per cent are unemployed. Of India's youth, 57 per cent suffer some degree of unemployability. It is estimated that a sum of Rs. 480,000 crores will be required, over two years, to repair this skill deficit. While ninety per cent of employment opportunities require vocational skills, unfortunately, at the same time, ninety per cent of our college/school graduates do not possess adequate practical knowledge. In the age group of 15 to sixty years that is employed, almost forty per cent of the population is not literate. Only seven per cent of the population in the age group of 15 to 29 years has received some form of vocational training. It is estimated that 300 million youth will enter the labour force by 2025, and 25 per cent of the world's workers in the next four years will be Indians.

Unless basic and specific strategies are set in place and integrated into the system to raise the employability of the growing work force, the mirage of a large pool of skilled labour in India will continue to obstruct our economic growth. The unfinished product from an inadequate educational system will else be vulnerable to anti-social tendencies, leading to greater social instability and inequality. To repair this skill deficit, we may need six to eight per cent of our GDP. However, capital by itself, without incorporating a structural change in our educational system at the school level and in higher education, will be ineffective. For optimum efficiency, the pyramid so constructed by the Indian educational system must be based on a strong and vibrant school education system, supported by a refined higher educational system. Only when that happens can we expect an output of a superior nature from the school system for the higher education system, which will ultimately deliver a suitable workforce for the construction of a knowledge society.

• • •

An issue of paramount concern today is the appeal that IT/ITES services hold for today's youth. In more than 1000 engineering colleges around the country, approximately 150,000 students opt for courses on Computer Science, Information Technology, ECE and EE courses alone, with all the other courses attracting fewer numbers of students. Indian industry requires trained students, currently a remote possibility with the lack of well-trained teachers and an ambient infrastructure. The current employability rate of graduating engineers is approximately 25 per cent. It is estimated that the IT industry will incur training costs of over US $ 2.6 billion over three years. According to a NASSCOM-McKenzie report, Indian industry will require over nine million suitable graduates for the IT/ITES sectors and Business Process Outsourcing (BPO) by 2010, which in turn will create six million employment vacancies in the sectors of construction, retail and transportation. Besides this, the growing Knowledge Process Outsourcing (KPO) industry in India, which is expected to be worth around US $17 billion by 2010, will require additional human resources. By its very nature KPO, as an industry, demands superior human resources and advanced services with unique skills from across disciplines such as commerce, law, humanity, finance, investment, infrastructure, agriculture and manufacturing.

The IT Industry has identified avenues for entry-level engineers in areas that require a solid foundation of technical knowledge, for those proficient in English and with soft skills, those skilled in process orientation, and for those with critical thinking abilities. In addition, it has been observed that another set of students opts for management studies, with ninety per cent of students at the IIMs from engineering backgrounds, and well over fifty per cent from the IITs. Given this scenario, it becomes imperative to assess the status of graduates in the humanities, commerce, the arts and science, and other engineering disciplines for which IT courses hold an irresistible appeal.

The IT industry is expected to grow at a sequential growth rate of around 25-27 per cent, but is projected to deliver merely US $ 60 billion as export business by 2010. However, as this growth is perceived to be inadequate, to increase our software export to US $ 200 billion by 2015 we must adopt multiple innovative strategies. The existing profile of IT products of outsourced projects must transform itself to that of the development of innovative knowledge products, and from that of IT-enabled services to knowledge-based services. Inevitably, this must exert additional pressures on the requirements of skilled manpower across all disciplines.

For instance, apart from our national e-governance plan with 25 mission mode projects in G2C domain, we also need to implement G2G services across governmental units. Moreover, the proposed State-Wide Area Network (SWAN) has to be established by 2008. The planned computerization of over nearly 15,000 district and subordinate courts is due to be completed, along with the government's introduction of over 100,000 Common Service Centres across the nation that will provide e-governance services to its citizens. Solutions for these tasks would inevitably need to be provided by the IT industry within the next three to five years.

Given these requirements, one may well question the opportunities available for students who graduate from other disciplines, and how they may be best moulded to meet national challenges.

• • •

I will now list several national missions and challenges for which our university system would need to provide skilled human resources.

The agriculture and food processing industry's mission is to generate 400 million tonnes of foodgrains given conditions of reduced land, water and with a straitened workforce, from the present 200 million tonnes. New technology is urgently required in this sector – ranging from seeds to improved cultivation methods, food processing and marketing. Regenerating this entire chain will enable large-scale employment, particularly in rural areas.

One of India's aspirations is to build 100 million homes within the next ten years. The development of essential infrastructure in metropolitan and tier-two cities needs to be enhanced in the form of new bridges, marketing complexes and industrial units. Forty per cent of rural areas require all-weather roads, in addition to the essential doubling of the present national highways ratio per every 100 square kms. Simultaneously, we are in the process of developing ports, railway systems and airports. For example, the Indian construction industry employs over 31 million people for its asset-generating activity of over Rs. 3,10,000 crore, which includes an expenditure of Rs. 2,00,000 crore incurred by the government. This will need the development of specialized human resources in every sphere of construction activity. It will also require a reorientation of our educational system for generating world-class skills in our youth; these skill sets will enable higher productivity which, in turn, will result in increased competitiveness. Another essential goal that our educational system must pursue is to ensure that the remainder of students should, at the very least, be equipped with a secondary school qualification with training for employment in the agriculture or service sector.

Another national goal that India hopes to achieve by the year 2030 is that of energy independence. It is estimated that when our population touches 1.4 billion people, the corresponding demand from the power sector will surge from the existing requirement of

130,000 MW to approximately 400,000 MW, assuming an energy growth rate of five per cent per annum. Electric power generation in India currently relies on four basic energy sources: Fossil fuels such as oil, natural gas and coal; hydro-electricity; nuclear power; and renewable energy sources such as bio-fuels, biomass, and energy from the sun, wind and ocean. To generate over 1,20,000 MW by 2030, we require a major thrust in the development of solar energy and wind energy. Similarly, it is proposed to harness over 65,000 MW from hydro-power sources.

Over fifty per cent of India's population does not have access to safe drinking water. We are currently engaged in the major mission of the 'Interlinking of Rivers' in the nation and the statewide creation of waterways, which will act as a reservoir to accommodate floodwater and enhance irrigation, navigation and tourism.

In the field of healthcare, India envisions a programme for 'Health for all', and 'Vision 2020' for eye care, providing tremendous opportunity in the primary, secondary and tertiary healthcare sector. We are also in the process of establishing tele-medicine centres that function on connectivity via satellite, terrestrial and wireless links in the primary health sector of two lakh panchayats.

In the sector of aeronautics, India plans to launch a mission for the design and development of passenger jet aircraft that will create several opportunities in the sectors of aerospace engineering, technology, and manufacturing and marketing.

The automobile industry in India accounts for a business volume of US $ 45 billion with a potential to grow more rapidly through both Indian manufacturers and several reputed international companies, which have established huge facilities in the country. We are poised to increase the business volume to US $ 200 billion by 2016 with an export component of at least US $ 50 billion.

India today builds ships for oil exploration, service vessels, port operations, self-propelled barges for river transports and cargo ships up to 92,000 DWT. In addition, we have facilities for building combat ships for the Indian Navy. By 2008, we will have three shipyards for building vessels of a capacity of 100,000 to 150,000 DWT, but also need to create facilities for vessels ranging from 150,000 DWT to 300,000 DWT.

• • •

In a country such as India, where the development of the rural sector is crucial, the government, private and public sectors have failed to work in tandem towards rural development. For example, activities such as the setting up of educational institutions, healthcare centres, the laying of roads, building of houses, the construction of a marketing complex, and providing communication links in a particular rural area has been attempted in the past as individual activities. To facilitate a synergy between these various activities a rural development programme, PURA (Providing Urban Amenities in Rural Areas) was devised, which envisages an integrated development plan with employment generation as the focus, driven by provisions of the habitat, healthcare, education, skill development, physical and electronic connectivity and marketing. For example, the Women's Engineering College of Periyar Maniammai University has pioneered the Periyar PURA involving a population of 1,00,000 from 65 villages in Vallam, Tanjore, which resulted in creating employment potential in that cluster.

Seven thousand PURAs encompassing over 600,000 villages have been planned for the whole country. Besides concentrating on the reinforcement of agriculture, the objectives of PURA will emphasize agro-processing, the development of rural craftsmanship, dairy farming, fisheries and sericulture, in such a manner that the non-farm revenue for the rural sector is enhanced, based on the core competence of the region. Rural economy will be driven by renewable energy such as solar, wind, bio-fuel and the conversion of municipal waste into power.

These programmes contain social, research and technological content along with substantial business opportunities that will lead to increased economic growth in the globalized scenario. Several challenges face us today: How do we prepare our higher education system to meet these challenges? What strategies must universities employ to draw students towards disciplines that have been discussed so far? How can vice chancellors inspire school students and attract them towards these national missions?

• • •

Our universities presently generate three million graduates and postgraduates every year and the number of students seeking employment after the completion of Class 10 and 12 is around seven million per year. Thus, nearly ten million youth are injected into the employment market every year. A huge chasm exists between the actual requirement and the availability of employable skill. One strategy that may be employed to bridge this gap is the provision of an interface between school curriculum and the requirements of the three sectors of the economy. At present, India's youth under the age of 25 – a number expected to grow till the year 2050 – is 540 million. Keeping this resource in view, universities and educational systems should create two cadres of personnel: one, a global cadre of skilled youth with specific knowledge of special skills; and, two, another global cadre of youth with higher education. These two cadres will be required to power the manufacturing and services sector of India as well as for fulfilling the human resource requirements of various countries.

Thus, the universities and secondary school education system will have to work towards increasing their turnout from the existing 11 per cent to twenty per cent by the year 2020 and thirty per cent by the year 2030. This is reflected in the Eleventh Five-Year-Plan. Those who are not covered by the higher education system should be imparted world-class skill sets in areas such as construction, carpentry, electrical systems, repair of mechanical systems, fashion design, para-legal, para-medical, accountancy, sales and marketing, software and hardware maintenance and service, software quality assurance, *et al.* Ideally, no Indian youth should be without either a world-class higher education or without world-class skill sets. Therefore, it is imperative that we begin without any delay to realize this goal since the overall time available for such a planned growth in education is short. A National Policy for creating a 'Global Human Development Cadre for India' must emerge, and, certainly, it is here that vice chancellors may study and contribute their inputs towards achieving this mission.

• • •

: A.P.J. Abdul Kalam

If we are to progress towards a knowledge society, we need to nurture the diversity of talents inherent in the wide cross section of our nation by promoting innovations, and the ability to compete successfully in an international market. The success of our industry in the fields of IT, biotechnology, pharmaceuticals and precision manufacturing is based on competitiveness that is cost effective, and the timely supply of quality products. For example, the productivity per employee of the Maruti automobile industry is $ 200,000, whereas that of the Indian IT industry is only $ 32,000 to $ 80,000.

To ensure the success of this national mission, vice chancellors have been entrusted with the responsibility to inspire the youth of India to study subjects of their interest be it poetry, music, art or philosophy, commerce, literature, finance and all the disciplines of engineering, along with support from the government in creating well-funded institutions in different subjects. Rather than creating new institutions in engineering and technology alone, the existing 300 universities and affiliated colleges should be empowered with autonomy and funds to transform themselves into world-class institutions.

To begin this process a vision is urgently needed for discussion and for realizing all aspects of the educational system that will enable it to generate the quality of human resource for meeting its developmental goals. The stakeholders for implementing this vision are the Planning Commission, Human Resource Development, ministries of state and central governments, National Knowledge Commission and the universities themselves. The universities will thus be in equal partnership in the Developed India Vision 2020. That is the India, which will be beautiful, prosperous and safe. We must all work together towards this endeavour for which we will be remembered.

•

# Adjusting to a Knowledge Economy

In 2005, the World Bank published a report on India and the knowledge economy. The thrust of the World Bank report is on education's role as enabler of the knowledge economy, and the knowledge economy's requirement of a new set of skills and competencies. In a simple sense, a country's per capita national income is nothing but the average productivity of its citizens. With aging populations in developed countries, and even in countries like Russia and China, there has been talk of India's demographic dividend. That the demographic dividend argument works, is known. For East Asia, several studies suggest that between 25 to 40 per cent of the East Asian miracle was due to the demographic dividend. Other than East Asia, it has worked in Japan in the 1950s, China in the 1980s, and Ireland in the 1980s and the 1990s.

By **Bibek Debroy**

Several factors explain the demographic dividend. First, there is the obvious increase in working-age populations, with a reduction in dependency ratios, and the direct impact of a larger quantity of labour input. To take one dramatic number, between 2001 and 2026, India's total population will increase by 371 million and 83 per cent of the increase will occur in the age-group of 15-59 years. Second, the quality of the labour input can increase and this is reflected in what economists call total factor productivity (TFP) growth. Third, when dependency ratios decline, savings rates increase, leading to increases in investment rates and higher rates of GDP growth. Fourth, if the decline in dependency ratios is at the lower end of the age spectrum as a result of fertility declines, female work participation rates increase.

However, there is no automaticity about a demographic dividend leading to sustained high growth rates. Among other things, one requires an improvement in health and education indicators, with a shortage in required skills already being felt. Nor should one forget the regional dimension, since high absolute and relative growths in population will happen in states like Assam, Bihar, Delhi, Haryana, Madhya Pradesh, Rajasthan and Uttar Pradesh. When the education system has to adjust to tap the demographic dividend and opportunities thrown up by the knowledge economy, one must have in mind Bihar, Jharkhand, Madhya Pradesh, Chhattisgarh, Uttar Pradesh, Rajasthan, and Orissa, and India's 150-odd backward districts.

In December 2006, the Planning Commission produced the Approach Paper to the Eleventh Five Year Plan (2007-12). This has a sub-title on faster and more inclusive growth. The introductory chapter states, 'It is important to recognize that better health and education are the necessary pre-conditions for sustained long-term growth.' There can be no quarrel with this statement. Further down the chapter we have:

> A key element of the Eleventh Plan strategy should be to provide essential education and health services to those large parts of our population who are still excluded from these. Education is the critical factor that empowers participation in the growth process, but our performance has been less than satisfactory, both overall and in bridging gender and other divides. Overall literacy is still

> less than seventy per cent and rural female literacy less than fifty per cent with corresponding rates even lower among the marginalized groups and minorities. While the *Sarva Shiksha Abhiyan* has expanded primary school enrolment, it is far from providing quality education. Looking ahead, we cannot be satisfied with only universal primary education; we must move towards universal secondary education too as quickly as possible.

This is also almost generic, though question marks can be raised about success indicators like increased primary school enrolment and the degree to which Sarva Shiksha Abhiyan can alone obtain the credit. Still further down the chapter, we have extensions of this argument.

> While both education and curative health services are available for those who can afford to pay, quality service is beyond the reach of the common people. Other privately provided services are of highly variable quality. In this situation, access to essential services can only be through public financing. In most cases this means public provision or partnership with non-profit and civil society organizations. A major institutional challenge is that even where service providers exist, the quality of delivery is poor and those responsible for delivering the services cannot be held accountable. Unless such accountability is established and cutting edge service providers trained, it will be difficult to ensure significant improvement in delivery even if large resources are made available.

Although this statement is about education at a very general level, some additional points have now been flagged. First, there is a question of access to the relatively poor. Second, flowing from the first argument, a case has been made for public financing, which is then equated with public provisioning, without making the jump from the one to the other at all clear. Third, an implicit argument has been made about regulation. Fourth, another implicit argument has been made about lack of accountability in public expenditure.

• • •

Let us go back to the World Bank report on India and the knowledge economy. This sets out the main issues, as perceived by the Bank, in strengthening India's education system. Paraphrased, these issues are – (a) improving efficiency in use of public resources; (b) making the education system responsive to market needs; (c) ensuring that access doesn't mean crowding out of the relatively poor; (d) ensuring quality, relevance and practical skills; (e) in higher education, shifting the focus of the government from administrative management to regulation; and (f) relaxing entry barriers and accreditation systems for private players, including foreign ones. In its chapter on strategic initiatives for inclusive development, the Approach Paper divides the education discussion into five segments – elementary education, secondary education, technical/vocational education and skill development, higher/technical education and adult literacy. Since education is a continuum and access to higher education is a function of access to school (elementary and secondary) education, such water-tight compartmentalization doesn't always make sense. However, if the expression 'higher education' is used, most people would interpret it as technical/vocational education and higher/technical education, probably the latter. Once one has pinned down the expression, one should ask how the World Bank's six issues should be addressed for this sector.

If we interpret higher education as higher/technical education, to the exclusion of technical/vocational education and skill development, this is what the Approach Paper tells us.

> India has a well-developed and comprehensive higher education system which has served us well thus far, but is now inadequate. The extent of access it provides is limited. Only about 10 per cent of the relevant age group go to universities whereas in many developing countries, the figure is between 20 and 25 per cent. There is an overwhelming need to undertake major expansion to increase access to higher education. The system also suffers from a serious problem of quality. While some of our institutions of higher education have the potential to become comparable with the best in the world, the average standard is much lower. High quality institutions are finding it difficult to get quality faculty given the

> enormous increase in private sector opportunities for the skills most in demand.

These points are not being flagged for the first time. For instance, in 2002, the S.P. Gupta Special Group constituted by the Planning Commission stated,

> It should be noted, however, that on the average the skilled labour force at present is hardly around 6-8 per cent of the total, compared to more than sixty per cent in most of the developed and emerging developing countries.

In 2001, the Montek Singh Ahluwalia Task Force, again constituted by the Planning Commission, stated:

> Only five per cent of the Indian labour force in this age category has vocational skills whereas the percentage in industrial countries is much higher, varying between sixty per cent and eighty per cent, except for Italy, which is 44 per cent. The percentage for Korea, which has recently been categorized as an industrialized country, is exceptionally high at 96 per cent. The developing countries listed have percentages which are significantly lower than the developed countries, but they are still much higher than India, e.g. Mexico at 28 per cent and Peru at 17 per cent. Differences in definition may make inter-country comparison somewhat unreliable, but the level in India is clearly far too low.

However, both these quotes have more to do with vocational education.

On higher education proper, the present regulatory and control structure is a maze. Although the Ministry of Human Resource Development is involved, directly or indirectly, there are multiple layers. First, there are twenty Central Universities, funded by the Centre and therefore under direct central control. Second, there are 109 deemed universities under the UGC Act, five institutions established under State legislation and 13 institutes of national importance established under central legislation. Till 1976-77, higher education was in the State List of the Seventh Schedule. The 1976-77 amendment moved it to the Concurrent List. Third, in addition to Central universities and deemed universities, there therefore exist 222 State universities and colleges, with the coordination function supposed to be exercised by UGC and the Central Advisory Board of Education (CABE). There are 18,064 colleges, including 1902 women's colleges. Fourth, some universities are affiliating, others are unitary. Some are single campus, others are multi-campus. Fifth, several forms of professional education are regulated by statutory councils like All India Council for Technical Education (AICTE), Distance Education Council (DEC), Indian Council for Agriculture Research (ICAR), Bar Council of India (BCI), National Council for Teacher Education (NCTE), Rehabilitation Council of India (RCI), Medical Council of India (MCI), Pharmacy Council of India (PCI), Indian Nursing Council (INC), Dentist Council of India (DCI), Central Council of Homeopathy (CCH) and Central Council of Indian Medicine (CCIM). This creates multiplicity and confusion, the artificial distinction between diplomas and degrees in the same subject and for the same duration being a case in point.

On the base that existed at the time of Independence, the numbers, including those on student enrollment and number of teachers, represent an impressive increase. But a few uncomfortable questions need to be asked. How many of these institutes of higher education are of requisite quality? Even if one ignores international rankings of universities and colleges, which can be subjective and therefore exhibit different rankings across different surveys, why is it that most of India's universities and colleges have excess and under-utilized capacity, while only a few have excess demand? Why is it that a large number of Indian students head abroad, and not just to the United States? Incidentally, this exit option is only available to the relatively richer segments of society. Why has there been a decline in the number of overseas students who come to India to study? Through WTO (World Trade Organization), there are no commitments right now in higher education. However, eventually, higher education is bound to be opened up. Are Indian institutes equipped to handle that eventual challenge and have the supply-side changes occurred? Why are legitimate and better foreign universities not allowed to operate in India while lesser known ones function through a grey area in the law? Why are Indian institutions of higher education more interested in setting up shop overseas (the Middle East, South-East Asia, even China) than in India?

One looks to the Planning Commission to provide answers to these uncomfortable questions and answer policy issues. Yet, if one reads the Approach Paper, all that one finds is concern over regional divides. The clichéd answer is that more colleges and universities must be set up, presumably through public resources. There must be reservation of seats for deprived segments (identified through collective identities like caste instead of individual identities like class) in institutions of higher education. This is in line with the standard prescription that public expenditure on education, including higher education, must be increased, a point that is also made by the National Common Minimum Programme (NCMP).

•

Institute of Chartered Financial Analysts of India (ICFAI), Hyderabad.

Courtesy: *Outlook*

# Of Grades and Graduates

Higher education has made a significant contribution to economic development, social progress and political democracy in independent India. Nevertheless, there is serious cause for concern at this juncture. The opportunities for higher education in terms of the number of places in universities are simply not adequate in relation to our needs. Large segments of our population simply do not have access to higher education. What is more, the quality of higher education in most of our universities leaves much to be desired.

The National Knowledge Commission (NKC) believes that an emphasis on expansion and reform of our school system is necessary to ensure that every child has an equal opportunity to enter the world of higher education. These concerns about the higher education system are widely shared. There is a clear, almost unanimous, view that higher education needs a systematic overhaul, so that we can educate much larger numbers without diluting academic standards. Indeed, this is essential because the transformation of economy

By **Sam Pitroda**

and society in the twenty-first century would depend, in significant part, on the spread and the quality of education among our people, particularly in the sphere of higher education. Moreover, it is only an inclusive society that can provide the foundations for a knowledge society. The objectives of reform and change in our higher education system, as has often been stressed, must be expansion, excellence and inclusion. Meaningful reform of the higher education system, with a long-term perspective, is both complex and difficult. The challenges that confront higher education in India are clear. It needs a massive expansion of opportunities for higher education and it is just as important to raise the average quality of higher education in every sphere. At the same time, it is essential to create institutions that are exemplars of excellence at par with the best in the world. In the pursuit of these objectives, providing people with access to higher education in a socially inclusive manner is imperative. The realization of these objectives, combined with access, would not only develop the skills and capabilities we need for the economy, but would also help transform India into a knowledge economy and society. It is universally accepted that a meaningful reform of the higher education system, with a long-term perspective is both complex and difficult. Yet, it is imperative.

• • •

The higher education system needs a massive expansion of opportunities, to the tune of around 1500 universities nationwide, that would enable India to attain a gross enrolment ratio of at least 15 per cent by 2015. Ideally, the focus would have to be on new universities, but some clusters of affiliated colleges could also become universities. Such an expansion would require major changes in the structure of regulation.

The present regulatory system in higher education is flawed in some important respects. The barriers to entry are too high, with the system of authorizing entry very cumbersome. There is a multiplicity of regulatory agencies where mandates are both confusing and overlapping. The system, as a whole, is over-regulated but under-governed. The NKC believes that there is a clear need to establish an Independent Regulatory Authority for Higher Education (IRAHE). The IRAHE must be at an arm's length from the government and independent of all stakeholders including the concerned ministries of the government. The IRAHE would have to be established by an Act of Parliament, and would be responsible for setting the criteria and deciding on entry. It would be the only agency that would be authorized to accord degree-granting power to higher education institutions, and also be responsible for monitoring standards and settling disputes. It would apply exactly the same norms to public and private institutions, just as it would apply the same norms to domestic and international institutions. In addition, the IRAHE would be the authority for licensing accreditation agencies. The role of the UGC would be re-defined to focus on the disbursement of grants to, and maintenance of, public institutions in higher education. The entry regulatory functions of the AICTE, the MCI and the BCI would be performed by the IRAHE, so that their role would be limited to that of professional associations.

The expansion of our system of higher education is not possible without enhanced levels of financing. This must necessarily come from both public and private sources. Since government financing will remain the cornerstone, government support for higher education should increase to at least 1.5 per cent of GDP, out of a total of at least six per cent of GDP for education. Even this would not suffice for the massive expansion in higher education that is an imperative. It is essential, therefore, to explore other possibilities that can complement the increase in public expenditure.

Most public universities are sitting on a large reservoir of untapped resources in the form of land. It should be possible to draw up norms and parametres for these universities to use their available land as a source of finance. Furthermore, while it is for universities to decide the level of fees, as a norm fees should meet at least twenty per cent of the total expenditure in universities. This should be subject to two conditions: first, needy students should be provided with a fee waiver plus scholarships to meet their costs; second, universities should not be penalized by the UGC for the resources raised from higher fees through matching deductions from their grants-in-aid. Other sources of financing such as philanthropic contributions, alumni contributions and licensing fees should be encouraged by creating supportive institutional mechanisms. It is also essential to stimulate private investment in education as a means of extending educational opportunities. It may be possible to leverage public resources, especially in the form of land grants, to attract more (not-for-profit) private investment.

It is perhaps the right time to create new institutions in the form of National Universities that would become role models as centres of academic excellence. The creation of fifty National Universities is recommended, that can provide education of the highest standard. As exemplars for the rest of the nation, these universities would be required to train students in a variety of disciplines, including humanities, social sciences, basic sciences, commerce and professional subjects, at both the undergraduate and postgraduate levels. While the number fifty is a long-term objective, in the short term it is important to begin with at least ten such universities in the next three years. National Universities can be established in two ways: by the government, or by a private sponsoring body that sets up a Society, Charitable Trust or Section 25 Company.

Since public finance is an integral constituent of universities worldwide, most of the new universities would require significant initial financial support from the government. Each university may be endowed with a substantial allocation of public land, in excess of its spatial requirements. The excess land can be a subsequent source of income generation. Exceptions need to be made in existing income tax laws to encourage large endowments. Further, there should be no restriction on the utilization of income in any given period or in the use of appropriate financial instruments. Moreover, these universities should be allowed the autonomy to set student fee levels and tap other sources for generating funds.

The National Universities thus proposed would admit students on an all-India basis. They would adopt the principle of needs-blind admissions, which would require an extensive system of scholarships for needy students. Ideally, undergraduate degrees in the National Universities, in a three-year programme, would be granted on the basis of completing a requisite number of credits, obtained from different courses. The academic year, therefore, would be semester-based and students internally evaluated at the end of each course. Transfer of credits from one National University to another would also be allowed. An appropriate system of appointments and incentives would be put into place to maximize the productivity of faculty in these National Universities. Strong linkages would be forged between teaching and research, universities and industry, and universities and research laboratories. The National Universities would be department-based, without any affiliated colleges.

• • •

A sweeping reform of existing institutions must necessarily be an integral part of our endeavour to transform higher education, at the moment a seemingly insurmountable task. Even so, the reforms in the following spheres, along the lines earlier suggested are not only possible, but would also make a tangible difference.

Of utmost importance is the requirement that all universities revise or restructure curricula at least once in three years. Annual examinations, which test memory rather than understanding, should be supplemented with continuous internal assessment, which could begin with a weight of 25 per cent in the total, to be raised to fifty per cent over a stipulated period. In this regard, a transition is proposed to a course-credit system where degrees are granted on the basis of completing a requisite number of credits from different courses, which provides students with choices. It is imperative that universities become the hub of research once more in order to capture synergies between teaching and research that enrich each other. This requires not only policy measures, but also changes in resource allocation, reward systems and mindsets. Alongside, a conscious effort must be made to attract and retain talented faculty members through better working conditions combined with incentives for performance.

The criteria for resource allocation to universities should seek to strike a much better balance between providing for salaries or pensions and providing for maintenance, development or investment. It should also recognize the importance of a critical minimum to ensure standards and strategic preferences to promote excellence. The elements of infrastructure that support the teaching-learning process, such as libraries, laboratories and connectivity, need to be monitored and upgraded on a regular basis. There is an acute need for reform in the structures of governance of universities that do not preserve autonomy and do not promote accountability.

It is clear that much needs to be done, but two important points deserve mention. The appointments of vice chancellors must be freed from direct or indirect interventions on the part of governments, for these should be based on search processes and peer judgment alone. The size and composition of University Courts, Academic Councils and Executive Councils, which slow down decision-making processes and sometimes constitute an impediment to change, need to be reconsidered on a priority basis. The endeavour should be to create smaller universities, which are responsive to change and easier to manage.

The system of affiliated colleges for undergraduate education, which may have been appropriate fifty years ago, is no longer adequate or suitable and requires urgent reform. Indeed, there is an imperative need to restructure the system of undergraduate colleges affiliated to universities. The most obvious solution that suggests itself would be to provide autonomy to colleges either as individual colleges, or as clusters of colleges, on the basis of criteria that have been stipulated earlier. However, this would be a viable solution only for a limited proportion, or number, of undergraduate colleges. Some of these affiliated colleges could subsequently be remodelled as community colleges, which could provide both vocational education and formal education. To aid this process, a Central Board of Undergraduate Education should be established, along with State Boards of Undergraduate Education, which would set curricula and conduct examinations for undergraduate colleges that choose to be affiliated with them. These Boards would serve to separate the academic functions from the administrative functions and, at the same time, provide quality benchmarks. New undergraduate colleges could be established as community colleges, or perhaps affiliated with the Central Board of Undergraduate Education or State Boards of Undergraduate Education, or alternatively, could be affiliated with some of the new universities that would be established.

An important function of the higher education system would be to provide for accountability to society and conversely, to create accountability within. A system of expansion of higher education, which would provide students with choices and create competition between institutions is going to be vital in enhancing accountability. There should be stringent information disclosure norms for all educational institutions such as their financial situation, physical assets, admissions criteria, faculty positions, academic curricula, as also their source and level of accreditation. Evaluation of courses and teachers by students as well as peer evaluation of teachers by teachers should be encouraged. Equally important would be a focus on upgrading infrastructure, improving the training of teachers and a continuous assessment of syllabi and examination systems. It is particularly important to enhance the ICT infrastructure. Websites and web-based services would improve transparency and accountability. A portal on higher education and research would increase interaction and accessibility. A knowledge network would connect all universities and colleges for online open resources. It may be necessary to rethink the issue of salary differentials within and between universities along with other means of attracting and retaining talented faculty members. Such salary differentials between and within universities could be effective without being large. It is necessary to formulate appropriate policies for the entry of foreign institutions into India and the promotion of Indian institutions abroad, while ensuring a level playing field for foreign and domestic institutions within the country. The system of higher education must recognize that there is bound to be diversity and pluralism in any system of higher education, and avoid a uniform one-size-fits-all approach. This sense of pluralism must recognize, rather than ignore, or shy away from such diversity and differentiation.

• • •

It is a universally acknowledged fact that education is the fundamental mechanism for social inclusion through the creation of more opportunities. It is, therefore, essential to ensure that no student is denied the opportunity to participate in higher education due to financial constraints. To this end, it would be unlawful for educational institutions to take into account any financial factor while deciding whether or not to admit a student. In addition, there must be a well-funded and extensive National Scholarship Scheme targeting both economically underprivileged students and those from historically socially disadvantaged groups.

A major aim of the higher education system must be to ensure that access to education for economically and historically socially underprivileged students is enhanced in a substantially more effective manner. Reservations are essential, but they are only a part, and one form, of affirmative action. Disparities in educational attainments are related to caste and social groups, but are also strongly related to other indicators such as income, gender, region and place of residence. Therefore, we need to develop a meaningful and comprehensive framework that would account for the multi-dimensionality of differences that still persist. For example, a deprivation index could be used to provide weighted scores to students and the cumulative score could be used to supplement a student's school examination score.

• • •

The recommendations set out by the NKC require action at three different levels: reforms within existing systems, changes in policies, and amendments in, or the introduction of, new statutes or legislation. The suggested changes would also be implemented at three different levels: at the universities, state-government level and the central government. In conclusion, it is important for us to recognize that there is a quiet crisis in higher education in India, which runs deep. Futhermore, the time has come to address this crisis in a systematic, forthright manner. NKC recommendations constitute an important beginning. The changes suggested in these recommendations are essential and would make a real difference. Of course, the process of reform and change is continuous, and there is more to be done. In the last two years the NKC has submitted its recommendations on about twenty issues. These include recommendations in the sphere of professional education for medicine, engineering, law, management, as also vocational education, open and distance education and more recently, school education.

The Eleventh Five-Year-Plan places high priority on education as a central instrument for achieving rapid and inclusive growth with specific emphasis on expansion, excellence and equity. This is reflected in the proposed allocation of Rs. 3 trillion, a five-fold increase over the Tenth Plan. The share of education in the total plan will accordingly increase, from 7.7 per cent to twenty per cent, representing a credible progress towards the target of six per cent of GDP. The vision of the prime minister and support of our leadership from across the political spectrum is indeed laudable. This is a landmark initiative in the history of government planning. There is an urgent need, therefore, to build consensus at all levels to ensure speedy implementation of these ideas. The education agenda outlined in the Eleventh Plan is a critical step towards realizing the objective of an equitable society. It is also fundamental to our continuing growth, employment generation, infrastructure development and other developmental priorities. NKC believes that given the demographic reality of a young India, expansion, inclusion and excellence in higher education can drive economic development and social progress. Indeed, what we do in the sphere of higher education now can transform economy and society in India by 2025.

•

: Sam Pitroda

A management course is considered the acme of Indian higher education.

# Cities and Universities

A university used to be a city – not an enclave, but certainly a domain identifiable not only by its architecture and a particular arrangement of spaces, but also by its own distinct rhythms, of life, of scholastic and cultural activity. In the best instances it was a city at the heart of the larger, 'real' city: a substantial institutional anchor amongst other civic landmarks characteristic of late colonial urbanism – the High Court, the Secretariat, the Civil Lines, public parks and gardens and the cantonment.

Even today, these university buildings or campuses have not lost their place at the metropolitan core, and are inseparable from the city's image – as for example in Bombay, or even in lesser cities such as Baroda, Lucknow or Allahabad. But their urban significance seems to have more to do with nostalgia and, in today's context at least, in the exotic appeal of revivalistic architecture, rather than any strong connection with the life of the city.

In the meanwhile, cities have grown five- to ten-fold, or even more; education, including higher education, attracts investment from the

By **Mohammad Shaheer**

high-profile industrialist world, as well from businessmen who wish to venture into this new and booming market. 'Knowledge Parks' and institutional zones occupy large tracts of formerly agricultural land in the distant suburbs of large cities, as for example in Greater Noida or Gurgaon, or even in remote rural sites as an adjunct to new industrial or commercial zones. Everything has changed – from public to private, and in urban planning terms, from the centre to the fringe, or perhaps to another developing centre.

These universities of the late nineteenth to early twentieth centuries owe their genesis to a colonial imperative, especially the Presidency universities and those at Lucknow, Allahabad and Agra, which were established in the aftermath of the independence struggle of 1857. In the light of what has transpired in the last fifty years, and some hints of the future glimpsed in fragments, it is probably still too early to determine which of these events has had a greater impact on life and culture, at least in the cities in which they flourished, if not in the then United Provinces.

Alumni of a certain generation would confirm the grandeur of these establishments, to be counted amongst the best in India, if not in the Asian region. Allahabad was especially renowned for academic excellence. It was a completely different academic culture. I remember having been able to gather some idea of life at the university through my father, who graduated from there in the mid-1930s. Old photographs in the family album show young undergraduates smartly dressed in the fashion of the period – three-piece suits in tweed or worsted, beautifully knotted ties, lounging in some expansive garden on a mild winter afternoon, sometimes their sartorial glory embellished with a felt hat or scarf, or a casual pipe. That was a time when cigarettes came in round tins of fifty, and pipe-smoking was an affectation of the sophisticated. In other scenes, there might be a photograph with the same people lined up for the studio camera in elegant *sherwanis* and *churidars*, and patent-leather pump shoes gleaming with high polish. Many of the students at university were the sons of 'a social elite which modelled its behaviour pattern and life style on that of the British and the landed aristocracy of the Rajas and Maharajas…'[1]

In their own way, these vignettes were Indian versions of an English original, just like the campuses in which they appeared. Everything about these universities, at least till we knew them up to the mid-twentieth century, was shaped by a particular perception of the English model (represented probably by Oxbridge and others): the buildings, spaces, and of course, academic schemes.

From the architectural point of view, they showcased the best available at the time, in design as well as material. It is quite evident that the building shapes are the result of considerable agonizing over style, material and detail, and a very conscientious desire for them to be not only of India, but also sympathetic to the particular architectural tradition of the city in which they find themselves. 'Indo-Saracenic' is the term used to describe this architecture, but I think there is more to it than that; the sheer extent of building volume, the differences in architectural style from one city to the next, the attention paid to detail and workmanship, and the visual impact of the whole assemblage deserves a more specific descriptive terminology. Expansiveness and generosity was the hallmark of these campuses, whether it was the large spaces between buildings, the quadrangles, or the wide arcades and verandas, there was no meanness or disproportion in the planning; hence, they exuded in their best days, the sense of dignity, reflection and repose appropriate to institutions of higher learning, which we strive for in new campuses today, but seldom achieve.

Yes, they were elite establishments, well supported and patronized by the local *taluqdars*, and they set standards consonant with what the Imperial establishment expected of the native educated elite in the country they ruled. The British didn't know it at the time, but rather than colonial administrators, these universities would produce the future academics and administrators of independent India. And naturally, because of the ambiguity between intention and actual result, our educated elite would be under what we cheerfully know as 'the colonial hangover' for at least two generations.

The aristocratic connection is often reflected in the style of architecture – the buildings are reminiscent of palaces. In Allahabad there is a rather heavy monumentality, owing more to Europe than India, but in Lucknow, the lighter brick and plaster style is in harmony with Avadh architecture. About this, Francis Robinson,[2] describing Harcourt Butler's term of duty as governor from 1918 to 1922 writes,

> he had driven the legislation establishing the University of Lucknow through the Senate of Allahabad University and the UP Legislative Council. Moreover, 250,000 pounds sterling had been raised in large part from the *taluqdars*; Sir Edwin Lutyens had designed the building...

which could be an exciting discovery, were it not that other sources have Sir Swinton Jacob as the architect.[3]

My memories of Lucknow span the late 1950s to the mid-1960s. One was familiar with the university, and close by, the fashionable shopping centre of Hazratgunj. But I became aware of their planned relationship and larger significance in the city many, many years later, even though for a year towards the end of my school education I cycled every morning and afternoon up and down the axis joining them, and which Imtiaz Ahmad has called the central vista of Lucknow[4]:

> 'Hazratganj', the street of the respectable, refers to a part of a central vista, which runs from the bungalows of the senior bureaucrats of the Secretariat... at one end and Lucknow University and Isabella Thoburn College at the other...

The route was from La Martiniere College to the suburb of Mahanagar, approximately aligned north to south and covered a distance of some five or six kilometres. The presence of the university campus registered itself as an area of leafy calmness, expansive greenery and very well-proportioned pale yellow buildings, with cusped arches surmounted by a skyline of a variety of quite elegant onion-shaped domes. It was different from every other area in Lucknow. In fact the whole street, right up to Isabella Thoburn College, a distance of about two kilometres, I would imagine, had at that time a distinctively pleasing appearance and feel. It was an interesting event on the journey, anticipated for the visual delight it offered everyday. It was, in a sense, an academic street, right in the middle of the city: Isabella Thoburn College at one end, Lucknow University on the eastern side of the street and the large campus of Colvin Taluqdar College opposite, on the west.

There was a strong social connection between the colleges and Hazratgunj; there had to be, with a large student population in close proximity. This relationship manifested itself in a phenomenon unique to Lucknow, known in local parlance as 'gunjing', a sort of promenade up and down this spacious shopping street, in the company of one's friends. Imtiaz Ahmad describes it nicely: '...it came to denote a compulsive urge to go to Hazratganj for a couple of hours in the evening as an act of personal recreation. It was a common sight to see hordes of youngsters walking up and down, cracking jokes, chatting and engaging in mild taunts... Even in homes where boys and girls were brought up in strict discipline and denied the freedom to stay late out of doors, an allowance was made for them to spend a couple of hours dawdling about Hazratganj.

Nothing is the same any more. Is it a coincidence that the glory of these academic palaces didn't last for more than a decade or two (at best) after Independence? Perhaps the way they had been conceived didn't fit well with the economic and social changes initiated in the 1950s, which gathered momentum in later decades and of whose effects most of us have first-hand experience of today. Certainly the interest of youth in politics and vice versa took its toll; whilst these institutions were entering a kind of academic stasis (other, perhaps socially destructive, kinds of life went on), the 1950s saw new prototypes, the IITs and later, the IIMs which were to flourish and thrive from year to year and acquire international stature. Was it because they were born in independent India, free of colonial perceptions and preconceptions? There are probably many other reasons.

The impetus to university education was part of a concerted reconstruction, rehabilitation and development plan of the British for two decades after the widespread destruction and carnage of 1857, in the hope of consolidating their Imperial project.

Today's explosive growth in the higher education sector has come about after almost three decades of relative somnolence; it promises unlimited possibilities, but are some opportunities for creating new kinds of academic environments being missed? Some things we can certainly remember in our Knowledge Parks and institutional zones: an institution is not an enclave or a gated community, its rightful place is not in a zone of commercial or industrial establishments in some far-flung suburb, just because it is profitable or expedient in real estate terms. An educational zone comprising many separate institutions does not have to be planned like a plotted industrial estate. Unfortunately, these are the kinds of shapes many of our future academic environments are now acquiring.

Institutions are vital to the life of a city; easily enough said, but what does that mean, and how do you ensure that it happens, so that you get better cities and better institutions? There are implications of access and inclusiveness, of built-in planning linkages in the form of common spaces, pedestrian movement and other infrastructure to encourage social interaction, recreation and community life. These kinds of objectives are possible only with a nuanced, socially conscious planning approach, which sees the full integration of university campuses with the social and physical fabric of the city as a desirable goal.

•

ENDNOTES:

1. Imtiaz Ahmad; 'Through the Eye of a Street', *Lucknow: Memories of a City*, Violette Graff, editor, Oxford University Press, 1999.
2. Francis Robinson, 'The Re-emergence of Lucknow as a Major Political Centre', *Lucknow: Memories of a City*, Violette Graff, editor, Oxford University Press, 1999.
3. *Lucknow*, compiled by The American Women's Club, Lucknow, Lucknow Publishing House, 1968.
4. Imtiaz Ahmad, *ibid.*

PHOTO ESSAY:

# Campus Styles: Presidency Universities, 1857-2007

PHOTOS COURTESY: **The National Archives of India, New Delhi**

# ACT No. XXII of 1857.

PASSED BY THE LEGISLATIVE COUNCIL OF INDIA.

*(Received the assent of the Governor General on the 18th July 1857.)*

AN ACT *to establish and incorporate an University at Bombay.*

Preamble.

WHEREAS, for the better encouragement of Her Majesty's subjects of all classes and denominations within the Presidency of Bombay and other parts of India in the pursuit of a regular and liberal course of education, it has been determined to establish an University at Bombay for the purpose of ascertaining, by means of examination, the persons who have acquired proficiency in different branches of Literature, Science, and Art, and of rewarding them by Academical Degrees as evidence of their respective attainments, and marks of honor proportioned thereunto; and whereas, for effectuating the purposes aforesaid, it is expedient that such University should be incorporated; It is enacted as follows: (that is to say)—

Incorporation.

I. The following persons, namely,

The Right Honorable JOHN, LORD ELPHINSTONE,
Governor of Bombay.

The Honorable Sir WILLIAM YARDLEY, Knight,
Chief Justice of the Supreme Court of Judicature at Bombay.

The Right Reverend JOHN HARDING,
Doctor of Divinity, Bishop of Bombay, *Ex-officio.*

The Honorable SIR HENRY SOMERSET, Lieutenant-General,
Knight Companion of the Most Honorable Order of the Bath,
Commander-in-Chief of the Forces in Bombay, *Ex-officio.*

COURTESY: THE NATIONAL ARCHIVES OF INDIA, NEW DELHI

**1. Act No. XXII of 1857**

A page from the Act establishing and incorporating a University at Bombay, 18 July 1857.

**2. Elphinstone Circle, Bombay**

: The National Archives of India, New Delhi

COURTESY: UNIVERSITY OF MUMBAI

Later renamed Horniman Circle, it was designed on the lines of London's Park Crescent, in a neo–classical style.

COURTESY: UNIVERSITY OF MUMBAI

**3. Rajabai Tower, Bombay**

Inspired by Gietto's Campanile in Florence and now the university library, this 280 ft. tower is offset with 8 statues that represent the Indian castes.

: The National Archives of India, New Delhi

COURTESY: UNIVERSITY OF MUMBAI

**4. Detail of Rajabai Tower**

The strong Gothic style, with elaborate arches and gargoyles are a distinctive aspect of Rajabai Tower. Detail of a statue that adorns the building.

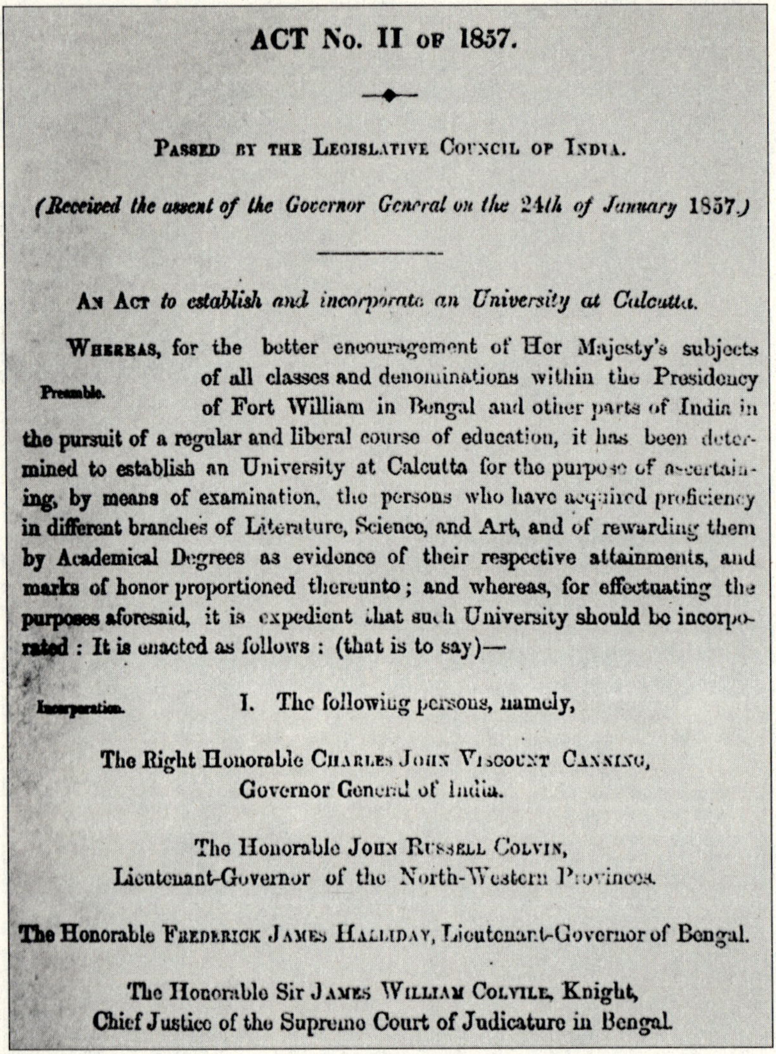

# ACT No. II OF 1857.

PASSED BY THE LEGISLATIVE COUNCIL OF INDIA.

*(Received the assent of the Governor General on the 24th of January 1857.)*

AN ACT *to establish and incorporate an University at Calcutta.*

Preamble.

WHEREAS, for the better encouragement of Her Majesty's subjects of all classes and denominations within the Presidency of Fort William in Bengal and other parts of India in the pursuit of a regular and liberal course of education, it has been determined to establish an University at Calcutta for the purpose of ascertaining, by means of examination, the persons who have acquired proficiency in different branches of Literature, Science, and Art, and of rewarding them by Academical Degrees as evidence of their respective attainments, and marks of honor proportioned thereunto; and whereas, for effectuating the purposes aforesaid, it is expedient that such University should be incorporated: It is enacted as follows: (that is to say)—

Incorporation.

I. The following persons, namely,

The Right Honorable CHARLES JOHN VISCOUNT CANNING,
Governor General of India.

The Honorable JOHN RUSSELL COLVIN,
Lieutenant-Governor of the North-Western Provinces.

The Honorable FREDERICK JAMES HALLIDAY, Lieutenant-Governor of Bengal.

The Honorable Sir JAMES WILLIAM COLVILE, Knight,
Chief Justice of the Supreme Court of Judicature in Bengal.

COURTESY: THE NATIONAL ARCHIVES OF INDIA, NEW DELHI

**5. Act No. II of 1857**

A page from the Act establishing and incorporating a University at Calcutta, 24 January 1857.

: The National Archives of India, New Delhi

COURTESY: UNIVERSITY OF CALCUTTA

**6. Presidency College, Calcutta**

Illustration: Rathin Mitra

Founded in 1817 as Hindu College, it was renamed as the Presidency College in 1855; one among the first group of constituent colleges of the University of Calcutta.

COURTESY: UNIVERSITY OF CALCUTTA

**7. The Senate House**

Illustration: Rathin Mitra

Erected in 1872, the Senate House was the first habitation of the University of Calcutta. It used to provide the venue for Senate meetings, the chamber of the vice chancellor, offices of the registrar and also examination and lecture halls. It was demolished in 1960.

: The National Archives of India, New Delhi

COURTESY: UNIVERSITY OF CALCUTTA

**8. Asutosh Building–College Street Campus**

Illustration: Rathin Mitra

Opened in 1926, this gracious building accommodates the postgraduate language and literature departments and the department of commerce.

## ACT No. XXVII OF 1857.

PASSED BY THE LEGISLATIVE COUNCIL OF INDIA.

*(Received the assent of the Governor General on the 5th September 1857.)*

AN ACT *to establish and incorporate an University at Madras.*

Preamble.

WHEREAS, for the better encouragement of Her Majesty's subjects of all classes and denominations within the Presidency of Fort St. George and other parts of India in the pursuit of a regular and liberal course of education, it has been determined to establish an University at Madras for the purpose of ascertaining, by means of examination, the persons who have acquired proficiency in different branches of Literature, Science, and Art, and of rewarding them by Academical Degrees as evidence of their respective attainments, and marks of honor proportioned thereunto; and whereas, for effectuating the purposes aforesaid, it is expedient that such University should be incorporated: It is enacted as follows: (that is to say)—

Incorporation.

I. The following persons, namely,

The Right Honorable GEORGE FRANCIS ROBERT, LORD HARRIS,
Governor of Fort St. George.

The Honorable SIR CHRISTOPHER RAWLINSON, Knight,
Chief Justice of the Supreme Court of Judicature at Madras.

The Right Reverend THOMAS DEALTRY,
Doctor of Divinity, Bishop of Madras, *Ex-officio.*

The Honorable SIR PATRICK GRANT, Lieutenant-General, Knight Commander of the Most Honorable Order of the Bath,
Commander-in-Chief of the Forces in Madras, *Ex-officio.*

COURTESY: THE NATIONAL ARCHIVES OF INDIA, NEW DELHI

**9. Act No. XXVII of 1857**

A page from the Act establishing and incorporating a University at Madras, 5 September 1857.

: The National Archives of India, New Delhi

COURTESY: VINTAGE VIGNETTES

**10. Presidency College, Madras**

The handsome buildings of Presidency College into which the students moved in 1870-71. To build this Indo-Italianate building is why Robert Chisholm came to Madras. This early twentieth century picture was taken long before the centenary dome and clock 'capped' the building.

**11. Law College, Madras**

: The National Archives of India, New Delhi

COURTESY: UNIVERSITY OF MADRAS

Law college, whose students moved from Presidency College in 1891-92 into these buildings that had been designed for them in the Indo-Saracenic manner by Henry Irwin. Law classes started in Presidency College in 1855, but Law College began functioning in May 1891 from the same campus.

COURTESY: SIMON FELTON/UNIVERSITY OF MADRAS

**12 & 13. Queen Elizabeth II at University of Madras**

: The National Archives of India, New Delhi

COURTESY: SIMON FELTON/UNIVERSITY OF MADRAS

Queen Elizabeth II and Prince Philip visited the University of Madras in February 1961 and were warmly received in Senate House by a large invited audience. She was ceremoniously led in (left) and then presided over a sumptous tea (right).

COURTESY: UNIVERSITY OF MADRAS

**14. Meenakshi College**

A majestic view of the Meenakshi College founded in 1920 near Chidambaram and affiliated to the University of Madras.

: The National Archives of India, New Delhi

COURTESY: UNIVERSITY OF MADRAS

**15. University of Madras**

The Library and Clock Tower blocks in the Chepauk campus.

**16. University of Madras**

: The National Archives of India, New Delhi

COURTESY: UNIVERSITY OF MADRAS

All ablaze in light and colour, the Senate House of the University of Madras still dominates the city's skyline.

# 2: The Scaffolding

# Declining Simplistic Narratives*

The American writer and performing artist Garrison Keillor used to have a radio show featuring a Malgudi-like imaginary town called Lake Wobegon, which he repeatedly referred to with the trademark refrain: 'where the women are strong, the men are good looking and the children are all above average'. Going by the overall tenor of the Fourth Review Committee's report on the Indian Council of Social Science Research (ICSSR), Indian social science research today is so woebegone that it has become a place where 'the institutions are weak, the research looks bad and the researchers are all below average'.

This is not what the review report is really saying, at least not exactly, but even if it were, not many would feel moved to protest. And

* First published in *Economic and Political Weekly*, 2 February 2008.

By **Satish Deshpande**

those that do would limit themselves to the counter-claim that there are at least some and perhaps many good researchers, or some such qualifying proviso. The truth is, it takes little effort to evoke a gloomy response where Indian social science – or even higher education in general – are concerned. We know that there is much to be gloomy about; it is the odd case of optimism that requires explanation.

• • •

But surely the very ubiquity of poor opinion should give us pause as social scientists and awaken the principled scepticism that counts among the most useful tools of our trade. Because the 'decline narrative' is so much a part of the Indian higher education scene today, we need to be careful not to take it at face value, at least not prematurely.[1] One may not necessarily disagree with the review report's verdict that virtually no Indian research institution is 'vibrant'. However, it would have been both interesting and instructive had the report provided some comparative descriptions and data on institutions that could indeed be so described. Given the inevitably strong 'you know it when you see it' element in notions such as vibrancy, it is all the more necessary to think about the empirical (but not only quantitative) signs by which they may be recognized. If something is both important and absent, and if its absence forms the main criterion for an evaluation, then it is only fair to provide a contrast class; if only as a brief illustration. This may actually be more important for those who agree with an adverse evaluation than for those who disagree, because it would reveal the amount of care taken in arriving at the judgment.

A second, and more important, concern is the overall solution to the ICSSR'S problems that is suggested by the report. While it is to be commended for its boldness in proposing a radical solution – in effect, the virtual dissolution of the council in its present form – the report seems unduly sanguine about the proposed alternative.

The fact that we have ourselves been responsible for many of the ills that we deplore, including the erosion of autonomy vis-a-vis the state, is a bitter pill for academics to swallow. If it is our own colleagues who have been complicit in creating or exacerbating problems in the past, how will we ensure that this does not happen again with the proposed Indian Academy of Social Sciences? This may well be one of those rhetorical 'who will guard the guards?' questions which cannot really be answered. It would nevertheless have helped to take it seriously and to think about possible safeguards, beyond and different from those implied in the summary of the organizational structure of the proposed Academy on pages 71–72.

Although its mandate is restricted to the ICSSR and its institutes, the report does begin with a broader view. Moreover, it comes at a time when the Eleventh Plan is primed to pump unprecedentedly large sums of money into the higher education sector. And while the Moily Committee's report may have faded from public memory, the major changes that it has proposed are probably only dormant rather than extinct. The University Grants Commission, too, is initiating bold moves to reinvigorate research in the universities. Foreign universities and other private initiatives are intensifying their efforts to become significant players in the Indian higher education scene. All in all, this is a good time to be thinking about higher education and research.

• • •

The first question to be tackled is that of priorities, and it is not an easy one. Do we want to ensure the production of good research, or do we want to nurture good research institutions? It may seem strange to pit two seemingly inseparable objectives against each other, but this is indeed the essence of the choice that globalized higher education forces upon us. It is not necessary to debate the meaning of 'good' in this particular context; whatever one may mean by it, the point is that the global present tends to stack the odds in a particular way. The key factor here is that good research need not be done in good institutions, specially if it is project-driven. 'Virtual' institutions – intellectually empty administrative shells that house a succession of projects, or that function as 'field offices' for institutions located elsewhere – are perfectly capable of producing good research of almost any variety. In fact, they have been doing so for a long time, and are also far better adapted to current intellectual trends and funding fashions.

It is even possible in these global times for a handful of individuals to choose the 'independent scholar' route, which used to be mainly an imposed identity in the past. This allows incumbents to exercise intellectual authority while divesting oneself entirely of all institutional responsibility. As with other locations in the intellectual field, this one too has its attendant pros and cons.

Research institutions – as different from research products – suffer from decisive disadvantages in this evolutionary race that is being played out in electronic rather than biological time. We know much more about how to produce good research than about creating and sustaining good institutions. Much of our wisdom about the latter tends to be both retrospective and tautological; institutions work when they do and do not when they do not.

Faced with this difficult terrain, it is easy to be tempted by the robust common sense of simple, strong remedies. Decreasing security of tenure and increasing funding are the most common, and it is understandable that they duly make their appearance in the ICSSR review report as well. Is there enough evidence, however, to establish that the shortcomings of research institutions are due mainly to excessive job security or lack of funds? The answer may seem self-evident in these liberalized times, but the question deserves further scrutiny.

• • •

Try this thought experiment: How many good research proposals – not great ideas or dream projects, but worked out proper proposals – do you know of that remained unborn for want of financial support? If you can think of some, try to analyze all the reasons why they never took off. In the hierarchy of numerous problems in social science research, the lack of good research proposals has always ranked much higher in recent times than lack of funds per se. And as for the virtues of insecurity, would you or other competent researchers you know prefer a short-term terminal contract to a secure job, even if the former pays more? If you are able to think of any such researchers, count the number that do not fall in the following categories: (a) freshers looking for their first academic job; (b) retired academics seeking remunerative short-term assignments; (c) faculty members of foreign universities on sabbaticals; or (d) local bureaucrats or university faculty on study leave.

This is not to deny that the State ought to spend much more on social science research, or that our universities and research institutions contain lots of dead wood. But these are not the primary reasons why they fail to be 'vibrant'. Every successful institution would have had its share of funding and personnel problems. We need to understand the possible reasons why they manage to prevail despite such difficulties. And what we need even more are good critical descriptions of such success stories that go beyond the nostalgic pleasures of golden age narratives and black box invocations of brilliance.

One of the paradoxes (or is it principles?) of policy-making is that we tend to plan for the extreme end of the spectrum, i.e., the best possible outcome. As the saying goes, life is what happens to you while you are busy planning for it. Even though we know that most people and most institutions live most of their lives in normal rather than inspired mode, when making plans we tend to plan only for the latter. But it is the ordinary times between bouts of inspiration that keep individuals and institutions going. Perhaps the key to understanding extraordinary events and brilliant individuals lies in intimate knowledge of the everyday and the average. It is not helpful to describe the average as 'not brilliant' or 'below expectations'; we need detailed evaluations of the concrete content of the average, for there are better and worse ways of being so.

• • •

It is often lamented that both researchers and research in India are far less 'professional' then they ought to be. There is a well known and largely justified series of complaints: Deadlines are not met, budgets are under spent or overrun, work is shoddy, and so on. Even though struggles with these frustrating features have been such a familiar part of our professional lives, we still seem to lack good, objective (dare one say professional?) descriptions. Useful descriptions of this sort are hard to produce for they lack the convenience and certainty of numbers as well as the gravity and glamour of important or extraordinary events. At the same time, it is always tempting to slip back into different versions of the 'they are like that only' essentialism.

With the benefit of hindsight, it is clear that periods of intellectual effervescence tend to be associated with larger societal moods and movements. But since such things are obviously independent variables we must concentrate on those that we may hope to influence. Perhaps the most critical of these are the elusive mediating factors that allow the channelizing of societal energies into realizable intellectual projects. It is not as though we live in less interesting times than our predecessors. But to understand the possible reasons why the academy remains largely impervious to the tumult around it we need to review recent social trends. Two of these are changes in the social composition of the academy and intergenerational shifts.

• • •

It is hardly news today that new castes and classes are entering the world of higher education for the first time. Their entry is overlapping with the unrelated exit of the old elites who now prefer the western academy and tend to migrate there much sooner than they did earlier, i.e., at the undergraduate or even high school levels rather than the postgraduate or doctoral levels common until the 1980s. The influx of the non-metropolitan and non-elite entrants is creating frictions in institutions long accustomed to smooth functioning lubricated by social homogeneity. The entry of women in larger numbers is another important process of change with its own distinctive profiles. While the 'feminization' of some elite enclaves of higher education with the entry of upper caste/class women is made much of, it is important to remember that the process is very uneven and far from complete when one looks at social science research as a whole. However, the kinds of friction caused are different because of the different caste/class composition of women entering higher education.

Like the old elite, the new entrants too come in search of credentials and careers rather than causes and vocations. But because of the mismatch between the teaching body and the student body, and because of the changes in the larger environment, it is harder for these institutions to do the mediating work by which at least a few are inspired to choose social research as a 'paid vocation'. Once this begins to happen, one can perhaps expect a shift in intellectual agendas and research projects as the new incumbents deploy their mix of acquired and inherited skills. Trying to figure out how institutions can connect with their new publics is clearly a very big challenge. But while much is heard about those who are voting with their visas or succumbing to corporate greed, one hardly comes across any suggestions for constructive engagement with the new groups coming into the academy. One indication of how far we have to go is the rarity of significant collective efforts at working with Indian languages in both teaching and research.

• • •

Another unexamined issue is that of generational change. To be more precise, this is actually about different stages in the life cycles of institutions. The generations that entered public institutions including the academy in the 1950s and 1960s were, by sheer historical luck, part of a once only experience. They were the generation that occupied new, expanding – and 'empty' – state structures. Resources were not plentiful and times were tough in many ways. But there was room and to spare at the top. The more successful segment of this generation retained positions of authority, power and eminence for nearly three decades. Their own predecessors were few and were part of a very different colonial era; whatever the length of the intellectual shadows they cast, they could not 'crowd' the younger generation in organizational or career terms.

By contrast, later generations have had to move in a much more resistant medium and, share intellectual and institutional space with much larger numbers. Perhaps this is one structural reason why earlier generations of intellectuals seem so much more 'singular'. How did these contingent facts of national and organizational history, influence research agendas and the health of institutions? This is hardly a rhetorical question, for it is not as though either the advantages or the disadvantages were all on one side.

It is questions like these that we need to address afresh if we wish to understand the present and specially the future of social science research in Indian institutions. But what we need above all is to cultivate a critical self-reflexivity – an awareness of who 'we' are and where we stand when asking and answering such questions.

•

: Satish Deshpande

ENDNOTE:

1. See 'Decline and Crisis', Chapter I of P. Chatterjee, *et al*, *Social Science Research Capacity in South Asia: A Report*, SSRC Working Paper Series, Vol. 6, Social Science Research Council, New York.

# A Different Degree

The concept of the Indian Institute of Technology (IIT) originated at a time when India was yet to gain Independence shortly after the end of the Second World War. At that crucial juncture, we were fortunate enough to have a visionary of the stature of Sir Ardeshir Dalal on the Viceroy's Executive Council. With rare foresight, Sir Ardeshir anticipated that the future prosperity of India would depend not so much on capital as on technology and proposed the setting up of the Council of Scientific and Industrial Research (CSIR). In order to man those laboratories, he persuaded the U.S. government to offer hundreds of doctoral fellowships under the Technology Cooperation Mission (TCM) programme. He was aware that such assistance would be merely temporary, and we would eventually need to learn to train our own technologists. Today, few recall that Sir Ardeshir Dalal was the true progenitor of the concept of an IIT.

By **P.V. Indiresan**

*My sons Quit India last year—went away to the US, the UK, Australia...!*

Dr. Humayun Kabir, a tsar of education, mooted Sir Ardeshir's proposal for an IIT to Dr. B. C. Roy, the chief minister of Bengal, perhaps prompted by Sir J. C. Ghosh, then director of the Indian Institute of Science, Bangalore. As was usual in government, Dr. Kabir appointed a committee to prepare a proposal, and appointed Sir N. Sarkar as the chairman. This was virtually an all-Bengali clique, but a respectable one. Like most committees, the Sarkar

Courtesy: R.K. Laxman / *The Times of India*

Committee too took its own time, but as Dr. Roy was in a hurry he did not wait for the committee to finalize its report. On the grounds that Bengal had the highest concentration of engineering industries, the draft report of the committee had suggested that an IIT may be set up in that state. Roy used that fragment of a report to persuade Pandit Nehru to push through a special Act to establish an IIT in Bengal. As an inducement, the Hijli Jail in Kharagpur was offered as a readymade location for the Institute. Thus was born the IIT at Kharagpur.

The Sarkar Committee never submitted its final report, yet the premature institute at Kharagpur was lucky in that it had some remarkable midwives to assist its birth. Unlike the usual run of bureaucrats who tend to cling to power, L. S. Chandrakant and Biman Sen in the Ministry of Education produced a blueprint for a level of autonomy, the like of which has not been seen since then in our country. Due credit must also be given to Sir J. C. Ghosh, the first director of IIT Kharagpur who used his exalted stature and the liberal provisions of the IIT Act by making the IIT truly free of the nitpicking interference of babus. It is to his credit that till today, directors of IITs are able to exercise authority to an extent unheard of almost anywhere else in the government. They are virtually free to select faculty, apportion the budget, and make purchases as they judge best. Except for a couple of aberrant occasions, they have been left free to manage academic programmes without political or bureaucratic interference. However, these days, there is increasing political interference in admitting students, and lately even in faculty appointments.

It is logical to suppose that there must have been some resistance within the Sarkar Committee to the recommendation to locate the IIT in Bengal. To counter such criticism, the Draft Report suggested the location of a second IIT in the western region to serve the process industries concentrated there. This draft report contained a few pages of sensible proposals along with a hundred pages of how a hydraulic laboratory should be set up! Apparently, at the instance of this erudite expert, it added that a third IIT should be considered for the north to promote the vast irrigation potential of the Gangetic basin. As an afterthought, unwilling to leave out the south, the Draft Report hinted that a fourth one might be considered for that region. However, unlike for the other regions, it offered no specific economic justification for the same. Curiously enough, in technology development, it is the south that has forged ahead of the other regions. In course of time, the pressure began to build for a second IIT in the west. In response, Nehru suggested seeking Soviet assistance and Krishna Menon, who was closest to the Russians, and also then our defence minister, appointed Brigadier Bose as the first director of IIT, Bombay. Bose superseded the local expert, Dr. Kelkar, who was quite naturally miffed. Fortunately, as a fallout of the prevailing Cold War, the Americans offered to help to set up yet another IIT. On the suggestions of the Sarkar Committee, this one was located in the north, in Kanpur, with Dr. Kelkar as its first director.

Naturally, the south could not lag behind. At that time, the Germans had run up large trade surpluses, and they were persuaded to support an IIT in the south. The Germans had all but decided on Bangalore as the location and, purely as a matter of form, visited Madras. There, they were in for a surprise. C. Subramaniam, the Tamil Nadu education minister took them around the governor's estate, with deer frolicking among hundreds of venerable banyan trees, and offered them the space across the table. The visiting German team was bowled over, Bangalore was forgotten, and Madras acquired the fourth IIT.

About this time, Chandigarh was being developed as a fully planned city with R. N. Dogra as its chief engineer. Being upright and honest, Dogra fell foul of Chief Minister Pratap Singh Kairon and shifted to the new college of engineering that was coming up in Delhi. He soon realized that the IITs were a class above a mere engineering college. So he persuaded Professor M. S. Thacker, then Member of the Planning Commission, to set up an IIT at Delhi. Dogra's argument was that the country was divided into five regions, and every region but the northern had an IIT each. (UP and Madhya Pradesh constituted the central region. Hence, officially, Kanpur was located in the central region, not the northern one.)

• • •

The commonest criticism once levelled at the IITs was that most of its students emigrated. Fortunately, a greater acceptance of globalization, and the realization that IIT expatriates have made some useful contribution to national economy and even more to national prestige have mellowed such critics. In fact, IITs are undoubtedly the best-known Indian brand across the world. However, it is a commonly held belief that the blame for the phenomenon of the brain drain lies squarely and exclusively with the IITs. Few appreciate the fact that it is the professional and economic environment that makes talented youth – whether they are graduates of the IITs or carpenters or nurses – emigrate. They also fail to remember that a significant majority of IIT graduates choose to remain in India, and many have attained exalted positions against heavy odds. The chiefs of some of the country's largest firms – Hindustan Lever, ITC, TISCO, Tata Industries, the NIIT – are all IIT graduates. Among their alumni is one cabinet minister at the Centre; a former chief minister of Goa; the much admired philosopher entrepreneur, Narayana Murthy; the highly vocal Kiran Bedi, two high profile sanyasins, and a top musician of Carnatic style. Several IIT alumni have effaced themselves and are working in conditions of great hardship promoting rural welfare. Considering that the IITs constitute barely 0.1 per cent of India's higher education system, that is an impressive roll call indeed.

IIT graduates are often criticized for forsaking their profession and/or the country they were trained to serve. But perhaps, in all fairness, we should also admit that it is we who often drive them away. Though India has, in recent times, has elevated an engineer to become the president of India, in general, the status of engineers in India is very pitiable. For instance, whom would you prefer as a son-in-law: a design engineer perfecting the cryogenic engine for ISRO or a marketing executive of a multinational? At best, Information Technology has some glamour; other fields command little respect. It is little wonder that IIT graduates opt out.

The migration of talented youth has been the norm in all countries and in all ages. There is a deep-seated economic reason why poor countries export talented people. It is all due to a fundamental principle known as the Law of Comparative Advantage. To take an example, it costs Rs. 1,000,000 to train an IIT graduate, and Rs. 50,000 to buy a notebook computer. That is, in India, one IIT graduate equals the price of twenty notebook computers. In the U.S., it costs 200,000 dollars to train an engineering graduate and only 1000 dollars to buy a notebook computer. Hence, in the U.S., a first-rate engineer equates to 200 notebook computers. Then, consider the exchange of one IIT graduate with sixty notebook computers from the U.S. India will then be three times better off: it will get three times more notebooks for each IIT engineer traded. The U.S. too profits – it gets slightly more than three times more engineers in return for the notebooks it sells. Thus, both countries benefit financially when India exports engineers in exchange for computers. This peculiar transaction is the result of the U.S. valuing engineers high, while valuing notebooks relatively low. In contrast, we value notebooks high and engineers low. So long as this disparity prevails, the natural flow will dictate the migration of Indian engineers and of notebooks being imported.

Those who are exercised about brain drain should first rectify this bias, and start valuing and honouring engineers more. As Christiansen, long-time editor of the journal of the Institute of Electrical and Electronics Engineers said:

> A country that trains its engineers and technologists well, then rewards them with both real and psychic income, should have little trouble competing in a world economy that thrives on trading high quality, high-tech products over international boundaries.

Such a country would also have little cause to worry about brain drain.

The IITs have succeeded in an ocean of mediocrity because, by and large, they have enjoyed the three basic freedoms of an educational institution: freedom to choose whom to teach, who will teach, and what to teach. The IITs also enjoyed full-cost budgetary support. However, it is important to remember that the IITs will remain successful only so long as these amenities are allowed to remain. Also remember that the IITs can state with full confidence that not once in fifty years have they had any significant student problem. IIT students never ask for holidays, nor complain about 'tough' question papers. IIT faculty take on chores and responsibilities that few teachers elsewhere would bother to undertake with no complaint about the workload. That is why both IIT teachers and students are accepted as models in academic culture.

• • •

It is nobody's argument that our IITs are perfect, or even that they are proper role models for universities to follow. At the same time, it is widely accepted that the IITs are performing better than most universities. So, it follows that the IITs must have some useful features that ought to be worth emulating. By all accounts, Indian universities are unwilling to learn.

In terms of size, IITs are small; the output from all IITs taken together is barely a hundredth of the national output of engineering graduates. The earnings of IITs through research grants, consultancy and endowments are substantial, approaching Rs. 100 crores a year in some cases. Considering how minuscule the size of any IIT is, with enrolment a small fraction of a typical university, all these add up to a creditable record of achievement. IIT graduates are prominent even in the IAS and dominate equally in admissions to the Indian Institutes of Management (IIMs).

In the U.S., every year about a hundred young scientists are selected for what is known as the President's Young Scientists' Award. Year after year, around ten per cent of them have gone to IIT graduates. That is a disproportionately large share even after taking into account the large number of IIT graduates who study in the U.S. Recently, the prestigious American journal, *The Business Week* ran a cover-page story about the extraordinary success of IIT graduates in American boardrooms where several IITians have become chief executives. Several IIT graduates have done well as entrepreneurs too; some of them are self-made near-billionaires. The U.S. Congress has gone so far as to pass a special resolution commending the IITs for their contribution to the progress of the U.S.

There are several basic reasons to which we may attribute the success of the IITs. For instance, classes are held regularly from day one till the last day of each semester. It is a rule in the IITs that each semester *must* complete a specified number of teaching days. If, for any reason, classes are not held on any day, that must be compensated by working an extra day during a regular holiday. That is why IIT students never ask for holidays; they know that will merely mean their losing a scheduled holiday. In contrast, it is not unknown for some colleges to complete not even 30-40 teaching days in a year. Next, examinations and tests in IITs are continuous and results are announced promptly, generally within a couple of days. In contrast, there are universities in India where results are delayed for more than a year. IITs update syllabi regularly; no semester ever passes by without some innovation or other in the design and content of the courses taught. A significant number among the faculty are engaged in research and consultancy.

All these bespeak a high level of internal discipline. Strange as it may appear, all that discipline is not the result of tight control but due to enormous freedom, as the faculty at every IIT enjoys an exceptional degree of autonomy. In general, they are free to set their own syllabus, set their own test papers, are even free *not* to hold a conventional examination at all, and instead, adopt other methods for evaluating students. They enjoy considerable financial autonomy too – even junior faculty are free to accept large research and consultancy projects worth millions and operate those funds with a freedom denied even to principals of most colleges. IIT faculty are free to take off, on an average, one day a week for their own consultancy work and keep most of the earnings themselves – there is no upper limit to what they can earn.

Even the worst critics of the IITs would have to concede that academically, the IITs are outstanding institutions. Have they served the country well? On balance, yes! Most teachers in engineering colleges have been trained in the IITs, admittedly at the master's level. Through such teachers and otherwise, the IITs have set standards for all other engineering institutions to follow, and have contributed to making the quality of engineering education across the length and breadth of India as good as it is. It is entirely due to the excellence of the IITs that India has made the mark it has in software and in a number of other technologies.

The IITs pioneered and perfected the mechanism of impersonal entrance examinations for admitting students that has given them an enviable reputation for integrity and objectivity. However, of late, the system has shown signs of becoming out of date, with the Joint Entrance Examination (JEE) becoming trainable. A large number of coaching institutions have proliferated and are distorting the admission process by generating an unmanageable number of candidates. Even the finest institutions in the U.S., such as Harvard and MIT, admit barely one in ten among the applicants. In the IITs, that number is approaching one in a hundred. This is a disproportionately high number to properly assess the aspirants. One single mark can change the rank by several hundred places.

The popular view remains that one single entrance test should decide entry to professional institutions. Aspiring students and their parents as well as many educators feel that the multiplicity of entrance tests places an unacceptable burden on aspiring candidates, and that a common entrance test is the best way to normalize the varying standards of different school boards. They point out to the existence of such common tests as SAT, GRE, GMAT, *et al*, in the U.S. They forget that none of these tests are arbiters of admission: they are only guides.

There are several reasons for this and the fact remains that having one entrance test is akin to putting all one's eggs into one basket. For instance, any accident, such as the leakage of question papers – a situation that is bound to occur sooner or later – will throw the entire mechanism out of gear. Next, a common entrance test will have only a total of 400 marks, not sufficient to discriminate individually the 400,000 places that are now approved for engineering. Moreover, written tests are not sufficiently good criteria for identifying talent. Since the JEE has become trainable, it confers an undue advantage on the rich who can afford to pay for coaching classes.

Howard Gardner postulates that intelligence includes eight dimensions: factual, arithmetic, analytic, linguistic, athletic, artistic, intuitive, and emotional. Currently, IIT entrance examinations test only the analytic and arithmetic skills and, to a small extent, English language comprehension. It is indeed difficult to hold large-scale tests in the other dimensions of intelligence. Schools themselves are best equipped to do so. Unfortunately, admission exclusively through entrance tests sets a negligible value to the opinion of the schools in the selection of candidates.

This indifference to performance at the school level is peculiar to India. In other countries, recommendations from school teachers and the reputation of the schools themselves carry much weight. In contrast, the IITs are making a fundamental error by denying admission to the finest students by relying totally on an entrance test, with no value given to school performance and education. On the other hand, when their own students are admitted to Stanford or MIT, the recommendations of the faculty and the reputation of the IITs themselves serve as deciding factors.

Professor Parkinson, who analyzed the problem of selections in his own inimitable and humorous way, has explained why the admission criteria should be so set that the number of applicants is no more than the number of vacancies. His is an ideal; practically, admission criteria should be such that the number of applicants will automatically be no more than at the most, two-three times the number of seats to be filled. While it is true that devising such criteria is undoubtedly difficult, that is the direction in which the IITs should progress.

Although the suggestion is unlikely to be accepted at present, I recommend that the JEE should be treated the same way American universities treat ranking in GRE or GMAT. Just as American universities have a set of recognized institutions from where students are exclusively admitted, the IITs too should have a set of acceptable schools to which the task of short-listing will be delegated. When aspirants are short-listed partly by recognized schools, and by a nationwide test, the list becomes manageable. This system will also put paid to the pernicious system of coaching classes that are turning youngsters into automatons.

The selection of schools to be recognized under this scheme can be transparent with the IITs listing the schools from which a minimum number of students were admitted in the previous years. On that basis, each school may be given a quota of students that they can sponsor in proportion to the number of their students who had gained admission in the previous years. Then, the schools may create a short list about three times the number to be admitted, which will be a very manageable figure. Alternately, the entrance test may be conducted by district authorities who too will be provided a quota based on the past performance of past students from their respective districts.

Either way, this system of short-listing is self-correcting. Any school or district board that lapses from the highest level of probity will be automatically penalized in subsequent years. Short-listing up to three or four times the average number admitted in earlier years is more than adequate because, statistically, it is unthinkable that the number of candidates worth considering in any year from any school or district would suddenly go up more than that many times. Hence, the possibility of any deserving applicant being rejected may be safely ruled out. As for the IITs, they will now need to scrutinize relatively fewer candidates and this may be done so much more systematically than the mechanical way they are doing at present.

The World Bank has popularized the idea that higher education is a 'non-merit' good, with the argument that a college education enables a student to obtain better paid jobs that are more prestigious and more secure as well. Therefore, the student earns a 'private benefit' from higher education. Therefore, it is not fair to burden the taxpayer with the cost of such an education. So higher education does not merit a subsidy, or, at any rate, not much subsidy. In any case, if a student does not have the means to pay, loans may be arranged so that the burden still stays with the student and is not passed on to the taxpayer.

The Sarkar Committee has suggested that the IITs should meet their costs in the following three ways: one-third from student fees, one-third from consultancy earnings and sponsored projects, and the remaining one-third as a grant from the government. Although the Committee did not spell out the rationale for this three-way division, it appears to be logical: there are three beneficiaries of higher education – the students themselves, businesses and the society at large. As it is quite impractical to calculate the exact ratio of benefits among the three, this three-way equal division was as rational as it could be.

In the U.S., colleges such as MIT, Harvard, Stanford and Caltech have similar average fees of about thirty per cent of the American per capita income. India's per capita income is Rs. 50,000 and on that basis, Indian college fees (in prestigious institutions) should be around Rs. 15,000 a year. This figure of Rs. 15,000 is desirable but not realistic as Indian costs, relative to the country's per capita income, are far higher than in the U.S. To begin with, in the U.S. professors are paid about three times their national per capita income. On that basis, senior Indian professors should get no more than Rs. 12,000 a month. Indian salaries – in per capita terms – are several times the American practice. Even then, we are unable to attract the finest staff. Further, our colleges have to procure equipment at American prices, not at Indian ones. Therefore, in terms of per capita income, Indian fees cannot be as low as American ones, unless subsidies are raised substantially.

The cost of technical education in the U.S. is around $ 50,000 a year, and on the basis of the Purchasing Power Parity is around Rs. 500,000 a year in India. That is the order of cost per student for a technical education of international quality. By all accounts, China is providing this quality of education in select institutions and India would be well advised to do so. One may well ask whether India can afford to do so; one should ask instead whether India can afford *not* to do so at least for the numbers that match the economic demand.

In my opinion, this is where we are making a mistake. In the early 1980s, just before the explosion in engineering education took place, the annual intake of students in engineering was only 26,000, a somewhat excessive number even then. Since then, the economy has at the most trebled. On that basis, the Indian economy should entertain approximately 75,000 admissions, with a maximum of about 5,000 admissions in the IIT system. Instead, we are admitting nearly seven times the number with most graduates declared as unemployable in response to the jobless growth rate.

By international standards, the desirable expenditure on engineering education in the IITs should be Rs. 500,000 a year per student and approximately Rs. 200,000 a year in smaller colleges. Then, the total cost of subsidy for technical education would amount to about Rs. 8000 crores a year – not an impossible burden for the Indian economy. The government may support most of that cost for about 75,000 students a year – in the manner in which European governments do – and let unaided institutions manage any excess demand.

Harvard University is typical of the manner in which private universities attract and cater to bright students and it does so by keeping admissions and fees separate. Admissions are made on the basis of a complex set of criteria for merit (school reports, SAT scores, extracurricular activities, and such like). The fee to be charged to any student is decided separately on the basis of the student's ability to pay. Through this blind test, care is taken that no meritorious student is discouraged from joining merely because of the expense involved. Harvard offers large subsidies to bright students, even more than what public institutions offer. Recently, it has raised assistance to families with incomes of $150,000 a year – corresponding to about Rs. 400,000 a year for India. Besides, Harvard pays its faculty far better than state universities. It can afford to do all these because it has accumulated huge endowments. The IITs are unable to emulate American universities because our rich do not endow educational institutions the way the American rich do and also because our governments do not encourage endowments from the public.

• • •

The higher education debate in India is centred on three issues these days. Firstly, is higher education a non-merit good deserving little or no subsidy as some finance experts make it out to be? Secondly, should higher education be a democratic right open to all, or should it be confined to a select few? And third, if higher education is to be restricted to a few, should it be confined to those who are competent, or should it be the preserve of the politically privileged, or should it be purchasable by the rich?

India's parliamentarians have almost unanimously opted for reservation for 'backward castes' on the ground that it is the best antidote for backwardness. If that argument holds true and reservation is indeed the remedy, then after fifty years or more of its use it should have become unnecessary. The fact that people want even more of it means that reservation is not a remedy, but an addiction. This move turns the idea of morality upside down: Poor children of forward castes are deemed punishable for no reason other than their parentage; rich backward-caste children are deemed worthy of patronage for no reason other than that they enjoy overwhelming political power. Those that breathe casteism declare themselves as secular; those that plead for quality education are condemned as communal. It is indeed a repetition of the story of the wolf and the lamb.

IITs and IIMs that have been free of the communal canker in all the years of their existence will now become breeding grounds for the worst form of casteism. Just at the time that the country is about to take off economically, and take its due place in the world, this move will destroy the institutions that have contributed most for that progress. Their demise is not the true tragedy; that the nation is killing the goose that lays golden eggs is the real tragedy.

In this connection, it is pertinent to raise and answer a few questions. One important consideration is whether academic standards can be maintained at the present level. As the government has already ordered reservation for higher education (with the order held in abeyance for the IITs on account of a case pending in the Supreme Court), it is logical that reservation will be applicable for faculty selections too. In that case, why should world-class teachers join IITs or IIMs when they know they are liable to be superseded by less able teachers on caste grounds? Once the finest teachers stay away, the quality of education will undoubtedly suffer.

It has been suggested that these reputed institutions train the reserved candidates to raise them to the required level on par with regular students. On examination, this plan is not feasible as even the best institution cannot correct twelve years of bad education. Succeeding in the IITs and the IIMs is like playing first-class cricket where, however good the training or talent, few can make the grade after being starved all through childhood.

In addition, this move is unlikely to help underprivileged OBC students. It has been observed that family incomes of SC/ST students entering the IIMs are significantly higher than that of general category students. Very rich SC/STs tend to monopolize the opportunities offered by reservation to the virtual exclusion of their own underprivileged. Undoubtedly, caste-based reservation reduces the distance between the rich of the reserved and the rich of the general communities. Simultaneously, it greatly increases the internal distance between the rich and the poor within the reserved communities. In other words, reservation pampers the rich and neglects the poor; it increases internal disparities among the reserved communities.

• • •

Another suggestion that may be considered is that the fees charged for any student be linked to the fees paid by the same student while studying in the school between the 8–12 standards. That fee, adjusted to inflation, would reveal quite accurately the family's capacity to pay taking into account not only the formal declared income but other sources too. This rule has the advantage of simplicity, and has the additional benefit of being self-regulating. This rule will also be socially just: the rich will pay more automatically, the poor less. There will be a few aberrations such as a rich child studying in a Central School, which charges a relatively low fee. Even so this school fee-linked charge will be fairer than most other options.

• • •

Probably the gravest error in the latest budget is the proposal to build more IITs. While it is true that India does require many more such institutions, it is still not yet ready. Great educational institutions are not built by money, but by talented and dedicated teachers. Unlike financial capital, which can be obtained in a trice, human capital takes years to cultivate. As a populist move, one worse than the loan waiver for farmers, the government plans to have instant IITs forgetting that without a bank of dedicated teachers that is a remote impossibility.

The finance minister ended his budget speech with a quotation from Pandit Nehru and one could only wish that he had first studied more carefully that great man's thoughts and actions. When the IITs were first set up, Pandit Nehru took great pains to attract the best available talent, including foreign ones. The present Parliament is doing exactly the opposite: It is insisting that teachers should be selected not for their ability but on the basis of their caste.

It is worth pointing out that, soon after Independence, several state governments systematically destroyed their universities. Even Calcutta and Allahabad which, till then enjoyed the highest reputation across the world, were devastated. The central government is unfortunately causing irreparable damage to the IITs and the IIMs in the same manner. It took twenty years for the IITs and the IIMs to establish their reputation all over the world – it did not take as many years for Calcutta and Allahabad to lose their sheen. We can only pray that the reputation of the IITs and the IIMs will survive a little longer and, in the meanwhile, a more far-sighted Parliament will rescue them from certain disaster.

The IITs have done the nation proud. Whether they will continue to do so will depend on several factors such as how well their autonomy is protected, how well teachers are respected, and how sincere and steadfast top academics and scholars are. Unfortunately, our finest scholars are no different from the IAS officers of the Emergency Era – as the late Justice Khanna famously remarked, they crawl when they were merely asked to bend. I quote from my last convocation report as director of IIT Madras:

> (Our MPs) feel that our standards are too high. Some have gone so far as to say that what we need is an Indian standard and not an international standard of education.

Whether we need or need not be aware of the latest developments in technology, it is necessary to debate the fundamental question whether, just because a group of people cannot cope with a certain level of education, they should have the veto power to deny such an education to the rest; whether social justice should imply that there shall be no institution at all in the country where merit is the criterion and also while the socially deprived should have special privileges, the talented need have no right of their own.

A university – like a flower – is helpless; it can be easily destroyed and depends entirely on goodwill for its survival. Not so long ago, universities of Allahabad and Calcutta were the most prestigious in our country and honoured all over the world as the IITs are today. Looking at what has happened to them, we cannot but be concerned about our own future.

•

# Science and Conscience

From the very beginning of a formal university education in India, science education was one of the declared aims of higher education, though, as it happened, the Faculty of Science was added later to the four initial faculties of Arts, Law, Medicine and Engineering at the University of Calcutta. In 1947, the number of universities in the country was 25, and science was taught in almost all of them.

The founding fathers of our republic always recognized the importance of science and technology in nation building. In fact, the dominant ideology of the first two decades after Independence held that only science and technology could help India – a poor, underdeveloped nation – leapfrog to higher levels of economic and material well being. This is a reason why the 1950s were a decade of building steel plants, hydro-electric projects, fertilizer plants, refineries, *et al.* This was also the time when technical education

By **Shobhit Mahajan**

was enthusiastically promoted as IITs, engineering colleges and even polytechnics were set up in various parts of India. Science and technology was then seen not just as a remedy for economic backwardness but, more importantly, as a panacea for social evils. There was a naive belief then that the rationality of science would eventually overpower our superstitious and backward rural population and that as our people imbibed a scientific temper, social ills would magically disappear.

The Science Policy Resolution of the Government of India (1958) summed this up well:

> Science has led to the growth of diffusion of culture to an extent never possible before. It has not only radically altered man's material environment, but, what is of still deeper significance, it has provided new tools of thought and has extended man's mental horizon. It has thus influenced even the basic values of life, and given to civilization a new vitality and a new dynamism.

On the face of it, in the five decades since these words were written, there has been tremendous progress in the fields of science and technology in the country. We can boast of a huge scientific and technical human resource base, a handful of world-class institutions of higher learning and a large number of universities. Over and above this is the huge scientific research infrastructure in the form of CSIR, DRDO, ICAR and other organizations.

However, this quantitative growth, frequently touted by the policy mandarins, hides a very important fact: that Indian science is in a state of crisis. Whether it is the number of research papers published in peer-reviewed journals, the citations of these papers, international awards or even the number of patents, our huge science and technology infrastructure just does not measure up to the best. It has to be admitted that the state of scientific research in the country is dismal and unless something is done urgently, we will continue to lag behind not just the developed countries but even other developing countries, such as China and Brazil.

Several reasons for this state of affairs are well-known: bureaucratic (mis)management, the all-pervasive patronage system that continues to operate in academia, lack of focus in areas of research, and so on. However, one of the key reasons is the pathetic state of higher education in science in our country. Since scientific research is to be ultimately done by human beings, it follows that if there are lacunae in our training of scientists, it will naturally impact the quality of their scientific output.

The crisis in higher education in general, and in science education in particular, has recently been highlighted in several reports like the National Knowledge Commission Report and the Indian National Science Academy and Indian Academy of Science Reports. These reports illustrate the fact that despite the enormous reservoir of talent and pockets of excellence, the quality of higher education in most of our universities requires substantial improvement.

The fact that higher education is in a state of crisis is thus fairly well accepted now, and that a massive overhaul is required in the sector is also understood by the policy makers. Unfortunately, what is not so apparent to policy makers is how to set about remedying the situation. To successfully undertake this overhaul, the nature and causes of the crisis need to be clearly comprehended or else there would be little achievement despite an enormous increase in expenditure on higher education that has been allocated in the Eleventh Five-Year-Plan.

• • •

The bedrock of higher education is the undergraduate teaching institution, which in most cases is the undergraduate college where almost all of non-professional undergraduate teaching takes place. One of the peculiarities of the education system in India is that these colleges are almost always affiliated to a university. With little academic autonomy as the curriculum, the academic calendar and the examinations are all centralized at the affiliating university, these colleges merely function as locations where the actual teaching takes place. This centralization, which might have worked successfully when there were fewer colleges affiliated to each university, is now a major impediment to any planned improvement in the teaching of science. In this system, dons at the affiliating university almost unilaterally take a decision, or pass legislation, that a particular curriculum needs to be implemented, with practically no inputs from college teachers. Given the variation in the academic standards of the students, the infrastructure available, and indeed the teachers

*It's OK, sir. Anything is pleasant after answering those exam papers!*

themselves, this top-down approach invariably fails to achieve its purpose. Instead of each teacher – with his/her experience of actual students – deciding the level of academic preparation and what the students can assimilate, it is left to the university to decide what should be taught.

In most cases, the curriculum itself is outdated and uninspiring, and the introduction of new syllabi – most often a readymade one from another university – is implemented without the least sensitivity to requirements. The nature of the curriculum in most universities is such that a passive reception of knowledge is encouraged without any structural elements that call for the student to investigate, develop problem-solving abilities, or to think independently. As a result, science is taught in a manner, which is contrary to its basic principles: that of discovery, experimentation and application to different situations.

Yet another system that causes extensive damage is that of the examination, where 'anonymous' teachers set question papers that are then graded by other 'anonymous' teachers, leaving the individual who has taught the students throughout the year with no role to play in assessing them – a very peculiar situation indeed! The nature of these examinations is yet another issue as, in most cases, they test little more than pure memory. Significant facilities that are desirable such as the application of concepts, problem-solving abilities, and critical thinking are not assessed, and, as a result, a student without any proper understanding of the subject but with good rote-learning capabilities is assured reasonable results.

Clearly, the system of assessment that exists is disastrous, and it is particularly so for the teaching of science. Another unintended consequence is a negative feedback effect on the system of teaching and learning, with little incentive to the student and, to a lesser extent, to the teacher. Such a system does little to promote innovations of any sort either in teaching or learning, with the average student following the path of least resistance and maximum gains by doing just the bare minimum required to perform well in the examinations. It is cause for great concern that most students of even premier universities such as the University of Delhi are, by this token, unlikely to have solved a single problem in three years of undergraduate education! Regrettably, the system not only encourages this state of affairs, but actually rewards those who lack these abilities, merely reproducing facts from memory.

One way forward towards finding solutions to these problems is the decentralization of curriculum and assessment. Given the uneven standards of faculty in colleges, a complete decentralization in terms of curriculum may not be possible. One possibility is that the university could frame the broad guidelines and leave the details of what is to be taught to the individual teachers. Alternatively, the university could decide on a core component of the syllabi and leave the college teacher to decide from among a menu of options for the rest. The teacher could then tailor the curriculum to suit the actual conditions in the college in terms of infrastructure, the academic level of students, and his/her own expertise.

Another desirable change would be the decentralization of the system of assessment as, the world over, the evaluation of students is done by the individual who teaches the course. A major impediment to this has proved to be the mindset of bureaucrats dealing with education, who display a regrettable fetish for 'objectivity': the argument being that the teacher assessing his/her own students will be subjective, and that will inevitably lead to grade inflation. This lack of confidence is highly objectionable and reflects a fundamental distrust of the teacher's integrity. To counter this, a system of continuous internal assessment to replace the present end-of-the year examination would empower both students and teachers. This assessment could be graded by placing students on a scale relative to each other, which would obviate any need for grade inflation.

• • •

The other major problem that our colleges are faced with is a completely inadequate physical infrastructure: classrooms, laboratories, libraries, computing and Internet facilities are in an advanced state of decay. Classrooms, tutorial and faculty rooms are woefully inadequate resulting in an environment that is not conducive to learning and exploration. Libraries are under-stocked and laboratories are ill-equipped for carrying out any meaningful investigations or modern experimentation.

The Internet is a tremendous educational resource, the potential of which is still to be exploited to the fullest. Most colleges, with the exception of some well-endowed ones, are bedevilled by a lack of computers, that is compounded by an uninterrupted supply of power as well as limited connectivity. The role of the library needs to be redefined as an information dissemination hub. Public access computers with subscriptions to electronic resources such as journals and databases need to be installed in libraries. In order to achieve maximum efficiency, the government could negotiate the prices for hardware and subscriptions at a state or national level.

Those colleges that will benefit most from access to computers and the Internet are those situated in smaller towns and the countryside, where the need for information and reading material is the greatest. As providing broadband access to all parts of the country is one of the stated objectives of the government, this should be easily achievable with proper planning and implementation.

Infrastructural constraints in terms of physical infrastructure are only part of the problem with a far more serious problem evident in human resources. That teaching is conducted by teachers is perhaps self-evident; nevertheless, it is clear that our educational planners don't seem to have grasped the import of this. It is a universally accepted fact that any improvement in the quality of education is crucially dependent on the presence of competent, qualified and motivated teachers.

Unfortunately, teaching rates very poorly on the list of professions that attract our finest students. This discrimination may be attributed to huge salary differentials between the private sector and the teaching profession, the low esteem in which teachers are now held in the public perception and a perceived lack of future prospects. Inevitably, even at the entry-level stage, students who opt to teach are, in general, not the most outstanding ones. These problems are further compounded during the course of a career whereby the teacher, once employed, finds few opportunities for advancement in terms of either his/her career or intellectual growth. With employment guaranteed to be life-long, there are no checks and balances on performance: no carrots for performance or sticks for non-performance. Inevitably, this results in a paucity of good, capable and motivated teachers who can inspire their students.

• • •

Another aspect of undergraduate training that is usually ignored in our colleges is the integration of research and teaching. Frontline research in the sciences usually requires a familiarity with a large body of existing knowledge and, in the case of experimental work, fairly advanced equipment. It would be impractical to expect the average undergraduate institution to possess the expertise and the equipment for undertaking frontline research. A possible solution to this is to provide centralized, regional facilities which can be shared by several colleges in the neighbourhood. A crucial exposure to research at the undergraduate level will not merely enhance students' understanding of the actual practice of science, but also motivate them to consider science as a viable career option.

The problem of human resources, for which there is no quick and easy solution, may be tackled by implementing a long-term strategy of empowering teachers, of providing them with opportunities for career advancement and intellectual growth, and a system of performance-based rewards. It is hoped that the implementation of these strategies will bring about an attitudinal change in society thereby making the teaching profession an attractive career option once more that will draw the finest students.

• • •

Finally, there is the all-important issue of access. Language poses a major barrier for an education in science as English is not the medium of instruction for most high school students. On the other hand, there is almost no university in India where science is taught in any other language except English. This poses an insurmountable barrier for a large number of students, who, while otherwise bright, find themselves handicapped. In addition, most students are daunted by books written by non-Indian authors as they are written in a style, language and terminology that is alien to them. This leaves them with no recourse but to rely on cheap, badly written books; interestingly, this also holds true for many students who do read English, but even so find standard textbooks difficult to comprehend. The non-availability of excellent textbooks by Indian authors is incomprehensible given our huge scientific manpower base. The finest scientists in countries such as the erstwhile Soviet Union and China wrote textbooks, which went on to become classics and were translated into English, while one is hard put to bring to mind more than a handful of textbooks written by Indian scientists working in India that may be considered world class.

Although the issues discussed above are largely in the context of undergraduate education and teaching, almost everything that can be stated also holds true at the postgraduate level. In fact, given a further filtration of the finest students into streams such as Management and Computer Applications after graduation, the quality of the students and their motivation further deteriorates at the postgraduate level.

The quality of higher education, of science in India suffers immensely due to these factors. It is evident that unless these issues are addressed seriously, there cannot be any significant improvement in the quality of education. Unfortunately, despite recommendations by several committees and commissions, precious little has been done to improve the existing situation. The State finds it much easier to open up new institutions rather than to channelize resources into improving the existing ones, or to implement systemic reforms. New institutions obviously offer more scope for patronage in terms of contracts and appointments and hence are preferred by all the vested interests.

The government has announced its avowed intention of opening up at least one central university in each state and one degree college in each district. This kind of attention to higher education is indeed laudable and long overdue. However, it would be prudent and cost effective to also allocate some resources in terms of time-bound, directed programmes for specific use such as libraries, IT, infrastructure, etc. to the existing institutions to improve their standards. These enhanced allocations should be centralized facilities, which could be shared by several institutions so built so as to maximize efficient usage.

We have indeed come a long way from that moment in time when the first Faculty of Science was started at the University of Calcutta. However, if we as a country do not take steps urgently to rescue our higher education in the sciences from mediocrity, we will continue to be a nation of unrealized potential: nine per cent growth, mobile telephones and global leadership of our IT industry notwithstanding. What is worse, it would be difficult to maintain growth rates in sunshine sectors such as IT and biotechnology in the absence of world class institutions of science and technology.

•

# Trojan Horse

With the realization across the world that the global economy is going to be increasingly knowledge-based, science and technology have become the subject of discussion not just in their classical ministries but also in ministries as diverse as commerce, industry and finance, and in the case of the United States, even in the State Department. In India, the prime minister has made frequent statements about the need to step up scientific research in the country and entering the global economy as participants in the knowledge revolution, and the Knowledge Commission has identified this as an area of core concern.

Basically, the global demand for technology development has evoked two responses in India. One is the emergence of its own research agenda, and the other is the emergence of India as an international research hub for contracted research. Several large

By **Suman Sahai**

companies, including multinationals, are outsourcing research and development programmes to India. This is partly because scientists are cheaper in India dollar for dollar, but also because India has a large pool of scientifically trained manpower to back the research programmes.

Industry data show that research and development services are now the third-largest segment in India's export of Information Technology (IT) services. Foreign companies have invested over $1 billion in research operations in India from 1998 to 2003, according to a study conducted by the Technology Information Forecasting and Assessment Council (TIFAC) of the Department of Science and Technology (DST). In addition to this, another estimated $5 billion in research investments are in the pipeline. The United States is the biggest investor followed by Europe where Germany, France, Denmark and U.K. have invested the most. Japan and, surprisingly, China have also begun to invest in research programmes in India and another nine countries are reported to be planning research ventures in future. Most foreign investment is being directed to research in computer sciences, pharmaceuticals, molecular chemistry, drug discovery, engineering and automotive design and biotechnology, including plant breeding.

Whereas the flow of foreign investments has enthused research institutions that are targeted for collaboration, there is also cause for concern. The flood of foreign funds has alerted the government about the security aspects of foreign agencies getting involved in critical research areas. Although India now attracts considerable foreign investment in research and development, it has no system in place for assessing how this investment is affecting the country's technological development. Nor is there any mechanism to monitor the impact of such investment on aspects such as skill development, sectoral capacity building, job creation or export revenues. There is also no credible assessment of whether, or how effectively, technologies developed by foreign companies or agencies are being transferred to India's public sector. Do such foreign-funded research programmes benefit only the scientists and technicians engaged there as a result of better salaries and perks, or do they also produce benefits for the country as a whole? For the country to benefit, research programmes will have to contribute to the requirements of India's technological needs and to do this, research projects will have to work in synergy with Indian academic institutions and towards national objectives.

Given the global spread of terrorism and the sudden intervention of foreign agencies in a seemingly innocuous activity like research and education, raises a slew of security issues. Waking up to this reality, and to plug potential security gaps, the government had begun to draft security legislation that would bring foreign direct investment in research and development under the national security scanner. A panel has been set up comprising senior officials of the Department of Science and Technology, senior scientists and subject experts, experts on intellectual property rights (IPR) and representatives of industrial R&D units to make recommendations and develop a framework to monitor Foreign Direct Investment (FDI)-funded research. The government's aim is to draft legislation that would allow it to block foreign investments from agencies that could be security risks. Unlike the United States or Europe, India does not have a formal framework established to keep an eye on security concerns in economic decisions. Given the strategic sensitivity of sectors such as telecommunications, IT, genetics and robotics, it is crucial that India set in place monitoring and oversight mechanisms related to foreign investment in research in these sectors. The rise of terrorism has made it imperative that security restrictions must inform decision-making regarding research goals and investment in fields that could create security concerns. R&D projects between collaborators in India and abroad require data transfer and exchange of information on a regular basis, yet there is no security control over this kind of data flow. This has implications for internal security as well as for claims of intellectual property rights.

Foreign investments in research are coming in both from public and private sectors abroad. When foreign funds come from private sources, an additional problem here is to determine what results are being produced from this research and how objective these research data are. There have been several instances of bias and influence in the outcome of research studies if the work was funded by private sources, especially corporate sources. Often, the bias is such as to clearly benefit the sector that is investing. A recent 2007 study done on corporate investment in medical education programmes in the United States, showed that when drug companies invest in the education of medical practitioners, they tend to bias course content in favour of their own commercial interests to the extent that patient health can be endangered. One of the researchers analyzing the 2007 corporate-funded study programme calculated the ratio of positive to negative statements made about the drugs mentioned in the exercises. In 14 cases out of the 15 examined, he found that the highest ratio of positive references was made for the drugs that were produced by the company sponsoring the study. Another researcher found that drug companies that were funding the study, tended overwhelmingly to speak glowingly about the products produced by them, neglecting to mention side-effects or drugs that had better track records.

As an example of the corporate influence on research, let me cite a study done in the U.S. Medical practitioners in the U.S. are required to participate in a continuing education programme, to keep themselves up to date with developments in the field of medicine. Pharmaceutical companies often fund such educational programmes and sponsor courses. When funding Continuing Medical Education (CME) courses that qualified physicians are required to take, the pharmaceutical giant GlaxoSmithKline (GSK) was found to advocate testing and treating pregnant women for herpes virus. If physicians were to adopt this line after their training, GSK would potentially see a jump in sales of its herpes drug. The fact is that this is completely unethical and flies in the face of what expert panels recommend on pregnant women and herpes. About 25 per cent of women carry the herpes simplex virus but the chances of a pregnant mother infecting her child are very low. The Department of Health and Human Services in the U.S. advises against screening pregnant women for herpes since herpes drugs can cause serious side-effects in pregnant mothers.

As the government opens the doors to foreign investments in higher education and scientific research, not all the country's academics are pleased. The views of academics and researchers over the desirability of foreign funds in higher education and research are, in fact, quite sharply divided. This comes to light at policy meetings and internal reviews. When a paper on 'Higher Education in India and GATS: An Opportunity', exploring trade in education services, was floated by the Commerce Ministry a couple of years ago, academics, scientists and educationists were sharply divided on whether this was a good idea for India or not. The critics, amongst whom can be counted distinguished scientists and academics, argued that foreign investors in higher education had so far brought in commercial products and were more likely to bring in educational products, such as copyrighted courses and workshop modules in order to make money. They are less likely to bring in skills and expertise with the intention of adapting these to the needs of Indian students or the requirements of Indian science and research.

Those who argue against allowing foreign investment in research and education point out that the education system has been growing at a rapid pace in recent times and does not need foreign funds as much as it does focus and sustained support inside the country. Professor Anandakrishnan, chairman of the IIT Kanpur, makes the case that India has good institutions in almost every field. There are 357 universities in India, twenty of them central universities where the standards are high; there are 13 world-class technical institutions, such as the Indian Institutes of Technology; there are 217 state universities out of which about thirty per cent are rated very highly and 102 deemed universities in both private and public sectors, of which fifty will be considered outstanding. In addition, India has almost 18,000 colleges offering a variety of disciplines, such as science, engineering, agriculture, medicine, management and commerce. Critics argue that in the last ten years, professional and technical education has shifted to the private sector not because this was required but because the government has abandoned higher education. If there was adequate support to good institutions, research output would be of a high standard and there would be little reason to bring in large-scale foreign investments.

The Central Advisory Board on Education (CABE) has recently recommended that the education outlay should be increased to six per cent of the GDP, which should include one per cent for higher education. If the government accepts this, there should be quite a lot of money available for higher education, including for scientific research. Greater allocation of funds for research should provide a counter argument to those who are pushing for (FDI) in research on the plea that advancement in scientific research is suffering because of the shortage of funds.

We need to consider two points here: one, that India has good potential to conduct high-quality research and two, the track record of foreign investments in educational programmes over the last ten years has not been very impressive. Most programmes have been offered by second- and third-tier institutions, not the top institutions of their countries. Most investors have not devoted any funds to creating educational infrastructure, such as setting up a campus, but prefer to operate out of rented premises. In many cases, the programmes available in India are not even accredited in the host countries. A survey of the programmes offered by foreign institutions in India showed that about a third of these were not recognized or accredited in their own countries. So the question is: will permission to allow foreign investment in scientific research result in raising the standards of science education or will it result in the exploitation of gullible Indian students? The government has to be extremely careful in formulating a policy in this field and it should put in place stringent filters to determine what kind of programmes can be offered in our country and by whom.

Investment in scientific research must be allowed only after firm guidelines are put in place to set priorities and standards. We need to determine the areas in which we would like to invite investment; the rating of the institutions that will be permitted to invest and the modalities for sharing the fruits of the research. The government can even shortlist the better-known universities and research stations in those countries where scientific research of good quality is being done, as preferred investors. We should invite investment in fields of research where we have something to learn and where we need to build our capacity, not necessarily where we are leaders ourselves. For instance, India is already doing top-class research on stem cells and could collaborate with other top-class institutions, but not necessarily invite FDI in this field.

We could take a leaf out of Singapore's book in the matter of framing a policy for foreign investment in scientific research. Singapore allows only world-class institutions to enter, and that only when they bring their own money. For instance the Massachusetts Institute of Technology (MIT), a leading technical institution in the U.S., collaborates with the National University of Singapore. From Australia, a country with which it otherwise has close contacts on several fronts, it is only the University of New South Wales, considered a premier institution, which was permitted to establish a campus solely on the basis of its own investments. As a result of its policies on foreign investment in education, Singapore has successfully achieved two goals: one, to make itself an educational destination for neighbours in Asia who can now go to world-class institutions in Singapore rather than to Australia or the U.S.; and two, to bring in top-quality programmes and skills to upgrade their own research. Singapore keeps standards high by enforcing a rigorous process of selection and rigid monitoring of the education and research programmes that are being implemented.

Even after prioritizing the institution and the research field, India will need to be careful about many other aspects associated with allowing foreign investment in research, especially if this is in a strategic area. For instance, research in micro-organisms will have to be carefully monitored to see that it is not leading to products that could help advance the goals of bio terrorism. There is also the knotty issue of intellectual property rights to resolve. Who will own the IPR? How will benefits be shared? Will the Indian research agency agree to patents, the implementation of which will hurt public interest? On the other hand, there could be strategic considerations with respect to the location of the research, or the collection of research samples. We would need to be careful in areas of research that could have defence implications or implications for our food security. How will all this be monitored given that such kinds of research would be conducted in hundreds of laboratories distributed all over the country? Before rushing to invite foreign money indiscriminately, India must engage in due diligence and assess whether its research interests and the capacity of its scientific cadre will benefit from foreign investments in higher education and research.

Why, for instance, would India allow research investment in computer sciences? Not only is there a strategic sensitivity here, but India is already engaged in high calibre computer science research at home. However, this is not to say that there are no areas in which foreign investment would not be beneficial for Indian interests. There are many: one such field is textiles and apparel, the other could be food processing.

In the case of textiles, India has traditional skills but could use technologies through foreign research collaboration that would allow it to emerge as a global player in the apparel trade. Research collaboration in pigment chemistry could help India to scale up its skills in vegetable dyes to achieve a commercial scale and become a world leader in non-polluting, safe natural dyes for the textile and garments industry. India could also benefit from foreign investment in research on design tools, cutting and tailoring equipment and environmentally friendly man-made fibres.

Similarly, foreign technology in the processing of fruits and vegetables would be a welcome addition that would help to create higher farm incomes by adding value and shelf life to perishable products. India is the second-largest producer of fruits and vegetables in the world, but a third of the fruit and vegetable crop is wasted because of a lack of processing technologies. Although the Indo-U.S. deal on agriculture, also known as the Knowledge Initiative on Agriculture, mentioned food processing as an area of cooperation, the focus so far has been on accessing India's genetic resources and promoting agricultural biotechnology!

In conducting joint research with foreign agencies, we need to be aware about setting appropriate research goals and managing Intellectual Property Rights in a way that national interests are served, not hurt. Apart from this, we will need to be vigilant that 'dirty research' is not being brought in under the guise of collaboration. Caution will be needed to ensure that research programmes do not deal with ethically dubious subjects: for instance, human clinical trials for dangerous drugs or research on hazardous, environmentally dangerous substances. Research of this kind, which an aware citizenry in Europe or the U.S. is not permitting in its own backyard, must not find its way into India because we have lax laws, or because regulators and law makers in this country can be persuaded. India will need to develop its own citizens' watchdog bodies to make sure that scientific research serves our interests and contributes to furthering our developmental goals.

•

# Healing the Healer

Medical education in India could be said to have been initiated by the establishment of the first medical schools in the country in Calcutta in 1822, Bombay in 1826 and Madras in 1827. These early schools had a limited objective of training medical apprentices with minimal qualifications in some aspects of health care. The first full-fledged medical college was established in Calcutta in 1838 under the supervision of the General Medical Council of Great Britain. The period between 1838 and 1896 witnessed the establishment of 19 medical colleges. The governance and oversight rested with the General Medical Council till the Indian Medical Council Act was passed in 1933 following which the Medical Council of India (MCI) came into being in 1934.

The relatively small numbers of medical colleges and the overview provided by the General Medical Council and the MCI in its early days enabled a very high standard of medical education to be maintained in a number of medical colleges established during that

By **Ranjit Roy Chaudhury**

period, such as Lucknow's K.G. Medical College, Patna's Prince of Wales Medical College and the Grant Medical College in Bombay.

There was a rapid proliferation of medical colleges in India after Independence. This, accompanied by a lack of competent teachers and a decline in the standard of governance, heralded the deterioration of the standards of medical education in the country. The recent development of establishment of private medical colleges, where students are admitted after paying a large capitation fee, has made the situation even more complicated.

Let us first deal with the widely accepted feeling throughout the country that there has been a decline in standards of medical education. Table I shows the rapid spurt in the number of medical colleges in the country till 1991.

*Table 1: Medical Colleges Established*

| *Period* | *Increase in Medical Institutes* | *Increase in Enrollment* |
|---|---|---|
| 1947–65 | 17–87 | 1400–5387 |
| 1965–75 | 87–105 | 5387–11,911 |
| 1975–85 | 105–106 | 11,911–12,278 |
| 1985–91 | 106–129 | 12,278–13,714 |

The number of medical colleges in February 2007 was around 267. This number, I understand, has now risen to 271.

No country in the world can possibly cope with such an explosive increase in the number of students without a simultaneous increase in the number of trained teachers to impart quality training. Sadly, in India there was no such planned increase. The result is that today it is difficult to find any teachers in some of the basic medical sciences, such as physiology and biochemistry, to say nothing of specialty sciences, such as forensic medicine and community medicine.

A second reason for the deterioration is the quality of teachers. This can, of course, be a controversial issue, but the prevalent feeling among the majority of medical educationists I spoke to when preparing for this article, was that the standard of the teachers – except in a few centres of excellence – has significantly deteriorated. It has been repeatedly stated that one of the reasons for this is that the clinical teachers in a majority of government medical colleges and nearly all private medical colleges have a large private practice, which is naturally their first priority. Thus they neglect their duties in the college. While there is definitely some truth in this, this is too simplistic an argument. When the first medical colleges were established, teachers were allowed private practice and yet the standard of teaching was high. In the early years, medical colleges had teachers of the calibre of Sir Lakshmiswamy Mudaliar, Colonel Ameerchand and Dr. Givraj Mehta. I mention these three because, in the only selection committee I faced for appointment as Assistant Professor of Pharmacology at the All India Institute of Medical Sciences (AIIMS), these three illustrious medical educators together with 'big' men like Dr. R.M. Kasliwal, Dr. Dukhan Ram, Dr. B.B. Dikshit and Dr. C.G. Pandit formed the Selection Committee. Perhaps, as was suggested to me, this is a period when many 'small' people were in positions of importance in the field of medical education: the last of the older generation of greats were Dr. Tulsidas, Dr. Santokh Singh Anand, Dr. V. Ramalingaswami, Dr. K.S. Wig and Dr. P.N. Chhutani in north India. Other, equally brilliant, names were then to be found in the rest of the country.

The third reason for this deterioration is that – along with a declining level of governance – the MCI has also been associated with a lack of transparency. It is the prerogative of the MCI to grant recognition to new medical colleges as also postgraduate medical degrees being run by colleges. It is fairly commonly believed that considerations other than performance, need and quality of the newer medical colleges being recognized, play an important part in the decision making process. In any case, a Medical Council formed at a time when there were a few medical colleges with a smaller number of postgraduate degrees cannot manage to provide oversight of the standard needed for the quantum jump prevailing today, both in the number of medical colleges and the specialties for which postgraduate degrees are being awarded.

Without going into detail of the future of the functioning of the MCI, I would like to reiterate that both the Commission of Macroeconomics and Health (2005), co-chaired by the Minister of Finance and the Minister of Health and Family Welfare, as well as the Postgraduate Medical Education Committee set up by the Ministry of Health and Family Welfare, which I had the privilege to chair, have recommended that the MCI should restrict its activities to undergraduate medical education and not have anything to do with postgraduate medical education. A separate mechanism of oversight for postgraduate medical education has been strongly recommended.

There are so many facets to medical education in India – its achievements, weaknesses, constraints and challenges – that it is impossible to deal with all these factors in one article. However, the main issues facing us today will certainly be discussed. The subject of private medical colleges has to be dealt with since this comparatively new phenomenon, not envisaged by either the landmark Bhore Committee or the Mudaliar Commission, is playing an important role in medical education today.

The Bhore Committee Report laid down the foundations of our public health system for the country in 1953 and these are still in place. The Mudaliar Commission (1961) laid down the foundation of medical education in India, and the principles and policies enunciated therein have served the country well. The quality of doctors produced in the early years was such that the much acclaimed National Health Service system of the United Kingdom could only function because of the competence of Indian doctors – for years, they formed the bulwark of the scheme, occupying perhaps 75 per cent of the positions of Home Officers and Registrars at British hospitals. However, as times change and different needs arise, the policies need to change as well. This is something that we in India have not been able to accomplish. We recognize the need for change – we even know what changes need to be made – but both the government and civil society appear to be incapable of making them. This could be partly due to the fact that health is also dealt with by the states and is on the Concurrent List. However, that is no excuse. In the field of health and medical education we have had, since the Mudalier Commission in 1961, the Kartar Singh Committee of 1974, the J.B. Shrivastava Committee in 1975, the Indian Council for Social Science Research and Indian Council of Medical Research Committee headed by Professor Ramalingaswami in 1983, the Working Group on Medical Education in 1986 and the Expert Committee on Manpower Planning, Production and Management headed by Professor J.S. Bajaj. Yet, despite the very erudite and practical recommendations made by these committees, nothing much has happened to change the direction of our undergraduate and postgraduate medical education.

The Bhore Committee recommended that the country should have one medical college for every 50 lakh population. In order to come up to this norm the government allowed the establishment of private medical colleges. The first private medical college was the Manipal Medical College established by Dr. Pai. This private medical college set up very high standards maintained till today, employed several experienced teachers who were just retiring from government medical colleges and produced a large number of well-trained doctors under successive vice chancellors of the calibre of Professor S. Valiathan. The Christian Medical College, Vellore, has been a pioneer in medical education, service and research in the country. Had all private medical colleges followed this path, the country would have benefited enormously. However, perhaps because of lack of oversight by government and lack of transparency on the part of the MCI, things went awry.

When the Bhore Committee recommended one medical college for 50 lakh population I believe they felt, but did not specifically state, that these should be evenly established throughout the country. What happened in fact was that most private medical colleges were established in a few relatively well-off states. This does not help. The existing medical colleges are spread very unevenly over the country. Javed Choudhury, a former Secretary of Health and Family Welfare, has calculated that the four southern states (Andhra Pradesh, Karnataka, Tamil Nadu and Kerala) and Maharashtra have 63 per cent of the total number of medical colleges in the country and 67 per cent of the seats, whereas the northern states have a serious shortfall of medical colleges. The Commission in Macroeconomics and Health established by Smt. Sushma Swaraj, then Union Health Minister of the country, has pointed out this unfortunate situation and has calculated that sixty new medical colleges are needed in the country. They have also recommended that these should be set up in those states and parts of the country where there is a need and where no colleges exist. The Task Force on Medical Education of the National Rural Health Mission has recommended that at least one medical college shall be set up in each district of the under-provided states. The Task Force has gone to the extent of recommending released norms for recognition of such colleges. At the moment only 37 per cent of the medical colleges are in the public sector. The number of doctors produced every year at this time is 25,700 while about 10,000 post-graduates qualify every year as specialists.

In addition to this inequitous selection of centres for private medical colleges, it is generally felt that money has come to play a part in this whole system – more than is warranted, justified or ethical. Since these private medical colleges charge a large fee from their students, they do not get the best students, despite a mandatory cut off point. This fact has also been highlighted by the Knowledge Commission of India that has also recommended replacement of the Medical Council of India by another lady. The Medical Education Committee of the Commission had eminent persons like Dr. Sneh Bhargava and Dr. P.N. Tandon on the Committee. There is great concern about recognition of new colleges by the MCI and it is felt by the doctors at large that some colleges that should not have been recognized have indeed been recognized. There is, of course, a great shortage of teachers and private colleges and even government colleges sometimes bring in temporary teachers (and, I understand, temporary patients) on the day of inspection of the college by the MCI. Surely, this is a ludicrous situation and something drastic needs to be done – particularly as India expects patients to come here from different parts of the world for good quality medical care at one tenth of the cost in the West. A joint study carried out by the Confederation of Indian Industries (CII) and McKinsey has estimated that India's healthcare market could reach Rs.3.2 lakh crores by the year 2012. At the moment, it is Rs.1.03 lakh crores.

To attain this we need to set our medical education system in order and ensure that colleges will not be recognized unless they fulfil the total requirements, that teachers are not imported on the day of inspection, that financial considerations are not the paramount factor and that medical colleges are not a business – as is thought today – for making money. The Commission on Macro-economies and Health (2005) states:

> Hence, even in colleges reputed to import excellent education, the quality is declining because of shortage of teaching staff, inadequate laboratory facilities and budgets to libraries, lack of research, inadequate clinical load and lack of first hand experiences in examining and managing patients.

It also goes on to say that:

> Both private and government medical colleges have a shortage of teachers. Often governments resort to a mass reshuffle of teachers of different specialties from one medical college to another on a temporary basis at the time of inspection by the medical council of India. Keeping a fake roll of medical teachers and showing expenditure under the salary head is a common tactic adopted by managements of private medical colleges, which has an adverse impact on the quality of instruction. The problem of shortage of medical teachers is more accurate in the private medical colleges especially in pre-clinical specialties such as Anatomy, Physiology, Biochemistry, Pathology, Microbiology, Pharmacology, Forensic Medicines and Community Medicine.

We need to improve the working of both our government and private medical colleges and if this is not possible in the private sector, then no new private medical colleges should be allowed to be set up. The Commission, I would like to remind readers, was set up by the Government of India with Sri Chidambaram and Dr. Ambumani Ramadoss as co-chairs. A million dollars was well spent on this commission, which has brought the Report ably prepared by over 500 consultants and experts from all over India led by Ms. Sujatha Rao, then Secretary of the Commission. Its recommendations need to be implemented.

• • •

One of the most visionary developments in the field of medical education has been the establishment of autonomous institutes, created with parliamentary authority, to give its own degrees and set its own norms with its own governing bodies. Institutes, such as the All India Institute of Medical Sciences (AIIMS), and the Postgraduate Institute of Medical Education and Research (PGIMER), have changed the visible face of medical education in India. It is commonly accepted that standards of excellence have been maintained at these two institutions. Unfortunately, many of the graduating doctors from AIIMS are now working in the U.S.A., but that is a separate issue which will be dealt with later. The freedom to evolve their recruitment criteria meant that these institutes could recruit faculty, which would not have been possible if the norms set up by the MCI had to be followed. Professor Ramalingaswami, Professor Sujoy B. Roy, Professor Lazaro, Professor Keswani and Professor G.P. Talwar, giants at the Institute would have been ineligible for the positions they held if the MCI rules had been applied to these institutions. I, too, was fortunate to be appointed, at the age of 34, as Professor and Head of the Department of Pharmacology at the PGIMER, Chandigarh, with only two years' teaching experience as an Assistant Professor. Under the MCI regulations, I would not even have been granted an interview. The impact of these two institutes and later, of Thiruvanathapuram's Sri Chitra Institute of Medical Science, in the field of teaching, research and medical care has been tremendous and outstanding.

The proposed creation of six such AIIMS-like institutes in different parts of the country is a laudable move. However, what needs to be kept in mind is that, to a very large extent, the AIIMS and PGIMER reached where they did because their staff members worked full time and no private practice was allowed. This condition should also prevail on the faculty of the six new institutes coming up and suitable emoluments and living conditions should be provided for making up the loss in practice. If these facilities are provided, then great things will happen. Dr. K.C. Mahajan, Head of Academics at the Sir Ganga Ram Hospital, one of the 'greats' in the profession who has seen it all over the last sixty years said, when I interviewed him before writing the article:

> 75 per cent of our boys and girls in the medical profession are excellent. Give them the opportunity and the means and they will change the face of the country.

There has always been attrition of well-qualified doctors going abroad although this country provided them the training here, and over the years we have come to accept this. However, in recent years, the rapid growth of the corporate sector hospitals with high standards of providing care has added a new feature to this phenomenon. Many senior faculty members from AIIMS and the Central Government Health Services (CGHS) have left their centres to move over to the private sector further. This further depletes good medical teachers. I must add here that not many medical teachers have left the PGIMER, Chandigarh, to join the corporate sector, although some have gone abroad. The conditions of service, salaries and perquisites have to be improved to retain such persons in the teaching institutes. The need for better living and working conditions and better salaries for doctors has been repeatedly stressed over the last 25 years by Professor M.G.K. Menon, and more recently by Dr. Harsh Vardhan, former Health Minister of Delhi State who established the much acclaimed 'Delhi Model' of rational use of medicines, now internationally recognized, during his tenure as Health Minister.

In a far-sighted move, Dr. Ambumani Ramadoss has, for the first time, set up a committee to recommend specific ways in which faculty can be retained at AIIMS, the PGIMER and the CGHS. This committee has made several recommendations to provide some benefits to the faculty. These include the possibility of retaining some of the research funds they attract for their personal use (as is done in the CSIR and other institutions), an honorarium for every paper published in a peer reviewed journal, more academic and research freedom, and more opportunities to go abroad for a longer period of time without forfeiting their positions at their parent institute. Also, unlike recommendations of other committees, these are in various stages of implementation.

There is no reason, in view of the shortage of teachers, why doctors working in the private sector should not be allowed to do some teaching at our government colleges, which are struggling to find teaching staff. A person who has taught for 25 years at AIIMS, for example, suddenly finds on joining the corporate sector that he is not allowed any more to teach in a government college. Similarly, our students in medical colleges need, in this global world, to see the latest technology exclusively available (more often than not) in corporate sector hospitals. They should go to private hospitals and be taught there. Such an interchange between the government and corporate sector hospitals, if accepted and implemented, would improve our undergraduate and postgraduate medical teaching. In fact, if all the faculty needed are present and the facilities exist there is no reason why private sector hospitals could not start a medical college in addition to the already existing programmes it runs for a Diplomate in Medical Education.

Dr. D. Banerjee, former Co-ordinator of the Centre for the Life Sciences at the Jawaharlal Nehru Hospital and another 'great' in public health medicine, also stressed the importance of raising the emoluments of the doctors. Dr. Banerjee's book, *Health and Family Planning Services*, deals with many of the issues I have discussed here. He is positive and optimistic of the future if we can get things right. As regards the past he says with a sigh, 'A large number of small men took over and compromised medical education.'

• • •

The situation prevailing in the country regarding postgraduate medical education is confusing and needs change. The country awards two types of postgraduate degrees. The M.D. and M.S. degree is awarded by the universities and the standard of doctors who pass out varies from college to college, from state to state, and from university to university. A result of such confusion is that our postgraduate degrees do not have the esteem and credibility they deserve. India also awards the Diplomate of the National Board of Examinations. The Diplomate qualification was initiated after the National Board of Examination was established in 1975. Up till now about 20,000 doctors have attained the Board postgraduate qualification. Training for this avenue takes place in 550 accredited hospitals and universities. There is an intake of around 3500 candidates every year; the fact that two streams exist makes things quite confusing.

After studying the present situation, the Postgraduate Medical Education Committee (2007) has unequivocally recommended that there should be only one stream and one degree for postgraduate medical education in India and this would be the Diplomate of a new body – the Postgraduate Medical Education Board of India. This Board would replace the Medical Council of India as regards postgraduate medical education. The entrance examination, the courses and the examination system should all be uniform and organized by the Board. Medical colleges, private hospitals and corporate hospitals would be encouraged to train candidates for the degrees and there would be no differences as to who should train the candidates. If facilities and faculties exist, the training progammes leading to the degree could be initiated after early recognition of that centre as eligible to becoming a training centre. The doctors who acquire an advanced qualification in the system would be a Brand 'India' Postgraduate. It is hoped that this change will take place soon. This qualification will be the only postgraduate qualification that will be recognized nationally and internationally. If medical colleges continue to give the degree of M.D. and M.S. from a state university, this would be recognized only in that state. This was the unanimous recommendation of the Committee.

In the end, it is clear that if we want to improve medical education in this country we need to make changes. The decisions about the changes may be hard to make, but I hope that we have the courage and conviction to take these decisions.

•

# 3: An Unfinished Agenda

# Building Excellence

Public universities in India, especially those dependent on state governments, have for some years now been generally viewed as being in serious decline if not terminal decay. Political interference, poor governance structures, a dearth of adequate resources and a lack of academic and administrative autonomy have, it is often believed, ensured that the university system in India has been reduced to a sea of mediocrity with isolated islands of excellence. But my experience as vice chancellor of the University of Jammu, for over five years, suggests that it is possible to transform even a little-known provincial university into a vibrant institution as long as one can secure unfettered political support and remain in constant dialogue with the region's civil society. With these essential requirements in place, it is not very difficult to ensure that a critical group of stakeholders become real agents of change and work

By **Amitabh Mattoo**

towards building a world-class institution of learning; the raising of financial resources, surprisingly, is a relatively easier proposition. This, of course, is not the place to reflect in greater detail on whether the University of Jammu can serve as a model. Nevertheless, as in Jammu, the biggest challenge that most Indian universities will face in the years to come – even those who successfully overcome the bureaucratic and political challenges – will be to attract world-class faculty and to be able to retain capable teachers and researchers. This essay draws much from personal experience, but should probably hold true for a large number of public universities in the country.

• • •

It is clear then that the key to the success of the university lies in the quality and motivation of the human resources that the university employs along with the infrastructure it operates with and the milieu it functions under.

What determines the quality of human resources that a university hires? The list of factors that come to mind include emoluments, infrastructure, institutional flexibility (that includes academic and administrative governance) and the elimination of political interference. This, of course, is by no means an exhaustive list but serves as a useful guide to building a first-class university faculty.

In terms of salary structure, the emoluments offered to university teachers as a determinant of the quality of faculty developed and retained is, of course, is the first thing that comes to mind. This was not always so. Before liberalization, when the demand for skilled personnel was less dynamic than it is today, academia suffered from an abundance of riches when, relative to the supply of postgraduate students (the qualification deemed necessary to enter the university as a member of the faculty), faculty positions available were very few. However, the increasing political interference in education led to a situation where it was not always the best scholars who were absorbed as members of the faculty. Intra-institutional political partisanship too had the same effect. At the same time, the living conditions under all those who lived on a government salary declined all the way to the '70s as high inflation ate into the real incomes received, as salaries in money terms did not rise as fast.

Given the relative lack of opportunities elsewhere for those with a postgraduate education, academia was still placed with a considerable pool of talent from which the best could be picked. Additionally, it was also assumed that for those seeking entry into the universities money was not the primary motivation; the love of teaching and research was. It is another matter that those selected did not always share these ideals. While salaries of government officials (and college and university teachers) started to rise in a fairly impressive manner from the mid-'80s onwards, the salaries offered to the private sector employees rose much faster. This was coupled with a change in attitude: the middle class that was supportive of government policies at the time of Independence and looked to their children entering government service now favoured employment in the private corporate sector where salaries were higher.

Without the reputation that could have insulated higher education from the unattractiveness of lower salaries, it has started to become increasingly difficult to get quality faculty to teach those subjects where the job market is favourable. Programmes offering IT courses were the first to feel the pinch of faculty shortage that now afflicts subjects like economics as well. The reason is simple: private sector salaries in these fields are so many times more than in academia, that the best and the brightest are naturally drawn to the private sector. Compared to academia where standard pay scales are the norm without any provision to reward the more meritorious, the market pays very handsomely to the executives who deliver. The annual remuneration of the best executives is measured in crores. Indeed, fresh MBAs expect to receive initial offers that are several times the pay received by their senior professors.

Another factor that affects the universities' quest for quality faculty is that in a globalized world, where information is readily available, exceptionally talented faculty is often lured away to universities in the developed countries where salaries are many times more than the salaries Indian universities pay. Is pay parity with the private sector then the answer?

Before attempting to answer this question, it is worth reiterating that those who choose to seek academics as a profession do so with the knowledge that in all probability riches do not await them in this particular vocation. This not to impute to them a perverse attraction for penury and hardship, but rather to assume that the love of influencing minds through teaching and the pursuit of knowledge thorough research and the recognition that comes from their peer group and even beyond compensates for a more modest financial pay package.

Equally important is the fact that employment for 'regular' university faculty is secure. Their services cannot be terminated before the age of retirement except for the most serious of offences, none of which is linked to their performance at the workplace. This job security is almost absent in the private sector. Indeed job insecurity increases the higher one rises. Similarly, promotion rules ensure that most university faculty members attain the position of professor in the course of their careers.

As for comparisons with pay scales in foreign universities located in Western Europe, North America and Japan, a comparison with the rupee equivalent of salaries received in dollars or sterling is misleading. Purchasing power parity comparisons are more reasonable and reveal a more favourable picture although it has to be conceded that salaries paid in the West do allow for a far more comfortable lifestyle.

It may be argued, therefore, that while the level of salaries that may be needed to attract and retain a world-class faculty needs to be raised, parity with the private sector or foreign universities is unnecessary. Security of tenure compensates for a lower level of pay where the private sector is concerned while purchasing power parity considerations ensure that pay scales of foreign universities do not have to be matched. It is pertinent to add here that security of employment where university faculty is concerned must not be tampered with. Even in an age of outsourcing, corporations do not tinker with or outsource core operations. Even as operational and cost flexibility assumes paramount importance, companies ensure that employees associated with core operations are hired on a long-term basis. For the university, whose core functions are teaching and research, hiring faculty members associated with such functions on short-term contracts would be short-sighted. Under these circumstances where planning horizons of faculty remain short, goals will remain myopic with obvious consequences on the learning curves of universities.

Security of employment of core employees, which refers to faculty members where the university is concerned, is essential to develop

The interior of the magnificent Library, University of Mumbai.

: Amitabh Mattoo

: Courtesy: University of Mumbai

and retain a world-class faculty. Institutions that are designed to function in perpetuity can scarcely be well served by people whose planning horizons are made short term by the nature of their employment contract.

The future problem areas would lie in the increasing pressure for differential pay scales for different departments, with faculty for vocational courses demanding more pay in contrast to departments whose programmes are not 'obviously' job-oriented. This can be faced squarely by allowing for differential pay scales or indirectly by providing for equal pay, but also providing a liberal regime for consultancies such that teaching and research is not compromised. Self-financing courses may also be used to give participating teachers a higher salary. The last two options mean that no extra financial burden is borne by the State. What should be avoided is the splitting up of faculties into increasingly specialized institutions where the possibility of interdisciplinary learning and research becomes difficult.

• • •

University infrastructure is also an important determinant in attracting, developing and retaining world-class faculty. Educational infrastructure such as libraries, both traditional and online, laboratories, provision for ICT and multimedia services and support, IT-enabled teaching devices are essential for research and teaching. Quality infrastructure serves to amplify the ability and effort put in by teachers enabling them to deliver more with the same effort. This is particularly true for IT and multimedia infrastructure which serves as a great leveller especially when competing with world-class institutions. This is because Moore's law ensures that costs of IT hardware fall even as performance improves.

With adequate infrastructure of this kind where lectures can be stored and improved upon, continuous improvement, or *kaizen*, becomes eminently possible, which in turn reinforces the confidence of the faculty to compete with the best in the world. This feeling of confidence, which in turn evolves into institutional arrogance, is a vital factor in retaining a world-class faculty.

The impact on research is obvious – if faculty members feel that infrastructure is not a constraint in pursuing research on any topic, it is one less reason to leave. Indeed, as research findings enter the curricula enabling continuous updating of syllabi the quality and reputation of the programmes being offered improves with its impact on faculty retention. In addition, as cutting edge research is carried out and results disseminated, collaborative research becomes possible as other world-class institutions as well as corporations – whose core areas are technology-intensive – seek to pool resources both infrastructural and intellectual in order to eliminate duplication and create synergies. Indeed, joint courses too could be offered in collaboration with other universities.

Equally importantly, students too may use this infrastructure to be better informed and in many ways be equipped to compete globally as the field is levelled. It enables us to compensate at least in part for shortcomings in course/programme design and judge members of the faculty independent of labels of caste, region, seniority or party affiliation. The breakdown of hierarchy where knowledge production is concerned and the ability to appreciate the real creators of knowledge and where they actually stand in the world of academia is another important contribution that infrastructure makes that helps in retaining motivated faculty.

By and large, these developments brought about by infrastructure serve to boost capacities, capability and therefore morale adding to institutional arrogance. Institutional arrogance, an intangible quality is a vital tool to maintain standards and, when projected in an appropriate manner, even shields institutions from political pressure.

• • •

We had begun with the premise that a faculty that aspires to be world class does so not out of the desire to make money, but because of the love of teaching and research. It is imperative then that the institution grant university teachers all the necessary flexibility to frame their respective courses. Motivated faculty members will seek to upgrade their syllabi continuously and cumbersome procedures inhibit efforts at change. This is not to say that there should be no checks. A standards setting exercise that sets the floor for any course and which itself is upgraded from time to time ensures that the changes that are implemented are for the improvement of courses taught and not their debasement.

At the same time, there should be similar flexibility for programmes designed, especially those that are self-financing. As new programmes are designed, introduced and discarded depending on the changing needs and requirement of a knowledge society, it is clear that not all programmes will succeed. Nor will it be easy to predict which one will. Yet the ones which succeed will be rapidly duplicated. Thus, it is vital that this flexibility be the norm. This is also essential for raising the resources necessary to increase the emoluments of university teachers.

Again, it is necessary to set up a body to set and measure standards that may evaluate the devised programme, given the programme's stated aim and course content. This evaluation can serve as an indication/guideline to prospective students whether to opt for the programme, and to employers whether to look at the programme to source employees. Nevertheless, institutional flexibility is paramount if new programmes are to be designed. The design of a successful programme is a vindication of the efforts of university teachers not only to keep up with changing times but also be agents of that change. It is also likely that it is motivated teachers who will take the initiative to do so and that too in the company of other motivated teachers. Universities that allow faculty members to do so will find it easier to retain motivated staff united in their purpose and functioning as an integrated team. Bureaucratic hassles that inhibit evolution and innovation serve to kill initiatives and demotivate even the best faculty.

The administration should be so designed that academicians are not overburdened by excessive paper work when implementing research projects or travelling to conferences. Indeed, it is the university system more than project sponsors who make spending a more arduous task. The latter is more interested in the project findings, provided there are no cost over-runs. A less bureaucratic system means fewer non-core employees in the university system, which means more funds and attention can be diverted to the core operations of the university.

In the same vein, institutional inflexibility may serve to deny universities the services of some of the world's best faculty members. For example, rules currently exclude the possibility of faculty in India holding joint appointments, with an appointment in an Indian university as well as an appointment elsewhere. This serves to exclude the possibility of an Indian professor who holds a position in a world-class institution offering the same courses in an Indian university as he or she does in his/her institution. This is an inflexibility that only serves to deny the services of a world-class faculty to Indian universities available at a fraction of its cost abroad.

Political interference in university appointments has been the bane of higher education in most states as well as central universities. Political interference can be classified into the following kinds: cases where political interference attempts to ensure that only persons subscribing to an 'acceptable' ideology are selected; and cases where caste/regional biases enter the selection process, and cases of straightforward favouritism where political players push their candidates in return for favours, or an IOU to be harvested later.

The induction of teachers through this process, given its patent unfairness, can be thoroughly demotivating for those teachers who have the ability and inclination to develop and bring to fruition world-class programmes. Yet, at the same time, given the present framework, political interference is also extremely difficult to avoid. It may be argued that universities and indeed departments of repute who have carved a niche for themselves in the academic world and possess and project institutional arrogance are generally able to resist political pressure. The problems arise when this is not the case as it is for most universities and departments where the presence of deadwood serves as an excuse to accommodate some more. In this regard, parochial interests become very difficult to resist.

It is here that the support of those stakeholders be sought whose stake in meritorious appointments is the maximum and this is quite easily the student community. Seen through the narrow prism of self-interest, as consumers of a service called higher education, they have a vested interest in seeing that the best teacher is appointed. This enables them to be trained better and compete nationally and globally. Even disregarding arguments based on self-interest, it may be argued that as a class university students are far more cosmopolitan in their outlook than politicians who espouse parochial politics. Indeed this cosmopolitanism should be nurtured and encouraged as a bulwark against parochial interests.

As for curbing political interference of other kinds, it has to be borne in mind that this interference is, by and large, local. A simple mechanism can ensure that this is minimized: universities should desist from employing their own students till these students demonstrate that they have obtained permanent employment in other universities. If the number of universities that follow this policy is sufficiently large, then a job market for university teachers – at least at the assistant professor level – is created with provisions for both supply of trained personnel as well as presence of positions, with competition being fairer as, for each department, the prospects of choosing one's own candidate is ruled out. As the candidate to a post is likely now to be a non-local, political interference may be expected to be reduced. But a by-product of this process is the elimination of 'in-breeding'. Thus, this process, by keeping merit at the forefront, gives the entire selection process a degree of credibility which not only attracts genuine talent, but also reduces the risk of demotivation that arises when undeserving candidates enter the system.

One way of motivating universities to undertake this practice is to link the financial assistance required to give raised pay with the adoption of this practice. This tempers the opposition of most members of the teaching community as they are already 'in' and stand to lose the benefits of higher pay if they resist reform. It is also an incentive for them to teach and supervise research better as the students they teach and supervise have to be made ready to face competition elsewhere.

• • •

The challenges of developing and maintaining a world-class faculty where Indian universities are concerned is made very difficult in a milieu where most universities are characterized by low local politics, corruption, complete de-motivation and the predominance of local turfs dominated by local 'academic' worthies who use their position to dispense favours to followers. Many universities no longer possess either the moral authority, or the intellectual rigour for the government, or the media, or the people at large to engage them for advice of intellectual inputs. It may thus appear that some of the suggestions outlined seek to reward those who should actually be penalized.

That is why students' empowerment and involvement in university matters, especially evaluation of teachers, their courses, the programmes offered and research supervised, is of the utmost importance. This is all the more essential if students are made to compete nationally for jobs, which increases the urgency for quality education and instruction. This urgency is likely to be increased as students become aware of the programmes and courses that are on offer elsewhere including the best universities. Infrastructure, especially in IT, delivers this information in real time and enables them to compare courses, course material, programmes, and research findings, enabling them to evaluate their faculty.

In this context, populist tendencies by teachers to devalue their syllabi are unlikely to win support whereas teachers who run the risk of offering more rigorous courses get greater appreciation, especially from the lot of students who are more motivated. In this milieu, the community that creates knowledge comes together more easily. The appreciation derived thereof is the key to retaining motivated members of the faculty. Similarly when empowerment and participation is coupled with increased competition the stake that students have in better instruction, supervision and course design rises higher. In these circumstances, the demand for the best faculty is likely to trump parochial and political considerations.

To sum up, therefore, appreciation and flexibility brought about by a judicious mix of resources and administrative reforms is the key to developing and maintaining a world-class faculty. While salary structures do need to be improved, the administrators may discover that it is the empowerment of students as well as increasing the competitiveness of the milieu that they operate in that may be the key to attracting motivated faculty members.

•

# Equity vs. Quality

Higher education in India, thankfully, is beginning to accquire the importance that it deserves. Underlying this new commitment to higher education are at least three factors: one, the realization that power in the contemporary world is increasingly rooted in the knowledge economy; two, the well-springs of the recent growth story in India and the respect that it is beginning to command in the world are in no small measure due to the contribution of a few institutions of higher education – IITs, IIMs, selected universities, etc.; and, three, the vast majority of our institutions of higher education remain quite untouched by concern for quality and excellence; in fact, mediocrity seems to be their defining characteristic. There is very little that is not known about the ills that plague the higher education scene in India. These have been dissected and analyzed threadbare by a number of commissions and committees over the years – the latest being the National

By **B.K. Joshi**

Knowledge Commission – not to mention the numerous scholars who have studied the issue.

A summary measure of where we stand in the world in terms of the quality of our institutions is provided by the various lists of best universities in the world. A recent evaluation of the world's universities and research institutes undertaken by a university in Shanghai came up with the sobering (for us) finding that none of the Indian institutions of higher education figured in the top 300, while six Chinese institutions did. The Indian Institute of Science was placed in the top 400 (Basu, 2006). In the words of the National Knowledge Commission there is 'a quiet crisis in higher education in India that runs deep'.

The problems confronting higher education in India are generally classified into three categories: access, equity and quality. It would not be incorrect to claim that so far the emphasis has overwhelmingly been on access with equity becoming a second important concern during the last two decades. Quality as a characteristic feature of higher education, except in a few selected institutions, is usually relegated to the margins of the discourse. Thus, it is hardly surprising that the achievements of higher education are recounted in quantitative terms like increase in the number of colleges, universities, engineering and medical colleges and enrolment of increased access. Even in terms of access we are found wanting as evidenced by the following observation of the National Knowledge Commission:

> The proportion of our population, in the age group 18-24, that enters the world of higher education is around seven per cent, which is only one-half the average for Asia. The opportunities for higher education, in terms of the number of places in universities, are simply not enough in relation to our needs (National Knowledge Commission, 2007).

Faced with this fact, our response is that we have to increase enrolment before anything else. It should hardly come as a surprise, therefore, that a series of regional conferences of vice chancellors convened by the University Grants Commission for achieving inclusive growth during the Eleventh Five-Year-Plan has come up with the recommendation that the 'foremost priority must…be enhancing access to higher education such that the GER is raised to a minimum threshold level of about twenty per cent for sustained economic development'.

Inclusive growth, by definition, presupposes equity. The issue really boils down to the effectiveness of the instruments that we choose for promoting equity and the impact these instruments have on quality. So far we have relied almost exclusively on reservations for select social groups – Scheduled Castes (SC), Scheduled Tribes (ST), Other Backward Castes (OBC) – as the means to equity. The time has come to ask a few pointed, though admittedly sensitive, questions: What has been the experience with reservations in India? To what extent have they been successful in promoting equity? Are reservations the only, or best, mechanism of affirmative action and equity? Has the emphasis on access and equity been at the cost of quality?

Before proceeding any further I wish to clarify that I am not questioning the need or importance of either improving access or promoting equity. Both are very important objectives, but they should not be seen in isolation from quality. In fact, access, equity and quality have all to be promoted simultaneously. We cannot hope to either progress internally, or compete internationally, if we even remotely believe, as we seem to have been doing so far, that the three ideals can be pursued sequentially - let us ensure access and equity first and take care of quality later. That, to my mind, is the crux of the problem that we are facing in the realm of higher education. Higher education, or for that matter education in general, is best conceived as a triangular structure resting on the three pillars of access, equity and quality. The stability of the structure demands that the size and strength of each pillar should be identical. If the pillars are not of equal size or strength, then the structure will either become lop-sided or even collapse. Something of this kind seems to be happening to higher education in India.

Sticking with the structural analogy for the moment, it may not be too far off the mark to say that the way we have been building higher education, the three pillars are of different size and strength. The pillar of access appears to be the longest and strongest (though not necessarily as long or as strong as it ought to be, or so the National Knowledge Commission and the UGC seem to be telling us). This is followed by the pillar of equity, while that of quality is the shortest and weakest. Is it any wonder that the higher educational system is unbalanced and debilitated? Can we, therefore, think of retrofitting the structure to correct the balance between these elements, since the option of demolishing the existing structure and building anew is not really available to us?

We now turn our attention to the questions raised above. There is little doubt that reservations have provided access to higher education to many persons belonging to deprived and oppressed groups. It is doubtful if in the absence of reservation the number of persons belonging to SC, ST categories (since these two categories have had the longest benefit of reservations) getting the benefit of higher education, including technical and professional education, would have been what it is today. Thus reservations have certainly resulted in the inclusion of new social groups, which earlier had little or no access to higher education. Whether this has promoted equity or not is a debatable point.

Two things need to be kept in mind in this context. One relates to the nature of social (read caste) hierarchy in India. Though the terms Scheduled Castes, Scheduled Tribes and Other Backward Castes are convenient short-hand devices to refer to whole social groups, these are by no means undifferentiated categories with all members suffering from similar disability. They, in fact, share some of the hierarchical characteristics of the larger, especially Hindu, society. Thus even among Scheduled Castes, Scheduled Tribes and Other Backward Castes there are groups that are socially and economically better off and so in a better position to take advantage of reservations. That is why complaints are frequently heard that the benefits of reservation have gone disproportionately to specific caste or tribal groups. The second concerns the politics and political economy of the reservation issue. From time to time various groups have voiced demands and exerted pressure on the system to be made eligible for reservations. Equally, these demands have been resisted by other groups who do not want the benefits enjoyed by them to be diluted by inclusion of more social groups in reserved categories. This has resulted in the gradual expansion of the list groups eligible for reservation, especially in the OBC category in states. The success or failure of a group has less to do with any objective social criteria and more to their political and economic clout.

Doctors' Strike against Reservation.

: B.K. Joshi

: Courtesy: *Outlook*

The following example can help to clarify some of these issues. The Supreme Court in Indra Sawhney vs. Union of India, 1992 (Mandal Commission Case) directed that the 'creamy layer' should be excluded from the ambit of reservation. The Supreme Court left it to the government to decide the criteria for identification of the creamy layer within a period of four months of the judgment. As subsequent experience shows this has proved to be problematic and the power of the vested interests has been so great that the provision has not really been applied.[2] To quote another example, in certain states such as Bihar and UP a sub-category within the OBC called Most Backward Classes (MBCs) has been identified, and it is claimed that they deserve special consideration such as a quota within the OBC quota.

There have been frequent and regular demands from groups outside the pale of reservation to be included in one or the other category enjoying reservations. It is interesting to note that while in states such as Rajasthan the demand of the Jats to be included among OBCs has been conceded, a similar demand by the Gujjars, backed by a fairly prolonged agitation, to be categorized as a Scheduled Tribe has not borne fruit, and in fact has resulted in a counter agitation by Meenas, who have enjoyed ST status, protesting against grant of ST status to Gujjars. An interesting case of extending the benefits of reservation comes from Uttarakhand. Here the whole of Jaunpur Block in Tehri Garhwal district has been declared backward and eligible for reservation. As a result persons belonging to this block (not necessarily living here), irrespective of their caste identity, which means including Brahmins and Rajputs, enjoy reservation as OBCs.

The last example raises an important issue about reservations in India. In general, barring a few exceptions like the one cited, the basis of reservations has been membership of certain tribal or caste groups. The exclusion principle enshrined in the concept of the creamy layer, on the other hand, is not caste specific, but is wider in scope as it embraces social and economic domains. While the caste and tribal criteria cover the most ubiquitous forms of social backwardness in the country, they nevertheless leave out of their purview other forms of backwardness such as economic, or religion-based, or even area-based following from the example Jaunpur Block in Uttarakhand. The issue of specific religious groups being brought within the ambit of affirmative action has acquired prominence lately in the context of the Sachar Commission report on the status of Muslims in India. This question has come up in two different forms in the past as well. For instance, Dalits who have converted to Christianity and Buddhism have been asking for recognition as SCs for the purpose of reservation despite the fact that the religion of their adoption does not recognize caste. It has also been faced by state governments while drawing up lists of OBCs entitled to reservation. Specific Muslim 'castes' have been identified as OBCs in some states. The demand for inclusion of more such groups is ever being raised. Finally, there is the issue of the poor and economically backward among the so-called forward castes and their demand for reservation through a separate quota. In short, the issue of reservation has got riddled with the same complexities that characterize the caste system.

Given the complexities of the issue of reservation there are no easy solutions to the various problems thrown up by it. Perhaps the time may have come to think of other methods of affirmative action. One alternative that may be considered is an equal opportunity programme. According to newspaper reports, an expert panel headed by Professor N.R. Madhava Menon, set up by the Government of India last year, has proposed the setting up of an Equal Opportunity Commission. This commission will be accessible to anyone who feels discriminated on account of belonging to a particular social group and just those belonging to Scheduled Castes, Scheduled Tribes, Other Backward Classes, minorities, persons with disabilities, etc. The panel is reported to have recommended going beyond a purely formal approach to equality, use of a 'Deprivation Index' for judging the need for protection and publicly debated criteria of evidence for establishing equality of opportunity (*Indian Express*, 5 May 2008). There is a strong need to seriously debate these ideas, along with some other alternatives.

In our single-minded pursuit of reservations as the sole means of providing access to education and ending discrimination, we have not really looked at other ways of achieving the same outcome. One of the arguments used against reservations as practiced in India, especially in the realm of higher education, is that it goes against the merit principle. Reservation, according to this view, implies that a certain percentage of the places available have to be filled from among students belonging to the identified disadvantaged groups. As a result, these places are filled by students from the reserved categories even when in terms of merit they are placed much lower than their counterparts from the open or non-reserved category. To compound the problem, many students from the open category are not able to secure admission in institutions of their choice even though they may have been placed higher in the merit list than students from the reserved category. Inevitably, this results in resentment among the open category against the reserved category. Such a situation arises because, for one, the reserved category students compete only among themselves for securing admission; and, secondly, in general, there are no cut-off points prescribed for them. This, therefore, raises the fundamental question: What is the purpose of reservation in higher education? While providing access is fine, should we be providing access without any consideration to merit? Does such a course really serve the wider social purpose, as against the narrow interest of those who benefit from it? In the words of one analyst:

> Enhancing access, equity and diversity in higher education does not mean that all must be treated as equal or exactly the same. Nor does it imply equal or proportional representation in all areas of higher education and institutional operations. It simply implies being systematically fair. Consideration for all on an equal footing requires that inequities, when they occur, should be justified by overall benefit and gains to all concerned and that they should be in the public interest. Some alternatives to affirmative action should also be devised to strike a balance between equity and equality, on the one hand, and individual gain and public accountability, on the other. Greater accuracy, creativity and autonomy in the appraisal of the qualifications of prospective students are required to serve the individual, institutional, national and international interests (Gupta, 2006).

What, then, could be some of the alternatives to reservations? This issue is admittedly complex and highly sensitive. It requires careful handling being a zero-sum game in which the benefit to one group is at the cost of other groups. The losers are not likely to sit back and accept what they feel has been unjustly taken away from them. Moreover, being socially and economically better placed than the beneficiaries of reservation and affirmative action policies, they are likely to use all means at their disposal to undo what they perceive as the harm done to them.

The alternative is best visualized in the context of quality and excellence, which should be the hallmarks of higher education. It is a fact that persons belonging to Scheduled Tribes and Scheduled Castes are grossly underrepresented in the field of higher education. As for the Other Backward Castes, the jury is still out. It is doubtful if the explanation for this situation can be given purely in terms of discrimination at the level of higher education. A major reason lies in the absence of access to education opportunities from the primary level upwards. This is the result of the accumulated neglect of primary and secondary education during the past sixty years. While on the issue of lack of opportunities, we have to also recognize that the poor from among the so-called forward castes are not too much better placed with regard to access to higher education.

The situation, as it has evolved over generations, cannot be corrected overnight. Hence, some ameliorative measures will have to be undertaken in the short term as well. Reservation, it needs to be recognized, is the easy way out. It can be done by fiat. The manner in which we have implemented it means that the only follow-up measure that is taken is asking for periodic reports on the status of its implementation. The results may, perhaps, be different if we adopt a different approach. What is being suggested is a two-fold strategy. Part one of the strategy consists of equipping the students belonging to the vulnerable and deprived groups – SC, ST, OBC, minorities, persons living in remote and poorly served areas, the poor from all social groups – to compete on equal terms with others and enter institutions of higher education on merit. This should be done by the provision of free mentoring and supplementary and remedial education to such children by existing universities and colleges – including professional colleges – either by organizing regular classes, or through the distance mode. The State should meet the full expenses of this programme. When students belonging to the vulnerable and deprived groups enter institutions of higher education on their merit it will work wonders for their self-esteem. We often do not realize that an affirmative action device such as reservation can also have negative psychological consequences by nurturing feelings of inferiority. As one analyst of affirmative action points out 'affirmative action can harm the interests of the very disadvantaged people it is intended to protect by branding them as "inferior" or "incompetent" or both. In the long run, it may prove to be "doubly cursed" or "fulfilling negative prophecies". It may even lead to further polarization or stigmatization in some cases, despite the best intentions to the contrary' (Gupta, 2006). The second part of the strategy involves liberal payment of scholarships, bursaries, fee-waivers, student jobs and earn-while-you-learn-schemes to students belonging to the poor, vulnerable and deprived groups. The objective should be to ensure that no meritorious and deserving student is deprived of higher education, simply because he or she cannot afford it.

Reservations, it must be recognized, will have to continue for some time to come. They cannot be eliminated in one stroke. At the same time, they cannot continue indefinitely as at present. It bears repetition that the Constitution of India, provided reservations for only ten years, which has been extended every ten years. On the contrary, instead of being eliminated, as was the intention of the Constitution, their ambit has been widened. It would not be incorrect to say that reservations have acquired a life of their own in India. Thus, any attempt to eliminate or reduce their scope is bound to meet with stiff resistance. One would therefore have to tread very cautiously, yet resolutely. Perhaps what can be done is to reduce the scope of reservation gradually in stages once the alternative methods of meeting the three-fold goals of inclusion, equity and quality start showing results.

Above all, we need clarity at the policy level on what we want in the field of higher education. Are we satisfied with mere expansion in numbers of universities and colleges of indifferent quality churning out unemployable graduates, postgraduates and even doctoral students; or do we aspire to build an inclusive higher education system – and not just a few selected institutions – of world standards in terms of quality? Once we are clear on this issue we should proceed to prepare a detailed road map for achieving our goal and steadfastly follow that goal.

•

: B.K. Joshi

ENDNOTES:

1. Chief Justice K.G. Balakrishnan observed while hearing the reservation case recently, 'Will the creamy layer ever allow the disadvantageous class to come up? They are enjoying the cream. In short, creamy layer is like a higher caste who will not allow the really backward to come up.'
//economictimes.indiatimes.com/articleshow/2507001.cms Nov.1, 2007

REFERENCES:

Agarwal, Pawan, 2006, 'Higher Education in India: The Need for Change', International Council for Research on International Economic Relations, Working Paper No. 180. http://www.icrier.org/pdf/ICRIER_WP180__Higher_Education_in_India_.pdf.

Basu, Kaushik, 2006, 'India's Faltering Education System'. http://news.bbc.co.uk/2/hi/south_asia/4793311.stm.

Gupta, Asha, 2006, 'Affirmative Action in Higher Education in India and the U.S.A. Study in Contrasts', Centre for Studies in Higher Education (University of California, Berkeley) http://repositories.cdlib.org/cshe/CSHE-10-06.

Malik, Surendra, 1992, Supreme Court Mandal Commission Case, 1992, Lucknow: Eastern Book Company.

National Knowledge Commission, Government of India, 2006, Report to the Nation 2006, http://knowledgecommission.gov.in/reports/report06.asp.

University Grants Commission, 2007, National Conference on Development of Higher Education for Expansion, Inclusion and Excellence: Relevant Issues and Recommendations of Regional Conferences of the Vice Chancellors. http://www.academics-india.com/VCs'%20recommendations.pdf.

# Mortgaging the Future*

For Indians, higher education has been, in Stanley Wolpert's evocative words, 'the swiftest elevators to the pinnacles of modern Indian power and opportunity'. This realization, coupled with the severe limitations of publicly funded higher education institutions and the greater purchasing power of the middle class, means that Indians are prepared to pay rather than be denied. According to National Sample Survey (NSS) data, the government's share in overall education expenditure has been declining steadily, from eighty per cent in 1983 to 67 per cent in 1999. For states like Kerala, the decline is steep, from 75 to 48 per cent, while for Madhya Pradesh it is from 84 per cent to 68 per cent. Indeed, while private expenditure on education rose 10.8 times between 1988 and 2004, that for the poor rose even faster, by 12.4 times. Many students who formally enrol in publicly funded colleges and universities barely attend classes there. Instead, they pay considerable sums to the burgeoning private sector vocational IT training firms such as NIIT and the Aptech or in

By **Devesh Kapur, Pratap Bhanu Mehta**

new professions such as the 'Aviation University' being set up by the United Breweries (UB) group.[1]

However, the most noticeable trend has been the transformation in the provision of professional education, especially engineering, medicine and business schools. We analyzed data on all medical and engineering colleges in India to understand how the ownership structure has changed over the last four decades. Data for medical colleges was obtained from the Medical Council of India's website, which gives the year of establishment, an ownership classification as 'Government' or 'Private' (institutions set up under the Societies Act or as trusts), and the number of seats for each institution.[2] We examined data for 19 major states of India – Assam, Andhra Pradesh, Bihar, Chattisgarh, Delhi, Gujarat, Haryana, Himachal Pradesh, Jharkhand, Karnataka, Kerala, Madhya Pradesh, Maharashtra, Orissa, Punjab, Tamil Nadu, Uttar Pradesh, Uttaranchal and West Bengal. Similar data for engineering colleges was obtained from the All India Council for Technical Education.[3]

In the case of engineering colleges, the private sector, which accounted for just 15 per cent of the seats in 1960, accounted for 86.4 per cent of seats and 84 per cent of all engineering colleges by 2003. In the case of medical colleges, the private sector dominance is less stark, but the trend is unambiguous: the proportion of private seats has risen from 6.8 per cent in 1960 to 40.9 per cent in 2003. While we do not have precise data, the situation in more than 1000 business schools suggests that ninety per cent are private. Even in general education, there is now a mushrooming of private, self-financing colleges. In Kanpur University (in UP), the number of such colleges outnumber state-assisted colleges three to one, while in Tamil Nadu, self-financing colleges comprise 56 per cent of general colleges and 96 per cent of engineering colleges (Srivastava, 2007). Educational institutions, including private universities and coaching centres, have emerged as the largest advertising spending category in print media (which has the largest share of the advertising market in India).[4] Even as political parties rail against de jure privatization, de facto privatization continues unabated.

For long, it was taken for granted that private universities (as distinct from private colleges) needed approval from the UGC. After the break-up of Madhya Pradesh, the Ajit Jogi-led Congress government in Chhattisgarh saw a regulatory loophole and enacted the Private

University Act in 2002. One hundred and eight such universities came up in the state, with 94 in the state capital (Raipur) alone. After a new BJP government came to power, it passed the Private University Amendment Bill in 2004, under which proprietors of all private universities would have to deposit Rs. 2 crore with the government and prove that they have 25 acres of land for their institutions. Belatedly, the UGC came up with the UGC Establishment of and Maintenance of Standards in Private Universities Regulations, 2003. Each private university would now require a separate State Act conforming to the relevant provisions of the UGC Act. Interestingly, the private universities set up were using the state's regulatory largesse, and, even to the limited extent they were delivering educational services, were doing so outside the state, under the nomenclature of these being off-campus centres. The new UGC regulations try to curb this loophole as well. A university set up under a State Act shall operate 'ordinarily within the boundary of the State concerned,' and can open off-campus centres (outside the home state), off-shore (abroad) centres and study centres only 'after the development of main campus ... and after five years of coming into existence.' Even then, it would require the prior permission of the UGC and the government of the host state, and such approval would be forthcoming in unspecified 'exceptional circumstances'. On the other hand, the admission, fee structure and programmes of study of the private university will have to conform to the norms and regulations prescribed by the UGC and other statutory bodies.[5]

The degree to which states have allowed the establishment of private higher education institutions varies considerably. The number is greatest in the southern states and Maharashtra, and least in states like Bihar and West Bengal. However, most other state governments are now following suit. Caught between escalating demand and ballooning expenditure on higher education, even communist West Bengal has begun to reduce funds to meet the salary requirements of teachers and non-teaching employees for private undergraduate colleges in Calcutta (Mukherjee, 2004). Gradually, the State plans to eliminate its annual commitment of Rs. 350 crore on the more than 240 general-degree colleges run by private bodies. However, the state government has been adamant that any self-financed undergraduate general degree colleges be affiliated with the state-run Calcutta University.[6]

There are three key reasons for the expansive stance of political parties from all ends of the ideological spectrum: the state's fiscal limitations; partial diffusion of the reservation conundrum by expanding supply; and, with earlier sources of patronage exhausted, the search for new sources of patronage. The licence raj may have been dismantled in industry, but it is flourishing in higher education. The non-profit status allows for tax exemption and makes it easier to launder money; it also gives access to free land without inviting a PIL; and, given the demand, virtually any institution has a market.

The exit to private suppliers of higher education is a phenomenon not limited to India's borders. While the numbers are lower, the overseas purchase of higher education has much greater financial implications. In 2006, we estimate that there were more than 150,000 Indian students studying abroad – nearly 80,000 in the U.S., about 40,000 in Australia, 19,000 in U.K., and another 11,000 in Canada, New Zealand and Singapore. Pre-liberalization, the figures were barely one-fifth of this number. The main growth has been in undergraduate education and professional degrees (especially MBAs), both of which require students to put up their own money. We have two estimates of the amounts spent by Indians on consuming education abroad: invisible data from the RBI balance of payments and our own calculations based on average costs of education in these countries with allowances for scholarships. The RBI estimate was $1.06 billion in 2005–06, more than 10-fold the amount in 2000–01 ($95 million). This is a lower bound, since in many cases the money is paid from overseas. Our estimate for 2005–06 is about $3.5 billion, a staggering amount for a poor country whose own educational institutions are starved of resources.

Even more important than the financial costs are the implications for public education when elites leave. Indeed, the dilemma is a more basic one – the consumption of public services by elites has adverse distributional effects. But when elites exit, so does their voice. The big difference between the higher education systems of Pakistan and India is that elites in the former invariably sent their children abroad even for undergraduate education, and consequently had little stake in the system. The results have been disastrous for higher education in Pakistan. Could India face a similar problem?

This reality is lost to Indian policy elites, especially in the HRD Ministry which is strongly opposed to the GATS (although the

Commerce Ministry has been an advocate). The Indian policy is expressed by the HRD Ministry:

> The revised offer made by India at the GATS was to partially open up the Higher Education Sector under the condition that Higher Education Institutions can only charge fee as fixed by an appropriate authority and that such fees do not amount to charging capitation fee or lead to profiteering. The provision of the Higher Education services would also be subject to regulations already in place or to be prescribed by an appropriate regulatory authority' (MHRD, 2006–07)

– hardly the most welcoming policies to attract the world's best universities, especially when so many countries are vying for their attention.

• • •

Three key variables help understand the political economy of India's higher education: the structure of inequality in India; the principal cleavages in Indian politics; and the nature of the Indian state. While India is not exceptional by conventional measures of income inequality, it is an outlier when measured by educational inequality. Indeed, India is to educational inequality what Brazil is to income inequality (Kapur, 2007). Such extreme inequalities inevitably result in populist redistributive backlash. However, the specific redistributive mechanisms are conditioned by the principal cleavages in Indian politics and the nature of the Indian state. The growth of identity politics has sharply enhanced political mobilization around two key cleavages in Indian society: caste and religion. Consequently, redistributive measures follow these two cleavages rather than other possibilities such as income and class, region (urban-rural), or gender. Moreover, given the fiscal constraints of the Indian state and the shifting locus of rents, since the resources available for redistribution are very limited, redistribution focuses on much more 'visible' forms. This explains why India's poverty alleviation programmes focus on 'visible' club goods such as employment programmes rather than less visible public goods such as health and education. And this is also why in recent years Indian politicians have obsessed over reservations in elite institutions in higher education rather than improve the quality of primary, secondary schooling and the thousands of colleges of abysmal quality.

The battle over admissions to higher education institutions in India is as old as independent India. In 1951, a Brahmin girl was denied admission to a medical college in Madras even though she had scored sufficient marks. The student appealed to the Supreme Court claiming she had been discriminated only based on her birth (caste). The Court agreed and struck down the Madras government order.[7] Major agitations broke out in the state and the resulting pressure forced India's first constitutional amendment even before the Lok Sabha had been formed. The amendment (adding Clause 4 to Section 15 of the Constitution) now read: 'Nothing in this Article or in Clause 2 of Article 29 shall prevent the State from making any special provision for the advancement of any socially and educationally backward classes of citizens or for the Scheduled Castes and the Scheduled Tribes.' The unambiguity implied in 'nothing' combined with sufficient ambiguity of the term 'socially and educationally backward classes' would prove fertile terrain for political populism.

The social reengineering that began in Madras province gradually spread to the rest of the country over the next half-century. The confluence of identity and redistributive politics meant that higher education – the erstwhile preserve of India's upper castes – would inevitably become the battle ground of politics, especially as the 'silent revolution' empowering lower castes gathered force. Indeed the mismatch between new social groups holding political power and erstwhile dominant social groups entrenched in universities led the former to deliberately undermine state universities (exemplified in Bihar in the 1990s), since in doing so they were also undercutting the social power of old upper-caste elites.

The other cleavage of Indian politics – religion – is also manifest in higher education policies. The India Constitution (Articles 29, 30) provides special protection to linguistic and religious minorities in the country, allowing them to preserve their culture and traditions through minority institutions with few government controls. However, when government controls are circumscribed for 'minority' institutions but mount for all other private higher education institutions, the incentives for each group to classify itself as a minority are obvious. Meanwhile, those minorities for whom the original protection was put into place – Muslims – get little more than symbols. The HRD Minster Arjun Singh's declaring AMU 'a minority institution' – later declared unconstitutional by the courts – even when the Muslim community was not pushing for it, is a case in point. When the Sachar committee on the status of India's Muslims showed that the socio-economic status of Muslims was relatively lowest in the states ostensibly most committed to secularism – the SP-governed UP, and the CPM-governed West Bengal – the states rushed to announce the creation of special universities for Muslims. A day after the final exit polls for UP elections in 2007 showed the SP losing, the government of Mulayam Singh Yadav called a special session of the State Assembly whose sole agenda was to pass a bill granting minority status to the Mohammad Ali Jauhar University in Singoor in Rampur (the constituency of his Urban Development Minister, Azam Khan) and making Khan the University's lifelong chancellor. With the University having been accorded minority status, any irregularity in its functioning can now be probed by the University Grants Commission only after being cleared by a three-fourth majority in the Assembly. The theoretical point is that the entry barriers are a degree of regulatory control varies between communities: this is both bad politics and bad regulation for education.

In 2007, India's best known liberal arts college, St. Stephen's College announced a new reservation formula for Christians and the introduction of a separate quota for Dalit Christians citing the college's 'Christian foundation' and unambiguous identity as a 'mission college' to justify the new quotas. Forty per cent of the seats in the college will now be reserved for Christian students as against the earlier 32 per cent, and 25 per cent of these will be set aside for Dalit Christians. Quotas for SCs, STs, the disabled, sports and children of defence personnel will add another twenty-odd per cent. Only forty per cent will be purely on examination results – this, in an institution where 95 per cent of the funding of the college is from the Government of India (via the UGC). The creation of many new central universities is also driven by similar motives. The Babasaheb Bhimrao Amedkar University and Mahatma Gandhi Antarrashtriya Hindi Vishvavidyalaya have total enrolments of 435 and 200 respectively, a decade after they opened – hardly the sorts of numbers that would enhance the ostensible social goals underlying their creation.

Nonetheless, the choice of instruments used by the Indian state to advance the cause of 'backward classes' remain puzzling. Consider the recent extension of reservations to OBCs in the Indian institutes of Technology (IITs) and Indian Institutes of Management (IIMs) on grounds of helping India's 'depressed classes'. The total number of annual admissions in the IITs are just 5500 and the IIMs a further 1200. The second-tier national engineering colleges (the National Institutes of Technology (NIT)) have another 11,000. The number of engineering colleges in India nearly tripled in the last decade – from 562 in 1997–98 to 1522 in 2006 – while their annual intake grew from 134,298 to 550,986 (MHRD, 2007). Thus, although the IITs account for just one per cent of all engineering graduates, they attract most of the attention.

Prima facie, it may appear that equity goals may be better pursued in expanding the size and quality of the base. The dismal condition of public primary education is a stark testimony to the level of commitment to this ideal. However, it could be argued that even with the best of intentions the sheer magnitude of the task means that it would take a long time. Why not try something that would promise faster, though more limited results? If that were the case, then interventions at the secondary school level would be warranted. The gross enrolment ratio in Class IX–X is 51.65 per cent but drops sharply to 27.8 per cent at Class XI–XII. Even a modest reduction in the dropout ratio could significantly increase the potential college-going pool among the backward classes. But there has been little effort directed to this end. Let us suppose that there is an imperative need to immediately improve access to tertiary education to the backward classes. Clearly, sharply increasing the resources directed for this purposes would be a beginning. At the secondary level, the Annual Plan expenditure for the purposes of improving 'Access and Equity' is Rs. 3.9 crores while another Rs. 3.7 crores has been earmarked for 'Quality Improvement in Schools'. At the tertiary level, UGC's entire expenses to this end are Rs. 84 crores: Rs. 26 crores for special development grants to universities and colleges in backward areas; Rs. 25.6 crores for remedial coaching of SC/ST students and disadvantage minority communities; and Rs. 8.8 crores for coaching SC/ST students and disadvantage minority communities for entry into services. There is no evidence of the effectiveness of these programmes.

An insight that might explain the choice of instruments comes from Mani and Mukand (2007), who argue that a 'visibility effect' distorts governmental resource allocation and explains why governments neglect provision of essential public goods, despite their considerable benefits. Greater democratization widens the gap in resource allocation between more visible (such as specific poverty projects) versus less visible (such as malnutrition prevention) public goods, up to an intermediate level of democracy (after that this gap decreases). The specific instruments to address distributive issues in India illustrate this trend.

The university system in India is the collateral damage of Indian politics. The vast majority of government colleges in small towns offer dismal educational outcomes, the result of tight control of appointments, fees, curriculum, capital improvements. With fees in some of these colleges capped as low as Rs. 9 per month, and the State picking up salaries for civil service like faculty jobs, with little work burden, there are considerable rents around to get those jobs. Running government higher education institutions to the ground is not the result of limited resources, but a matter of deliberate strategy. For politicians, there are four benefits of the license-control raj.

First, old-fashioned rent seeking on contracts, appointments, admissions and grades: At the Centre the HRD Ministry appoints more than 100 heads of the key higher education institutions. There are hundreds of discretionary grants to government-aided institutions and building contracts. The situation is far worse at the State level as examples from just two states illustrate.

*Karnataka*. The credentials of the nominees of JDS (Janata Dal Secular)-BJP coalition government to the governing syndicate of Bangalore University were so dubious as to be rejected by the previous vice chancellor. A new, more pliable, VC has accepted all of them – and their power to steer contracts and appointments despite the Karnataka Universities Act, 2000, which requires all members of the governing syndicate of Bangalore University to be 'eminent educationists'. The first vice chancellor of the all-women Karnataka Women's University, Bijapur, has been indicted by the Justice S.R. Venkatesh Murthy Committee for large-scale misappropriation and maladministration. Despite this indictment she remains in office. In Tumkur University, which exists on paper, the vice chancellor is under investigation for running up huge personal bills on the university account. At the Rajiv

Gandhi University of Health Sciences, Bangalore, the Central Bureau of Investigation has recommended the filing of criminal charges against the vice chancellor, former registrar and thirty other officials for deliberately leaking question papers to favoured students writing the university's postgraduate entrance test and tampering with their answer papers.

*Uttar Pradesh*. In September 2005, the vice chancellors of four universities – Mahatma Jyotiba Phule University, Rohilkhand, Bareilly; Veer Bahadur Singh Purvanchal University, Jaunpur; Sardar Vallabh Bhai Patel University of Agriculture and Technology, Modinagar; and Chandrasekhar Azad University of Agriculture and Technology, Kanpur – were dismissed by state governor T.V. Rajeshwar Rao on corruption charges. In August 2006, Class V students were found grading the postgraduate answer papers of LLB, BCA, MCA and nursing students of Chaudhury Charan Singh University, Meerut.

Old fashioned patronage and partisan politics: The use of State resources on higher education directed for partisan purposes has been an accepted practice ever since Mrs. Gandhi put large resources into the creation of JNU to enlist the support of intellectuals of a specific ideological bent. In the last decade this has become more blatant, ranging from Murli Manohar Joshi's (the HRD Minister in the BJP led-NDA government) attempts to pack various ICSSR institutions with academically inept partisans to the Left Front government in West Bengal refusing to grant autonomous status to the venerable Presidency College, since it would then be unable to pack the faculty with its own supporters.

However, the demand-supply imbalance for affordable quality institutions has also led to bitter battles on the location of brand name central educational institutions. This includes not just the IITs and IIMs, but central universities. Recently members of the Left parties and the Dravida Munnetra Kazhagam – fellow travellers in the UPA government – nearly came to blows in the Lok Sabha over the introduction of the Indian Maritime University Bill, 2007 which sought to locate a national-level maritime university in Tamil Nadu (the state to which the minister belongs) rather than Kolkata (which has had a long standing marine engineering college).

New entrepreneurial activities: Parliament in independent India was initially dominated by lawyers. Subsequently, agriculturalists became dominant. Today 'educationists' are probably the most prominent. In many cases they have a direct interest.[8] In other cases, their names are used to signal protection, be it the Sharad Pawar University or the Arjun Singh Street in Jamia Millia University. The promotion of professional (medical, engineering, business management, and so on) colleges has become the private preserve of small-town politicians doubling as 'educationists'. It makes good financial sense to run government-run higher education institutions to the ground since it forces students and parents to look for more meaningful alternatives in the private sector – which are controlled by them. Politicians have emerged as the single largest provider of new higher educational institutions. The license control raj in higher education and the apparent horrified reactions to education becoming a commercial enterprise, result in capitation fees driven underground, thereby ensuring large amounts of untaxed income. And since the institutions are classified as Trusts and Societies, their reporting requirements are much less than if they were under the more transparent Companies Act.

Colleges as screening mechanisms for politics: It is usually assumed that an important function of higher education is to act as a signaling device to potential employers and labour markets. The better institutions indeed play that role in India. But the majority of government institutions (where the education is a farce) appear to serve a signaling role to an entirely different audience: political parties and politics. Since the education in these colleges – mostly in small towns and cities – have little effect in job markets, especially in the growing private sector, student politics serves as the signaling mechanism for aspiring politicians. The ability to win student elections and resort to street violence is an asset to all political parties.

• • •

Despite impressive reforms elsewhere, Indian higher education sector remains the most tightly controlled and least reformed sector. Deep ideological and vested interests have made reform in India's higher education sector all but impossible. It would not be an exaggeration to say that India's current system of higher education is centralized, politicized and militates against the production of general intellectual virtues. The fact that the system nonetheless produces a noticeable number of high-quality students is due to the sheer number of students and the Darwinian struggle at the high school level to gain admission into the few good institutions.

The most acute weakness plaguing India's higher education system is a crisis of governance, both of the system and of individual institutions. This is most visibly manifest in the acute shortage of qualified faculty. The generation that was inspired by a broad commitment to the public good has retired, or will do so soon. There is little likelihood of sufficient replenishment, given entrenched mediocrity in institutions with lifetime appointments, few competitive pressures and abysmal governance. The result has been the academic equivalent of Gresham's law – the bad drives out the good. The prevailing political ideological climate in which elite institutions are seen as anti-democratic, finds its natural response in political control to influence admissions policies, internal organization, and the structure of courses and funding. As quality deteriorates, students are less and less willing to pay the very resources without which quality cannot be improved. In India's case, the answer has been the growth of private sector higher education institutions and increasingly the consumption of education abroad.

Fundamentally, Indian policy makers have to recognize two things. First, the competition for talent is now genuinely global. If the design of institutions is not commensurate with this reality; if the freedoms, incentives and quality benchmarks on offer do not allow you to compete on a global scale, building quality institutions will remain a chimera. There is, in principle, no reason why India could not become a global education hub, if it got its regulatory system in order. Second, a vibrant system requires enlisting the energies of a whole range of actors. It also requires responding to a diversity of challenges and unexpected opportunities. Only a system that draws on the competitive energies of the market on the one hand, a flexible and supple state system on the other, and a genuinely committed non-profit sector as a third leg will be able to meet India's challenges. The scale of demand in India is such that it needs to draw resources and energies from all sources rather than engage in a politics that benefits incumbents, constrains supply and rewards mediocrity with regard to quality.

•

ENDNOTES:

* Abridged, from 'Mortgaging the Future? Indian Higher Education' by Devesh Kapur and Pratap Bhanu Mehta, to be published jointly by NCAER and Sage Publications.

1. According to Finance Ministry data cited in *The Hindu*, since its launch in 2001 the Education Loan Scheme has grown from roughly 50,000 accounts and Rs. 670 crore loans as on 31 March to approximately 1,53,000 accounts and Rs. 2,600 crores loan amounts on 31 March 2004. 'Education loan scheme simplified,' *The Hindu* , 11 August 2004.
2. See: http://www.mciindia.org/apps/search/
3. See: http://www.aicte.ernet.in/
4. Nivedita Mookerji & Pummy Kaul, 'Education tops ad spend in print,' *Financial Express*, April 18, 2005, p.1.
5. 'A private university shall fulfill the minimum criteria in terms of programmes, faculty, infrastructural facilities, financial viability, etc. as laid down from time-to-time by the UGC and other statutory bodies such as the All-India Council for Technical Education, the Bar Council of India, the Distance Education Council, the Dental Council of India, the Indian Nursing Council. 56 the Medical Council of India, the National Council for Teacher Education, the Pharmacy Council of India etc.'
6. The one condition on the self-financed colleges is that they have to offer courses in emerging areas like bio-technology, molecular biology and business administration. See: Mita Mukherjee, 'Privatisation kickoff with two colleges', *The Telegraph*, 4 April 2004.
7. Champakam Dorairajan challenged a Government Order issued by the government of Madras Province (as it was then called), earmarking admission of students to Engineering and Medical Colleges of the State strictly on the following basis: of every 14 seats, 6 were to be allotted to Non-Brahmin (Hindus), 2 to Backward Hindus, 2 to Brahmins, 2 to Harijans, 1 to Anglo-Indians and Indian Christians and 1 to Muslims.
8. The examples cited here draw from various issues of *Education World* as well as newspaper articles.

# In Defence of Liberal Education

There is a searingly powerful moment in Akbar Ahmed's recently published book *Journey into Islam*, an account of his travels across the global Muslim community. Ahmed, a devout Muslim who holds a chair in Islamic Studies and is a professor of international relations at American University, describes his travels through the Muslim world with his American students as an 'anthropological excursion'. When he visits Aligarh Muslim University (AMU) in India, an institution instrumental in shaping his liberal sensibilities, he is taken aback. Instead of finding in the AMU an academic beacon of liberalism he comes across students shouting slogans in praise of Osama bin Laden and ready to descend into mob violence at the sight of their American visitors. Ahmed's AMU encounter was even more disturbing than the group's visit to Deoband, an acknowledged centre of South Asian Islamism. For Ahmed, this may be a sad

By **Harsh V. Pant**

acknowledgement of the collapse of the 'Aligarh model' of liberal Islam, but for India this signals the collapse of yet another bastion of liberalism: its universities.

The Indian government is not unaware of this crisis. Inaugurating a national conference of vice chancellors, organized by the University Grants Commission, the Union Human Resources Development Minister, Arjun Singh, described higher education in India as a sick child and asked the assembled vice chancellors to define 'what should be the content, extent, methodology and basic ingredients of higher education'. Education has been placed at the centre of the forthcoming Eleventh Five-Year-Plan, described as India's 'education plan'. The outlay for education is being increased from 7.7 per cent of the total gross budgetary allocations in the Tenth Plan to more than 19 per cent in the Eleventh Plan with an unprecedented five-fold increase in education spending in nominal terms. Again, the prime minister has repeatedly emphasized the need for reforms in the universities and called for a 'new revolution in modern education' with an emphasis on 'a quantum jump in science education and research'.

The National Knowledge Commission, a high-level advisory body established by the prime minister to recommend changes in the higher education system 'with the objective of transforming India into a knowledge society,' has also underlined the need for a systematic overhaul of India's higher education system. Its of recommendations include creating more universities, changing the system of regulation for higher education, increasing public spending and diversifying sources of financing, establishing a number of National Universities that can provide education of the highest standard, reforming existing universities, promoting greater accountability and ensuring greater access among others. In line with these suggestions, the government has indicated that it plans to fund new central universities, Indian Institutes of Science Education and Research, IITs, IIMs as well as Indian Institutes of Information Technology. Not only will the science and technology base in universities be strengthened but more scholarships will be offered for the youth to enrol in science courses at the undergraduate and postgraduate level.

While these are noble goals, it is instructive to point out that the focus seems largely to be on quantity and on science and technology education. This is understandable for a number of reasons. Knowledge is the key variable that will define the global distribution of power in the twenty-first century and India has also embarked on a path of economic success, relying on its high-tech industries. While India's nearest competitor, China, is re-orienting and investing in higher education to meet the challenges of the future, India continues to ignore the problem as if the absence of world-class research in Indian universities is something that will rectify itself on its own. True, India produces well-trained engineers and managers from its flagship IITs and IIMs, but their numbers are simply not enough. There is also a growing concern that while private engineering and management institutions are flourishing due to a rising demand, the students they produce are not of the quality that can help India compete effectively in the global marketplace.

India has the third-largest higher education system in the world, and is behind only the U.S. and China in this area. Our higher educational institutions churn out around 2.5 million graduates every year. However, this caters to just about 10 per cent of India's youth and the quality of this output is considered below par. Apart from our premier institutions – the IITs, IIMs, AIIMS, the Indian Institute of Science, and Tata Institute of Fundamental Research, to name a few – our higher education sector is increasingly incapable of meeting the rising expectations of an emerging India. Indian universities, which should have been the centre of cutting edge research and a hub of intellectual activity, are more often in the news for political machinations than for research excellence. Years of low investment in higher education along with a mistaken belief that providing uniform support to all universities irrespective of their quality have led to a situation where neither our academics nor our students have any incentive to undertake cutting-edge research.

Higher education cannot be reduced to mere economic instrumentality with its sole focus on equipping students with the practical skills needed by employers. Nor should the purpose of our higher education be simply to produce engineers and scientists able to compete with the Chinese. Reduction of learning to job skills rather than an inquiry into the larger issues of life can be disastrous in the long run. Unfortunately, the government's response so far seems to signal that a democratic society like India no longer needs or requires liberal education to shape its intellectual foundation.

: Harsh V. Pant

In a 2002 essay, Mark Yudoff, then President of the University of Minnesota, observed that a university might succeed in competing in the academic market, but still lose hold of what makes it what it is: '...to remain a great learning institution, it will have to continue to nurture learning for its own sake...and to foster other less quantifiable and profitable – but still valuable features of the university'. One is unable to gauge whether either the government or the National Knowledge Commission is interested in such an overarching overhaul. Their emphasis appears to be on science, partnerships with industry, and advances in technology. So if there is to be a new dawn in Indian higher education, it seems as if liberal education is unlikely to be a significant part of it.

• • •

A number of factors have contributed to the mess that confronts the Indian higher education system today. India has never been good at providing a balanced higher education to its students to begin with. Immediately after their Intermediate examinations, students are asked to choose between the Sciences and the Arts, as if that is the most meaningful distinction in education. The importance of the three years of undergraduate education for a student as well as a society cannot be overestimated because, as Allan Bloom puts it, 'they are civilization's only chance to get him'. Sadly, all we offer our undergraduate students in our provincial universities and degree colleges is perhaps one of world's least stimulating educational systems. How can we expect our youngsters to have a passion for intellectual pursuits when for them higher education means listening to their lecturers drone on from notes that have not even been updated since they were first made? The result: the reputation of our universities has been so dented that ambitious Indian students no longer consider them even as a last resort.

We must also remember that universities do not exist in a vacuum. Since an educational system and a society have a symbiotic relationship, it may well be that we have today an education system that mirrors a broader national culture that no longer privileges learning as a means to improve oneself as a human being. A nation that seeks to define its progress by its ability to use modern technological gadgets – in sports, in politics, and in intellectual pursuits – is hardly likely to look at education in any other way other than as a means to become technologically competitive. In the absence of any serious stimulation, youngsters today tend to apply their imagination and intelligence to whatever is within easy reach. In fact, all of us, young or old, are equally susceptible to the culture of distraction spawned by television, video, and the web. Given today's emphasis on marketable products, measurable outcomes and business skills, it is unlikely that higher education will be able to expose students to larger issues of justice, truth and morality. The youngsters of today, hammering away at a Microsoft Xbox or obsessing about Facebook profiles, have no place for books. In this world of instant messaging, where is the time to lose oneself in a private world conjured by a writer for hours or even days?

The truth is that our higher educational institutions are making students too practical for their own (and their nation's) good. The really important questions – What is truth? What is morality? What is justice? – are no longer addressed. Yet it is such questions that determine who we are, both as individuals and as a society. An ultra-competitive environment and the rising cost of education foregrounds a utilitarian strain that has made it difficult for liberal education to make a case for itself. This is true of most other countries as well. It is important to remember that it was only after a great deal of hue and cry that the higher education system in the U.S. re-introduced the teaching of 'great books' and started to place an emphasis on service-learning so that students were made to engage with the outside world.

Matters have not been helped by the institutions we have created to administer our system of higher education. For instance, the UGC has tried to increase its control over the Indian higher education system, making it impossible for universities to shape their own courses and determine their research agenda. This top-down approach in the mistaken belief that homogenization of institutions will produce greater pedagogic creativity leaves no room for competition among higher education institutions. Indian universities have become moribund institutions run by cloistered, change-resistant bureaucracies where curriculi are not updated for years, teaching methods remain obsolete, and students are not exposed to cutting edge research and ideas. Political interference in selections, appointments and day-to-day administration of universities has become common, eroding autonomy to such an extent that a university is now considered a sort of government department. Our universities are being held hostage to the imperatives of identity politics, encouraging parochialism rather than countering it. Indian universities are seen today to be serving every conceivable social, political and economic purpose except the one that they were designed for: the cultivation of the intellect. The higher education system in India has ended up becoming another instrument for serving myriad socio-political goals and has lost sight of its true purpose, relinquishing any vision of the role of education in a liberal democracy.

• • •

The three components of a liberal democratic society – the market, civil society, and the State – have different expectations from universities. The market requires trained personnel for the technologically complex economies; the State requires a corpus of trained elite to run its apparatus; and civil society requires a liberal education to foster the deepening and broadening of democracy. While these competing expectations produce some conflicts in so far as the relative utility of liberal and professional education is concerned, both remain essential in a free society and are necessary for the development of an educated individual – an individual who can think and communicate effectively, make relevant judgements and ably discriminate among values. A balance between the two is therefore needed, not a sharp distinction between 'liberal' and professional training. If the purposes of liberal education are to instil knowledge, to cultivate intellectual skills and to nurture the traits of personality and character basic to a reasoned and responsible life, then it should be part and parcel of any professional education. The way our undergraduate education is structured, however, continues to be a major hindrance towards such integration.

Most students today find engineering, medicine or management the most lucrative options to study. At the same time, our education system has created an artificial divide between various streams. The result is that our engineers, doctors and managers are rarely exposed to the underlying liberal ethic of higher education. Social sciences and humanities are being devalued today vis-à-vis science and technology, which are bound to result in some serious consequences.

Democracy requires a questioning citizenry brought up on liberal education that gives its citizens the ability to interrogate and investigate the claims of authority. India's higher education has long ceased to ask big questions, the most important of which should be: What kind of citizens is the Indian education system producing?

A liberal education encourages us to ask probing questions and to think intelligently about the perplexities and challenges of human experience. It allows for the formation of the character quality of being considerate, respecting and loving other people, especially those who disagree with us. Critical thinking is an essential skill that such an education is well-equipped to provide whereby students analyze ideas, differing viewpoints, opinions, and in the process learn how to construct logical assessment, and defend their conclusions with facts and logical argument. Thomas Jefferson argued that education should 'enable every man to judge for himself what will secure or endanger his freedom'. It is liberal education that produces a thinking citizen, the backbone of a democracy. Higher education, if it is to have any real meaning, should be transformative, liberating students from the confines of their own backgrounds and prejudices and opening up a world with new meanings and purpose. Liberal education nurtures those intellectual and moral habits that form the basis for living the best life one can. More important, we need to understand that literature, art, philosophy, history, etc. should be studied for their own sake, without needing any justification. They should not be viewed as instrumental to some larger good. They are their own good.

It is not at all evident if our higher education is preparing students to be democratic citizens, a task that should continue to be the principal purpose of a liberal education. Indian higher education has all but abandoned the intellectual and moral principles that have traditionally informed and given substance to liberal education. Indian universities of today have become intellectually dull places imbued with careerism as opposed to the energy of contending ideas, limiting the questions the Indian academics ask and the conclusions they reach. Indian universities need to earn back social respect and reclaim their role at the centre of public life by embracing a culture of reasoned inquiry and debate.

• • •

: Harsh V. Pant

The critical role of liberal education for societies at large has been highlighted by various scholars. It has been suggested that liberal education increases innovation and economic fluidity, helps in the development of critical thinking and communication skills in a country's leadership and citizenry, extends participatory citizenship, promotes tolerance, reduces brain drain and generates cross-cultural understanding. All this makes it imperative to promote a system of higher education that contributes to greater social mobility and egalitarianism.

Since a university epitomizes the very spirit of free inquiry, Bloom, in his perceptive meditation on the state of higher education in the U.S., *The Closing of the American Mind*, concludes that 'a crisis in the university, the home of reason, is perhaps the profoundest crisis' for a modern democratic nation. Though the crisis that he was drawing attention to arose from a different set of issues facing U.S. academia in the 1960s and 1970s, the present crisis in Indian universities is equally profound and has the potential to directly affect the future of India. If the main goals of higher education are teaching students to think critically, broaden their intellectual horizons and promote self-awareness, then the Indian higher education system should be considered a comprehensive failure.

Indian universities have yielded intellectual and moral authority to the point where students are not taught values, and are not even allowed to discover them. Our undergraduates are not given a chance to understand the ideas that shaped the past with the result that they do not learn to think coherently about the present. They learn nothing about Indian heritage, its writers and poets, or its ancient texts for fear of offending sensibilities. It is imperative that we identify an essential core of knowledge for students and encourage our undergraduates to take a 'core curriculum' of philosophy, history, mathematics, literature, science, and a regional language along with English. There is a need to craft a meaningful agenda of what it means to be educated in today's intellectual and moral climate.

To be effective in a liberal democracy, a liberal education has to be highly subversive in nature, allowing the citizens of liberal democracies to question authority. While reflecting and reinforcing a modern, liberal and enlightened sensibility, a liberal education thus serves the highest form of democracy. The value of a liberal education comes from a distinctive quality of mind and character that it encourages the ability to explore moral and political questions from a variety of perspectives. In the words of political philosopher Leo Strauss,

> Liberal education, which consists in the constant intercourse with the greatest minds, is a training in the highest form of modesty, not to say of humility. It is at the same time a training in boldness: it demands from us the complete break with the noise, the rush, the thoughtlessness, the cheapness of the Vanity Fair of the intellectuals as well as of their enemies. It demands from us the boldness implied in the resolve to regard the accepted views as mere opinions, or to regard the average opinions as extreme opinions which are at least as likely to be wrong as the most strange or the least popular opinions.

The fate of liberal education, therefore, should be taken very seriously by Indians, especially if we are serious about preserving the liberal democratic socio-political order in India. And Indian academia has a special role to play in this regard. It is wrong to assume that academics can engage in politics of the day only by coming out of their ivory tower and protesting in the streets. The academia has a far more effective way of dealing with political issues: by conveying knowledge that provides individuals with a way to comprehend themselves and their surroundings and teaching them how to conduct themselves in the world. The future of India as a liberal democracy ready to face the contemporary world hinges on their success.

•

: Harsh V. Pant

Management students celebrating their graduation.

Courtesy: *Outlook*

# Where Did We Go Wrong?

The first colleges in India set up in the Western mode will be two hundred years old in the first quarter century of this millennium. One must, therefore, remember that India – unlike many other Third World or even First World countries – is an old player in modern education. Simply because the pioneers of this education were Englishmen or those inspired by them, it has suited later nationalists (and more recently the fashionable post-colonialists) to somehow conclude that this was a sinister ploy by the alien rulers to control the populace. Nothing could be further from the truth: Western-type colleges were crucial in retaining and enhancing the heritage of Indian languages and culture. Colleges teaching Sanskrit and Persian – and soon Hindustani and Urdu – were set up in late eighteenth or early nineteenth century. Several 'Hindu' colleges sprang up in Calcutta, Poona, Benares (as these cities were then

By **Meghnad Desai**

called) and elsewhere by 1825. They were the first secular abodes of knowledge where a student's caste did not hinder him from getting educated. Women's education, too, was pursued in face of 'native' disapproval by the Company in early nineteenth century and later by Christian missionaries.

Education in India was thus the first liberating force from centuries of caste oppression and a brahminic monopoly of knowledge. Were it not for British rulers of India, who had lived through the Enlightenment, a *vaishya* like Shyamji Krishnavarma would never have become a Sanskrit scholar, or a *mahar*, such as Bhimrao Ambedkar, a lawyer and economist of distinction. It was also the Western-educated elite in the colonial 'college towns' that defined the idea of India as a single nation with an identifiable history and culture. It was their education at home, and in England, which enabled this so-called westernized elite to make 'The Discovery of India'.

Sadly, the years since Independence have not furthered the liberating force of higher education. Designated a State subject, primary and secondary education have once again gone back into the clutches of caste domination. This is why the North Indian states of UP, Bihar, Rajasthan and Madhya Pradesh display such poor educational and human development indices. However, thanks to the anti-brahmin movement, education – and consequently, human development – flourishes south of the Vindhyas. Indian universities follow the same pattern: so that while the universities in the old port cities of Bombay, Calcutta and Madras have maintained their standards, the ones at Benares, Lucknow, Allahabad and Patna have virtually ceased to exist as educational institutions. The latter are now simply nurseries for breeding mafia-politicians in their student and teacher unions.

In the first two decades after Independence, the Ministry of Education was entrusted to distinguished academics and politicians. Turn now to the NDA and the UPA coalitions and the ministers who held this portfolio under them. Both have shown a total bankruptcy of vision and an immense capacity to inflict damage. But why blame individual ministers? Our political parties have helped to create student unions across universities that are not just anti-intellectual, but positively unintelligent and thuggish. The recent violence in Delhi University led by the Akhil Bharatiya Vishwa Parishad (ABVP) is not an isolated instance: Bhopal, Lucknow and Baroda are no different. Campus violence only reveals that whether 'secular' or communal, all parties encourage student violence. Lumpen behaviour is sanctioned by senior party leaders since they look upon university student and teachers' unions as effective weapons to be used in the vote bank war. Apex institutions, such as the University Grants Commission (UGC), which are supposed to guard the standards of academic excellence, are widely viewed now as obstacles to progress. They have proved helpless in halting the falling standards of our universities. Thus, while they can delay recognition for a new institution, they have never taken away the licenses once given.

All this is tolerated because of a peculiar change of attitude that has taken place in Indian society. What we witness in the 350 universities that now exist is an inverted pyramid. After letting loose the forces of populism on publicly maintained universities, the high elite of civil servants, politicians and rich businessmen have opted out of the university system. Their children now go to premier institutes such as the IITs and IIMs. The entrance to these institutes is fiercely competitive and it is no wonder that reservations and caste quotas for these elite temples are strongly resisted. Those who cannot get their progeny through these exams can always send them abroad. Little wonder then that the elite do not care what kind of higher education is given to the rest of the country. So, a lousy education is the price Indians pay for not being a part of the elite club that has power, privilege or money.

Our public sector universities are hopeless and likely to remain so because they have been kept under-financed since students are grossly under-charged. Teachers here need not teach, let alone keep up their knowledge base, or engage in research, since they are now little better than government babus who have no fear of being sacked. Promotions follow with age though wisdom seldom does. This is why, despite boasting of a youthful workforce and thousands of graduates, India is faced with the problem of skill shortage. The graduates of most universities need extra on-the-job training to be useful in their jobs. The under-resourcing of education is a cost for the private sector as well as for the hapless student. As India's young population grows, there is not sufficient educational infrastructure to equip them with even the rudiments of knowledge.

What, then, is the solution? Yes, we must have 1500 more universities as the Knowledge Commission has advised. In fact, we may need 15,000 more. But there is no point in doing this if they are going to replicate the existing template. The truth is that universities need to be given better resources. The first step to enable this is to make all higher education fee-paying and to have realistic fee levels. Education may be a public good at primary and secondary levels, but higher education is an investment in human capital, which enhances the recipients' earning power. There is no reason why the tax payer, often a landless worker, should finance the future middle-class income of the university student. Income contingent loans should be created (as in Australia and U.K.) so that students can pay the full cost of higher education.

The full cost of this education will require better-paid teachers, but with short contracts and incentives to perform better than at present. There should be no tenure except at the senior level after, say, twenty years of good performance or, in exceptional cases, outstanding research output. It will require better stocked libraries with good internet facilities and well-maintained buildings. I would calculate that roughly 75 per cent of these costs should be met from the fees, with the government providing the remainder. Even this remainder should be allocated strictly on the basis of research performance and indices such as a low drop-out rate, peace on the campus and a decent pass rate.

Since universities conduct their own examinations at present, it is difficult to check their standards. However, once fee-paying education begins, students will insist that there are GMAT-type tests that measure the educational achievements of students independently of their university teachers. Thus, for core subjects – such as English and math – universities should cease to be examining bodies and become purely teaching ones. If nothing else, this will sort out the sheep from the goats.

There will be a complaint that charging for higher education will make it unaffordable for the less well-off. This is the usual ploy of the populist politician whose own children will not suffer such education. As it is, not many less well-off go to university in any case and even if they did there is a response to such predictable objections. An income contingent loan means that no one pays up front, but only out of future income and at a rate depending on their income. At present, parents are willing to pay at private universities and for elite institutions such as IIMs. The same logic can be extended to all colleges. A proper cost of going to universities will at least make it expensive for those 'students' who hang around universities to further their political careers. It will also make their fellow students more protective of their education against disruption by thugs. Such money as is currently subsidizing fees in the public universities should be converted into a national fund for merit scholarships.

But there is much more to do beyond that. Higher education in India has followed the British model. Not as it is at present, but as it used to be – narrow, inflexible, elitist and subsidized. Now British education is aiming at getting fifty per cent of the 18 to 25 years cohort into higher education whereas 43 years ago, when I first started teaching at LSE, it was 12 per cent. However, the degree structure is still a rigid three-year one in most cases and British universities insist that students finish their entire degree in one university. The American system is, and has always been, more open and broad-based in terms of recruiting across the income and class spectrum. Americans allow colleges, which have a two-year Junior college status, where students can get a basic grounding and then go on to finish a degree only as and when they feel they need it. They allow students to transfer credits from one college to another and finish a four-year degree at their chosen pace. Significantly, America achieved the fifty per cent target for students of the young cohort getting access to higher education long before Europe did.

Americans consider education a democratic right and not – as the British once did – a class privilege. But that does not mean it is free. Students pay for their education by working while studying, taking loans or saving up before going to college. India needs to think much more along American lines. This means that any student – of whatever ability – who has finished secondary school or dropped out and later worked, can access higher education for at least two years at some institution. Moreover, this institution will, in return for a fee, provide her/him with education. Thousands of such colleges are needed. What is more, they should be allowed to flourish with minimal government interference. Students will know the difference between a good college and a worthless one. They will also realize which institutes give value for money and which ones are simply a waste of time.

: Meghnad Desai

Let us not forget that people already follow this logic when they pay to learn in schools which teach computing and professional skills of that kind. Anecdotal evidence says this is also how the moderate income earners in cities treat the question of their children's schooling. They are willing to pay for private schools than go to the free, but useless, public school.

Trusting the consumer is difficult for the babu whose raison d'etre is cultivating a climate of distrust to justify his paternalistic interference. It is worth remembering that both babudom and politics have failed Indian higher education. The Indian people must demand a new education structure, which caters to their needs in a friendly and flexible way. India needs a fifty per cent target for its young cohorts to go to higher education. The way to do this is to reduce the role of the State to one where it provides merit scholarships and a minimal regulatory structure. I am certain that the innovative energies of the Indian people will do the rest.

Let me briefly explain what I mean by that.

The last twenty odd years have shown that when freed of babudom and political interference, the Indian business sector is able to stand on its own feet. Today, this sector is competitive and world class. This was largely achieved by abolishing the 'permit-license raj' and cutting tariffs and other protectionist comforts. Indian business can now play a more prominent role in restructuring higher education to help make it world class. The crucial element here is to devise a testing scheme on the lines of GMAT or GRE that will grade all colleges across the country and then insist that when they recruit, it is these grades that will be considered evidence of academic achievement.

Since it has failed miserably to maintain standards or further the cause of higher education the government, on the other hand, should withdraw as the provider of higher education. Instead, it should finance higher education strategically by providing merit scholarships and funding research. It should also make a simpler regulatory framework to encourage the setting up of new institutions. Teachers should not be treated as government babus, since that is what rots the system, but made accountable to the students and universities they serve. In short, if the government is serious about improving the education system it should release this sector from its clutches.

•

# A Conversation with A.K. Damodaran

## *Madras University*

**A.K. Damodaran:** I spent my early years in the native state of Cochin, a small state, a promontory of Madras Presidency. Madras University had a large number of colleges affiliated to it all over the Presidency and Maharaja's College; Cochin was one of them. It was a very demanding type of university and our college was allowed to hold graduate classes only as late as 1924. I was quite happy to spend two years in Cochin's Maharaja's College. Then I went to Madras Christian College. I was not interested in what I was supposed to study, so I became a happy wastrel and thoroughly enjoyed myself. The All-India Students' Congress came later, but there was already a students' movement, and the nationalist movement as well. We all were very involved in these activities. I was a dazzling success as a speaker, but a total failure as a student. Mathematics and I did not speak to each other, so I came away and spent one more year in a small college, St. Thomas' College, in Trichur. In other words, I had an unusual exposure to Christian colleges: Madras Christian College and St. Thomas' College.

By **Ira Pande, Narayani Gupta**

**Ira Pande:** *You must have come from a very conservative Hindu family and I know many people of your generation who did this kind of shift, to Christian institutes, very seamlessly, where you preserved both your identities. Perhaps what made education in those days so rich in every respect was that you were really blending two traditions of knowledge. Would you like to say something about this?*

**AKD:** You are absolutely right. I would like to highlight the phrase 'really seamless'. The Maharaja's College was a government college but the principal was a former lecturer in a Christian college, not in a theological sense, but with a genuinely moral environment. The secular atmosphere of a Christian college is impossible to reproduce; I will give you just one example. I was once awarded a prize for debating and my teacher asked me to buy myself some books. The ones I bought were all by rationalists and free-thinkers. The Dean of my hostel, Professor T.G. Platten, was slightly upset but he did not say anything.

**Narayani Gupta:** *Could you tell us something about your mother, who was a great Sanskrit scholar and writer in Malayalam?*

**AKD:** I would love to talk about the beginning of women's education at this point. The young ladies who were born in the 1880s were the first ones in our family who went to school. My mother just escaped it, she never went to school. She studied Malayalam and Sanskrit at home. I don't know why that happened because all her younger sisters went to school and later became very distinguished scholars in English and Malayalam while she was a pure Sanskritist. The movement for university education for women comes at the end of the nineteenth century with the establishment of women's colleges. In Madras, it was Queen Mary's College and Women's Christian College.

**IP:** *Did it help that your own family was enlightened enough to send you to Christian institutes and that you yourself were exposed to Sanskrit and the classics at home?*

**AKD:** One of the most remarkable things about not just Kerala but the entire South Indian culture, is that there is a certain mutual tolerance between communities. For example, you can access good Malayalam in the Bible – a little eccentric but very good, nonetheless. And some of the finest poems in Malayalam

A handsome skyline of buildings that constituted the Madras Christian College and School after it had put down firm roots in George Town, across the way from the Esplanade. This picture dates to the 19th century.

: Courtesy: Vintage Vignettes

were written by Hindus about Christian themes.

**IP:** *I will skip many decades now and come to a much later period to ask you something about a lack of such tolerance in the north. Here, caste still remains a huge impediment, which perhaps is why North Indian universities have remained locked in a certain insularity. South Indian universities, I feel, are different in this respect. What are your views?*

**AKD**: One important point to remember here is that in Madras, for example, the anti-brahminical movement was an *internal* development within the upper castes, not a movement of Dalits versus the upper castes. It was led by the Nairs and the Mudaliars – the non-Brahmin upper castes against the Brahmins. This is perhaps a reason why the caste question in the south is different from the north. However, I find your point interesting because in Benares you get a great man like Madan Mohan Malaviya who founded a Hindu university. He was a great nationalist, but also a Brahmin, and a Hindu university was bound to be a little biased towards the Brahmin, don't you think?

**IP:** *So, university education in Kerala, due to its mixture of a Christian and Hindu population and tradition of mutual co-existence, was different.*

**AKD**: Yes, but please remember that in the first ten years of the century it was still not possible for a low-caste Hindu to get a job even in the south. For instance, Sir C.P. Ramaswamy Aiyar was the Diwan of Travancore and he set up the Travancore University. One of the most brilliant students who passed out from there in 1944 was K.R. Narayanan. He topped the MA exam in English but was told very politely by Sir C.P. that it would be impossible for him to be employed as a lecturer. So Narayanan came to Madras, and joined the *Hindu*. Later, of course, he rose to become the president of our country. This is typical of that period. It was at the time when I was a student in Maharaja's College that the second Dalit teacher was appointed. Before that there were only Brahmins or non-Brahmins, such as the Mudaliars, Menons and Nairs.

### *Lucknow University*

To return to the story of my education: My very indulgent elder brother suggested that, to make up for lost time, I should go to Lucknow and study for MA and LLB – MA in the morning and LLB in the afternoon. Allahabad and Benares also had provision for this, but they would allow you to write only one exam at a time. One had to come back and write the other exam later.... Between 1944–46, I did both an MA in English and an LLB from Lucknow University. I thoroughly enjoyed myself. Lucknow was lovely in those days with the Gomti and the Hazratganj. We enjoyed cycling through the city.

***IP:*** *Who were the eminent people in the university in your time?*

**AKD:** The most eminent, of course, was my own teacher – Prof. N. K. Siddhanth. Then, there was D. P. Mukherji, the two Sahni brothers and the two Mookerji brothers. The Sahni brothers were great scientists: one a palaeobotanist, the other a geologist. The Mookerji brothers were equally renowned: Radha Kamal, the economist, and Radha Kumud, the historian. One of my teachers later became president of India. This was Shankar Dayal Sharma, who taught us jurisprudence. When I met him once at Rashtrapati Bhavan, his eyes lit up, and he said, 'Roscoe Pound!' (the name of one of the great jurists of the last century).

***IP:*** *Did any cultural differences between the south and the north at that point of language, or social behaviour, strike you?*

**AKD:** No. Please remember that during the '30s we all picked up a little Hindi for two reasons: one, because we wanted to become nationalists and the Dakshina Hindi Pracharini Sabha in Madras helped here; and two, we were crazy about Hindi films! It was Ashok Kumar who taught us Hindi. (*Laughs*) There was no alienation as far as I can remember for this was a small university.... I don't think there was a single woman teacher in the university in Lucknow University. However, there were some very distinguished students in my time who later on made a mark. Names such as that of Ranjana Siddhanth, N.K. Siddhanth's daughter, come to mind. There was another woman, Kamala Shastri (nee Jaspal) who came to Delhi and looked after Indo-Japanese Cultural Relations. She was a victim of the sexist service rules of those days. She joined the foreign service, but had to resign when she got married.

**IP:** *Did you sense any division then between Hindu and Muslim students?*

**AKD:** There was some of it, of course. The politics was there. Lucknow University had a small number of Muslim students, though most Muslim students in those days went to Aligarh.

**IP:** *Your generation of university students took part in the political movement. Nowadays, several North Indian universities such as Lucknow, Allahabad and Benares have been destroyed by the involvement of students in politics. How did students in your times avoid being polluted by dirty politics?*

**AKD:** It is really a question of the absence of any such feelings. It is impossible to describe the total absence of interest in students' unions for example. It is so important now all over India not only in Lucknow, but that way we were completely devoid of any such thing. But the interesting feature of Lucknow was that it had a remarkably close link between the Congress Party and the Socialist Party.

**IP:** *What careers did the students of your time opt for? How many do you think went back into teaching?*

**AKD:** Most of them became lawyers, a few went into the civil services. The double degree system made it possible for them to be good law students and also articulate. So they would write the civil service examination and get in.

**IP:** *So up to this point, the university system was really flourishing in our country and very few people thought it necessary to go abroad except those who wanted to specialize in something. Indian university degrees were considered as good as anywhere in the world.*

**AKD:** Absolutely correct.

**IP:** *At which point do you think, and how and why, did this get reversed? Did you see in your time the seeds for future decline?*

**AKD:** In the late '40s, the British Council began encouraging students to go to England, but the big change began much later – in the mid-'60s, when American rules changed, and the U.S. Education Foundation came to India, and Fulbright scholarships were offered. The whole global system changed. In a sense, India and Japan were the chief beneficiaries of this.

### *Delhi University*

**AKD:** From 1946 to 1953, I was a teacher in Delhi University. I taught English in three colleges – Hindu, Commerce College [it was renamed Sri Ram College for Commerce (SRCC) after Independence] and Ramjas. The only difference, of course, was that the Commerce College was at that time unisex whereas both Hindu and Ramjas had co-education. In those days, Indraprastha and Irwin were the two women's colleges and St. Stephen's and Delhi College were the other colleges. By the time I left teaching, two new colleges, Kirori Mal College and Miranda House, had come up.

SRCC modified their curriculum, increasing the commerce component and reducing many of the English courses. I was a beneficiary of this change, because the principal, Gurmukh Nihal Singh, suggested that I move to his old college, Ramjas. Things were different then because English was the medium of instruction. I vividly remember how, the week after Gandhiji's assassination, I had to discuss Caesar's assassination while teaching *Julius Caesar*. The whole class became so emotional and so excited that the principal thought there was some trouble!

Another interesting fact I recall from those days is that most colleges had good college magazines. In the middle of 1948 we produced in Commerce College a whole issue devoted to Gandhiji.

***IP:*** *Were these college magazines an initiative of the students or something that you as teachers of English promoted?*

**AKD:** The teachers did most of the work, but the students cooperated willingly.

***IP:*** *By the time I reached the university (1968), politics was deliberately kept out of college magazines. This slowly killed the initiative of the students. Also, our times saw the cult of worshipping the toppers. Today, there is no place for the second best, or for the third best, or for those who do not aspire to even that level. When you were talking about your university days, you said that you had a wonderful time, you weren't especially interested in doing brilliantly, whereas nowadays in all campuses, attention is focussed entirely on results while the means have become immaterial to the goal. So, has that created some kind of a terrible disconnect between learning* *and knowledge and information? All students want from teachers now is a key to pass exams. Was it like this in your time?*

**AKD:** I don't think so. Of course there were a number of very good students apart from those who stood first, second and third, who did well in life. Please remember that even in the civil service examination, since I am a product of that, if you look at the results over the years, you will find that people who were in the first ten were not necessarily the best. They were good but that is about it. As the saying goes, universities polish pebbles and dim diamonds. Think of Rabindranath Tagore, who never went to university (though he founded one!).

***IP:*** *What are your views on university libraries?*

**AKD:** In my memory, university libraries are so wonderful. For example, Lucknow had a lovely library – the Tagore Library. I used to spend hours there and I used to sometimes read whole chapters and go back to read the rest. There were also one or two good bookshops in Hazratganj and they encouraged browsers.

### *Jawaharlal Nehru University*

***IP:*** *After a long and distinguished career in the foreign service, you came back to teaching – in JNU.*

**AKD:** Quite right. I was away from 1953–1977. Then, when I was a joint secretary in the ministry in 1977–78, I was invited to become a visiting professor at the School of International Studies at JNU.

***IP:*** *JNU is, in a sense, one of our youngest universities, created with great hopes and plans. So when you went there, what did you find was different – in the students, the atmosphere, the teachers, the curriculum?*

**AKD:** JNU was a purely central residential university and there was only one campus. That made solidarity easy to achieve. At the same time, the teachers were very bright and young. There was a certain charm in their Leftist bias and, as you know, the Yechury generation came out of that campus. But my own personal memories of that time are that it had a very good atmosphere. This, I think, was primarily created by the first vice chancellor, Parthasarthy, and his colleagues in the first five years, but it continued to flourish for a long time. Perhaps, things have changed now.

### *General Issues*

**IP:** *Do you think that the Mandal movement is a watershed, a point from which we began to take caste into education and reverse the process of liberalizing caste categories? Today, those who are privileged and moneyed or have the power and position, send their children abroad. In the earlier days, whether you went to a St. Stephen's College or to a government college... you considered yourself at par with the best. This is so no longer.*

**AKD:** This is a sad development. One primary reason for this, I feel, is the language factor. English is not really important in some mofussil universities. So the students there graduate without being able to speak in English.

**IP:** *So you think the great divider is English and the language?*

**NG:** *I would like to add a point. It was possible in the 1930s and '40s to have studied in school in the vernacular, with English as a second language, and yet be very good at expressing oneself in English in college.*

**AKD:** You are quite right. When I was in school, the medium was Malayalam, but there was an English class and by the time I was 10 or 11, I could read English fluently. At this point, I want to spend one minute on our professional colleges and universities, for engineering, medicine, and law. The most exciting development of the late '50s in India was the creation of the IITs and the IIMs. In the last twenty years, Indian Institutes of Law have come up in places such as Lucknow, Calcutta, Delhi, Bangalore and Bhopal. In our time there were only four engineering colleges worth attending: Guindy-Madras, BHU, Benares and Roorkee.

**IP:** *Perhaps these institutes have preserved a certain level of excellence because they have rigorous screening. Then again, there is the problem of subsidising university fees ad infinitum. Do you think that this is responsible for the decline of our campuses?*

**AKD:** I think so. We have to solve this problem and see how private sources can help to finance higher education.

**NG:** *But in the '50s, the prevalent thinking was that the university* *network should expand, everybody should be able to go to university, was it not?*

**AKD:** I know. Amartya Sen has often said that the real crisis is in our lower education, not in our higher education. But I would like to say that we could have done much better in the university education by emphasizing the quality of literacy, the whole concept of 'deemed university' has to be rigorously enforced.

***IP:*** *What about the Open University concept?*

**AKD:** The Open University idea is a really great concept. Before the Second War, there were only two or three institutions which offered correspondence courses, the Chartered Accounts education, the Federation of Secretaries. Later there were many more, and these correspondence courses are the beginning of the open universities. Of course, the most important one in India is IGNOU.

***IP:*** *What are your views on foreign partnerships with universities?*

**AKD:** It is a very difficult situation because while it is welcome, at the same time our less successful ones might suffer even more. I myself am for greater collaboration as far as possible and all that I can tell you is from my personal experience. In the '30s there was an influx of Jewish professors from Europe escaping from Nazi Germany to America. They founded the basis of modern American education. In the Fletcher School of Law and Diplomacy (part of Tufts University), where I studied, there were three or four of them: Leo Gross, Ernest Holm, Richard Neumann. Similarly, there is no question at all that foreign teachers will make an impact. Indians who are abroad might be welcomed back to teach. There is no alternative to excellence.

***IP:*** *We have so far kept our campuses insulated from the outside world. Yours is a rare example where you came back to teaching after serving in the foreign service, but this kind of movement is rare. If we could encourage a situation where, for example, a practising economist or the ex-governor of the Reserve Bank of India could go back to teaching, we could perhaps introduce new life to our campuses. This happens all the time in America. So many architects, for example, earn so well that it makes no sense for them to go back to teaching. We all agree that teaching is a vocation, but I think we pay our teachers so poorly that* *we make it difficult for many good people to come and teach. I don't know how we can work that out. To some extent in our professional institutes, they have started to look more liberally at people who have a visiting status. Our universities have still not explored this avenue.*

**NG:** *One way could be that people who have got to the stage of a comfortable pension can come back and do some teaching. Secondly, the salaries need to be increased. You will certainly get better teachers then. I remember in the 1970s, there was a pay hike and the new recruits included really good students who might have been lost to the IAS.*

**AKD:** I think that is important. You remind me of the telling lines, 'Excellence sits high amidst the rocks, remote and inaccessible/And a man must wear his heart out before he reaches her.'

**NG:** *Somewhere the sense of vocation has gone.*

**AKD:** This brings me to where we began. Please remember the great names of the pre-World War I universities. The most brilliant example, of course, is Ashutosh Mukherjee in Calcutta and of V.S. Srinivasa Shastri of Annamalai University. Then you have got Raghunath Paranjpe in Bombay who was actually one of India's few senior Wranglers in Mathematics. You have the zoologist, Sir K. Ramunni Menon, and the great doctor, Dr. Lakshmanaswami Mudaliar, people who were actually at the top of their professions. In Allahabad, there were stalwarts such as Amarnath Jha, Harivansh Rai Bachchan, and Firaq Gorakhpuri. Among the first lecturers in Aligarh, when it became a university, was K.M. Panikkar.

**IP:** *Thank you very much for speaking to us. It has been wonderful to hear of your experiences and views.*

•

# 4 : Off the Beaten Track

# Memories of Stephania

The editor's invitation to look back on my years at St. Stephen's College raises one awkward consideration at the very outset. After all, what does the very name 'St. Stephen's' convey to outsiders? Let's face it: to non-Stephanians, the term 'St Stephen's' conjures up three overlapping concepts, none of which is meant to be flattering – elitism, Anglophilia and deracination. One is obliged to confront this stereotype head on.

When I was given the rare privilege of delivering the 125th Anniversary Golden Jubilee Lecture at the College (the 100th anniversary had featured another old boy, Pakistan's then president, Zia ul-Haq), I was able to take for granted that few in the audience (which included serving and former cabinet ministers, ambassadors and generals, not to mention the assorted CEO and cricket star) would contest that there is a spirit that can be called Stephanian:

By **Shashi Tharoor**

most of us had spent three or five years living in and celebrating it. Stephania was both an ethos and a condition to which we aspired. Elitism was part of it, but by no means the whole. In any case Mission College's elitism was still elitism in an Indian context, albeit one shaped, like so many Indian insitutions, by a colonial legacy. There is no denying that the aim of the Cambridge Brotherhood in founding St. Stephen's in 1881 was to produce more obedient subjects to serve Her Britannic Majesty; their idea of constructive missionary activity was to bring the intellectual and social atmosphere of Camside to the dry dust plains of Delhi. Improbably enough, they succeeded, and the resultant hybrid outlasted the Raj.

The St. Stephen's I knew in the early 1970s was an institution whose students sustained a Shakespeare Society and a Criterion Club, and organized Union Debates on such subjects as 'In the opinion of this House the opinion of this House does not matter'. We staged plays and wrote poetry, ran India's only faculty-sanctioned Practical Joke Competition (in memory of P.G. Wodehouse's irrepressible Lord Ickenham), and invented the 'Winter Festival' of collegiate cultural competition, which was imitated at universities across the country. If that sounds deplorably effete, we invariably reached the annual inter-college cricket final, and turned up in large numbers to cheer the Stephanian cricketers on to their accustomed victory. (One of my few worthwhile innovations as president of the Union, aside from improving the mess food, was to supply throat lozenges free of charge to the more raucous of our cheerleaders at the cricket final. I am told this is one more Stephanian tradition that, along with our cricket team, has bitten the dust.) We maintained a careful distinction between the Junior Common Room and the Senior Combination Room, and allowed the world's only non-Cantabridgian 'gyps' to serve our meals and make our beds. And if the punts never came to the Jamuna, the puns flowed on the pages of *Kooler Talk* (known to Stephanians as 'KT', or 'Katie') and the cyclostyled *Spice* (whose typing mistakes were deliberate, and deliberately hilarious).

This was the St. Stephen's I knew, and none of us who lived and breathed the Stephanian air saw any alien affectation in it. For one thing, St. Stephen's also embraced the Hindi movies at Kamla Nagar, the trips to Sukhiya's *dhaba* and the chowchow at TibMon (as the Tibetan Monastery was called); the nocturnal Informal Discussion Group saw articulate discussion of political issues, and the Social

Service League actually went out and performed social service; and even for the 'pseuds', the height of career aspiration was the IAS, not some *firang* multinational. The Stephanian could hardly be deracinated and still manage to bloom. It was against Indian targets that the Stephanian set his goals, and by Indian assumptions that he sought to attain them. (Feminists, please do not object to my pronouns: I only knew St. Stephen's before its co-edification.)

At the same time, St. Stephen's was, astonishingly for a college in Delhi, insulated to a remarkable extent from the prejudices of middle-class Indian life. It mattered little where you were from, which Indian language you spoke at home, what version of religious faith you espoused. When I joined College in 1972 from Calcutta, the son of a Keralite newspaper executive, I did not have to worry about fitting in: we were all minorities at St. Stephen's, and all part of one eclectic polychrome culture. Five of the preceding ten union presidents had been non-Delhiite non-Hindus (four Muslims and a Christian), and they had all been fairly elected against candidates from the 'majority' community. But at St. Stephen's religion and region were not the distinctions that mattered: what counted was whether you were 'in residence' or a 'dayski' (day-scholar), a 'science type' or a 'DramSoc type', a sportsman or a university topper (or best of all, both). Caste and creed were no bar, but these other categories determined your share of the Stephanian experience.

This blurring of conventional distinctions was a crucial element of Stephania. 'Sparing' with the more congenial of your comrades in residence – though it could leave you with a near-fatal faith in coffee, conversation and crosswords as ends in themselves – was manifestly more important than attending classes. And in any case, you learned as much from approachable faculty members – like David Baker, Mohammed Amin, Ranjit Bhatia, P.S. Dwivedi, Vinod Choudhury and others too numerous to mention – outside the classroom as inside it. (It was at one of Amin-Sahib's Medieval History lectures that he memorably translated the words inscribed above the stage in the College Hall – Jesus said, 'I am the Light of the World' – as '*Jesus ne kaha, main Noor Jehan hoon*'.)

Being ragged outside the back gate of Miranda House, having a late coffee in your block tutor's room, hearing outrageous (and largely apocryphal) tales about recent Stephanians who were no longer around to contradict them, seeing your name punned with in *KT*, were all integral parts of the Stephanian culture, and of the ways in which this culture was transmitted to each successive batch of Stephanians.

Three years is, of course, a small – and decreasing – proportion of my life, but my three years at St. Stephen's marked me for all the years to follow. Partly this was because I joined College a few months after my 16th birthday and left it a few months after my 19th, so that I was at St. Stephen's at an age when any experience would have had a lasting effect. But equally vital was the institution itself, its atmosphere and history, its student body and teaching staff, its sense of itself and how that sense was communicated to each individual character in the Stephanian story. Too many Indian colleges are places for lectures, rote-learning, memorizing, regurgitation; St. Stephen's encouraged random reading, individual note-taking, personal tutorials, extra-curricular development. Elsewhere you learned to answer the questions: at College, to question the answers. Some of us went further, and questioned the questions.

Standing at the College on the 125th birthday of St. Stephen's, I remembered the values the college had taught me, in the classroom and outside it. St. Stephen's influenced me fundamentally, gave me my basic faith in all-inclusive, multi-spirited, free-thinking cultures, helped shape my mind and define my sense of myself in relation to the world, and so, inevitably, influenced what I have done later in life – as a man, as a United Nations official, and as a writer. Stephania encouraged the development of qualities that would stand me in good stead in each of these activities.

So when I look back at College today, I celebrate the secularism, the pan-Indian outlook, the well-rounded education, the eclectic social interests, the questioning spirit and the meritocratic culture that are the vital ingredients of the Stephanian ethos. These are what the idea of Stephania contributes to the idea of India I have described in my books and speeches around the world. The moment any of these ingredients is removed, St. Stephen's will no longer be St. Stephen's.

•

# An Old Banyan Tree

What could have been and what should have been are questions that most people are excessively fond of as they intrinsically carry within them the comfort of being concerned without the need for any affirmative action. These are easy questions to ask because we know that there can be no cogent or sometimes workable solutions – the debates and discussions stand testimony to our love of words and our indulgence in noble sentimentality. Visva-Bharati – its very idea and our perception of it – fits in very well with such rhetoric, punctuated with the lament of what could have been … and what should have been ….

Let us assess Visva-Bharati from the time it was transformed into a Central University by an act of Parliament in 1951, very soon after India's independence and a decade after Tagore's death. This transformation, however lofty the inherent intention of the Visva-Bharati Act, acted as levelling mechanism – the rules and regulations and their execution were guided by common and shared norms of higher education formulated to achieve the common good

By **Kumkum Bhattacharya**

of the nation. In addition, the programmes and courses that were offered in most universities, and which may not have been part of the original design of this unique university, were made available in Visva-Bharati. It is indeed difficult to maintain a sense of uniqueness because of the lack of any 'standardized' measure to 'assess' the very uniqueness of institutions. Perhaps, it is always more convenient to deal with factors and entities that have a common denominator.

Among the most noticeable changes that took place when Visva-Bharati became a central university was that from a place of vocation, it became one of occupation and employment, with its set pattern of agreed upon 'essential qualifications' being the sole criterion of entry. The admission process for students, too, conformed to national standards. The desire to maintain the cosmopolitan nature of its faculty and alumnus has, unfortunately, not been fulfilled in the manner envisioned by its founder, Rabindranath Tagore. One reason for this state of affairs is Visva-Bharati's geographical situation and the consequent pressures that act on it to accommodate regional faculty, staff and students. However, this is not to say that the problem cannot be overcome.

One of the many significant reasons for the creation of the nucleus of Visva-Bharati, the Brahmacharya Vidyalaya – now known as *Patha Bhavana* – was to provide an alternative to the then existing colonial system of education, as well as to demonstrate that a superior quality of all-round education was possible with the abundance of mind rather than of material. Tagore later established Visva-Bharati in 1921 with the motto in Sanskrit that translates as 'Where the world builds its home in a single nest'. At the inauguration of Visva-Bharati he had stated that '... not a mere school ... [but] a pilgrimage'. Although independent India retained most colonial structures and systems under the patronage of its own nation state, with the 'white' being replaced by 'brown', there remained very little choice but to join in the task of nation building along with the course of the mainstream. It was precisely the consequences of this short-sighted approach of not institutionalizing 'alternatives' and developing homegrown systems that Tagore had foreseen in our impatient quest for freedom.

Visva-Bharati was never robust, either in funds or in garnering widespread support on the ideational level, and this was true even in Tagore's lifetime. He must, indeed, have wearied of carrying the load of his best cargo. In the very early years of Visva-Bharati's transformation into a central university, it was its varied and multi-hued facets that attracted attention. For one, it showed a certain timelessness in maintaining a continuity with the tradition that was so creatively envisioned by its founder. The idea of separate schools was contained in the very foundation of the university where the curriculum stressed on the development of the creative aspects of its students, and everyone – staff, students, alumni and the neighbouring community – shared in the common tasks, joys and sorrows of *asrama* life. Moreover, the informality with which its chancellor/visitors/rector interacted with this community was based on the principles of a well-rounded education. The enlarging ripple effect of its village extension programme drew upon Tagore's philosophy of rural reconstruction, and the secular metamorphosis of religious festivals and occasions into aesthetically and ethically-oriented festivities and ceremonies – Basantotsav, Vriksharopana and Halakarsana – have been some of the landmarks of this institution and, fortunately, they continue till the present day. We are wont to hear that today in Visva-Bharati, these festivals and occasions are routine affairs rather mechanically conducted, certainly not the best way to pay homage to the mind that conceived of *Achalayatan* and *Raktakarabi*; Tagore, too, would have revolted against such intransigence.

It is evident today that Visva-Bharati has chosen the soft option of rigid observance of the rites and rituals that once affirmed the vibrant and dynamic ambience of this university. Growing aspirations for the good life, the common grand dream of success and its conventional measures, the ennui of the masses and the values associated with individuation have not left us all at Visva-Bharati inured – at least we are not so cocooned from all these markers of modernism.

This brings me to another point – does it behove only Visva-Bharati to carry forward the legacy of Tagore? Admittedly, we not only occupy the 'space' and are also the direct beneficiaries in most material terms of his legacy than others, and most certainly we cannot claim the prevailing social apathy or an undefined disaffection as our excuse. Tagore belongs not only to Visva-Bharati, but also to the entire nation, if not the world. In what ways has his legacy been fulfilled, or valued in other places? Why is it that the slightest news of something amiss in the abode of peace translates into very material returns? Does this not reflect contemporary society bred on the 'here-and now' syndrome of instant gratification? Alas, even this painful and scathing self-criticism displays its sado-masochistic aspects.

Let me now illustrate how the very idea of Visva-Bharati is alive and functioning even today. The two schools, *Patha Bhavana* and *Siksha Satra*, along with their nursery sections (Ananda Pathshala and Santosh Pathshala, respectively), continue to be the nuclei of Visva-Bharati, with emphasis on co-curricular and extra-curricular activities. The modern ideas of the idyllic school sharing in the task of community strengthening have been in practice almost since its inception. The efforts of the schools and their extension activities are evident in the villages around.

Sriniketan, with its commitment to rural reconstruction, displays a dynamism coupled with a quiet rhythm in its activities. Its underlying philosophy has always been comprehensive all-round development and rejuvenation in partnership with the rural communities, and the joining of forces with others engaged in developmental work. In the recent years, there has been a distinct spurt in the formation and activities of women's self-help groups who are provided necessary orientation and training to develop their entrepreneurial skills. The rural library movement has been a success and the rural libraries are developing into resource centres through the use of modern technology. The various institutes and departments situated in Sriniketan work in tandem with the block offices, panchayats and district administration. Over the years, Visva-Bharati has involved a significant portion of its students in the Pulse Polio Programme. I do not know of many other universities that reach out in this manner to communities around them.

It is this inclusive nature of Visva-Bharati that creates the space for everybody to think of themselves as stake-holders in the growth and development of the university. Their individual perception of what is the 'right' way leads sometimes to a situation of impasse. While it is true that all is not well with Visva-Bharati, there are innumerable ways to perfect the working of the university that Tagore had set up, and tackle its imperfections: drawbacks that Tagore himself, time and again, acknlowledged. We must all affirm our faith in Rabindranath Tagore and collectively work towards this goal, so that we can honestly earn the legacy that we have inherited.

•

Gurudev with Patha Bhavan Students. (c. 1935)

: Kumkum Bhattacharya

Courtesy: Mrinal Pande

# A College of One's Own

The changing personality, presence and voice of Indian women in the last decade or so leaps to the eye each time one turns on a TV set or opens a newspaper. It is unnecessary to name the thousands of Indian women who have earned a place for themselves in every sphere of our public life from space exploration to performing arts, academia, politics, industry, banking and sports. However, these myriad achievements of women have to be placed alongside the millions of women who have not had access to education. An important difference between the two sets of women has to do with the role of modern education in the lives of those who have had opportunities of college and university education. Even today for many women, going to college or university is a process of empowerment in itself. The power of education and the capacity of women to make positive changes are now widely acknowledged.

By **Zoya Hasan**

Amartya Sen has often argued that women's education plays a crucial role in facilitating radical, social and economic changes that are critically needed in our problem-ridden world. In the context of India, the obvious conclusion is that women's education is a powerful tool for transformation and necessary for modernity in an essentially traditional society.[1]

India possesses a fairly well-developed higher educational system, which offers facilities of education and training in almost all aspects of creative and intellectual endeavours: arts and humanities; natural, mathematical and social sciences; engineering; medicine; dentistry; agriculture; education; law; commerce and management; music and performing arts; national and foreign languages; culture; communications, etc. Based on a wide framework of Central Universities, State Universities, Deemed Universities, Institutes of National Importance and colleges affiliated to the universities (both government aided and self-aided), the higher educational system is now more mass-based and democratized with one third to forty per cent of enrolments coming from the lower socio-economic strata.

India has a large number of women's colleges, perhaps the largest number anywhere.[2] Whereas their numbers are dwindling in Western countries, statistics here show that during the past two decades, the number of women's colleges has significantly increased. In 1987, there were 781 women's colleges; by 1997, there were 1195; and by 2006 the numbers had gone up to around 1902. We also have quite a few women's universities. The SNDT (Shreemati Nathibai Damodar Thakersey) University in Mumbai, and its three other campuses enrol 45,000 undergraduate and graduate women, making it possibly the largest women's university in the world. Another four women's universities have been established, which include the Padmavathy Mahila Viswavidalaya at Tirupati, the Mother Teresa University at Kodaikanal, the Banasthali Vidyapith near Jaipur and the Avinashilingam Institute of Home Science and Higher Education at Coimbatore. In addition, there are two deemed universities.[3] By 2006, the number of universities had gone up to seven. The majority of women were enrolled in the humanities and social sciences and a minority in the natural sciences; only 12 per cent were enrolled in professional courses.[4] The Economic Survey of 2006–07 noted that the number of women students had risen from 2.45 million in 1997 to 4.04 million in 2004–05. In 1950, only 12.3 per cent students in higher education were women, whereas by 2007 they comprised some 40 per cent of the total enrolments.[5] Although the participation of women in all stages of education has risen rapidly in the last two decades, it is still below fifty per cent.

Historical forces over the past sixty years, demographic changes, societal trends, legislative advances combined with the rising numbers of working women and the fact that many of them have gained leadership positions in various sectors of public life has had considerable effect on the landscape of higher education, especially since the 1990s. Women's colleges have played a pivotal role in this process.[6] Many such colleges were founded when opportunities for education for women were severely limited. These were historically necessary for the advancement of women's education as many women would not have entered a college, but for the existence of such institutions. As elsewhere, women's colleges have also played a crucial part in encouraging women's career expectations, particularly women from middle-class families.

Women continue to face accumulated disadvantages and discrimination of various types at various levels of society, economy and polity, which makes the role of women's colleges in the promotion of education as an agent of change extremely important. In several countries including India, these colleges have encouraged women's focus on traditionally male-dominated fields of study, such as mathematics, computer sciences and physical sciences. In India, until recently, women were significantly under-represented in the physical sciences, medicine and other professional courses. Of the total enrolment for undergraduate studies, women constituted about 28 per cent in 1981 and 34–37 per cent from 1991 to 2000.[7] At the postgraduate level, the enrolment proportions were no different – 29 per cent in 1981 and 38 per cent in 2000.[8] Although there is no specific data available on the numbers of women obtaining PhD degrees in the natural sciences in recent years, trends in postgraduate enrolment in the sciences in particular show that women with doctorates may constitute about a third of the total national enrolment for doctoral studies as well.[9]

In the case of the United States, there is the evidence that women's colleges when compared with co-educational institutions conferred upon women equal or larger proportion of bachelor's degrees in traditionally male-dominated fields. In the Indian context, Vineeta Bal, Senior Fellow at the National Institute of Immunology, observes that women's colleges can help women to make choices and opt for natural sciences free of external constraints.

> Since I am a product of a co-ed school, college and professional training, most of my acquaintances were also from the same background. I thought that co-ed was the best way to get exposed to society and adjust to it. However, over the past few years, especially after I became a resident of Delhi and experienced the harshness of and pain elicited by the 'male gaze', I have reconsidered my views. I have met many more women from elite women's colleges in Delhi, and heard their views. I have also visited a women's engineering college in Jaipur and seen the freedom and happiness with which those young women were wandering around in the college premises. In the present state of the Indian society, where women are still looked at simply as a sexual object by many men, providing women a space of their own in women's schools, colleges and universities is not a bad idea. In these educational spaces women are spared from the prying eyes of men at least for a few hours a day, they have the scope to concentrate on their work. Many women from such institutions also say that being in a women's college also helped them in taking decisions which were not influenced by gender-based competition. If they wanted to opt for mathematics they did, without worrying whether being a student of mathematics will go down well with the boys around! In rural India also, educational places meant exclusively for women might help them gain the confidence which comes out of being educated, being potentially capable of earning, being independent.

Many think that women's colleges are redundant or outmoded and that they should become co-educational. Others argue that a women's college is the equivalent of Virginia Woolf's 'room of one's own', and that such a college is free of the inhibiting presumptions of the male-dominated world.[10] A glimpse into this 'women's only' world is provided by Geetha Nambissan, an alumnus of the Stella Maris College, Madras, and now professor at the Jawaharlal Nehru University:

> For most of us who came to Stella Maris in the early 1970s, this was our first residence away from home. In those days … colleges were known because older sisters and aunts or their acquaintances had been there or through 'word of mouth'. Parents were quite happy to send their daughters to institutions run by nuns because not so much I suspect for the quality of education that they imparted (this was taken for granted) but more so that they would provide a safe and sheltered environment for their daughters, many of whom would get married after they finished their graduation…. Without these colleges women's higher education in India would not have come even this far!

However, women's colleges are not about separating women from the world but about encouraging and empowering them to be active agents within it. Moreover, the significant issue is not with regard to the merits or demerits of women's only institutions, but the fact of going to college, whether women's only or co-educational. In India, attending an educational institution is in itself an important step: it helps to develop in women a sense of confidence, competence and agency. Publisher and writer, Ritu Menon, an alumnus of Miranda House observes:

> It didn't matter that Miranda House wasn't (and isn't) co-educational – it was enough that it was the oldest women's college on campus, a kind of sister-institution to St. Stephen's, and arguably, the premier women's college in Delhi University.

Menon points out they are exposed to 'intellectually challenging and transformative experiences' which enabled women to 'choose the lives, the life-styles, the vocations, careers and political engagements that define us now'. In the face of a male-dominated world of universities, women's colleges are a counterweight that helps develop confidence and skills of women and gives a choice to those who prefer to study unencumbered by the male gaze.

In an ideal world, co-educational institutions would be preferable to the continuation or promotion of single-sex educational institutions. Doubtless, it is good for men and women to study in co-educational institutions and have the opportunity to interact with each other from the undergraduate level itself. Yet, in a gender segregated society such as India, they play an important role in promoting access to higher education, especially in many small towns and rural areas. Among conservative families and communities in a predominantly traditional and patriarchal society, parents, fearful of their daughter's reputation and marriage prospects, are opposed to sending them to a co-educational institution. It is also important to remember that in many states, enrolment of girls in higher education is still low and the availability of women's colleges encourage parents to send girls to college. Even in metropolitan cities, middle- and upper-middle-class parents sometimes prefer to send their daughters to a women's college because they look upon it as a safe, trouble-free space. This is not to discount the individual prestige associated with many women's colleges, but it must be said that the enclosed space in the women's campus is seen by many parents as a protection against temptation and danger.

• • •

In a study of women's colleges in India, Jaya Indiresan suggests four reasons for the continued existence and proliferation of women's colleges. Social and cultural: within the traditional Indian society, conservative Indian parents do not approve of the free mixing of men and women. Academic: the availability of female-oriented courses and the perception that there is more effective teaching, more personal attention and fewer distractions and disruptions. Non-academic: greater opportunities for participation in extra-curricular activities and better counselling and greater security. Institutional: greater opportunities for availability of hostels and scholarships. Above all, many of these colleges now provided high quality education to women comparable to that in co-educational universities and colleges.

India's women's colleges are clearly very different from one another – some are of pre-independence vintage, others quite new; some large, some small; some comparatively privileged and others not at all, some located in metros, others in semi-urban and rural areas. There is also a great divide between the English medium, urban metro colleges such as Lady Shri Ram (LSR), Miranda House, Sophia College, Stella Maris among them, and the vernacular colleges such as the Mahila Vidyalaya, Lucknow; Vasanta College for Women,

Benaras; Vanasthali College, Jaipur; Maharani Science College for Women in Mysore; Maharani's Arts College, Bangalore and Government College for Women, Thiruvanthapuram. The crucial divide here is more along the lines of language and culture. The vernacular colleges are indeed firmly rooted in a regional context but, nonetheless, facilitate access of women to higher education, which, otherwise, they would not have. Many women studying in these colleges aimed for careers, whereas for others it was a brief encounter with freedom from family controls and responsibilities. We can see this in the frothy romantic comedies of the 1960s, when women's colleges were simplistically portrayed as locations where students and teachers regularly fell in love and students dodged their local guardians to hold romantic rendezvous. The classic movie of the college romance genre was the hugely popular *Mere Mehboob* set in the Aligarh Muslim University (AMU) campus of the 1960s. For years after its release, people imagined that every Muslim girl student looked like Sadhana and that every Muslim youth was a Byronic Rajinder Kumar who sang soulful ghazals at a *mushaira*.

Nevertheless, now the interesting trend is how vernacular colleges are increasingly mirroring lifestyles and attitudes visible in our metro colleges. In the metro discourse, appearances were often more important than the quality of mind. Recall the *behenji* category, which is a typical instance of this. The classic definition of a *behenji* was coined, in all likelihood, in the context of sophisticated metro colleges. The word brings to mind images of dowdy, unfashionable girls, not very articulate in English. Politburo Member of the Communist Party of India (Marxist) and Rajya Sabha, Brinda Karat, aptly points to this distinction:

> This is somewhat similar to the unstated difference between pass courses and honours students, with the latter feeling that they were most superior...This has less do with academic standards than just sheer snobbery, but it certainly helped me gain an insight quite early on in Miranda into the existence of the elite students from public schools and those from less privileged backgrounds, most of them day scholars in the pass courses sometimes referred to in a derogatory way as *behenjis*.[11]

However, this is changing rapidly with urbanization and exposure to trends in the metros, which students in these colleges want to replicate. Many of our vernacular and mofussil colleges were established to expose women to modern, liberal values, which were not governed by caste, communalism or religiosity. Increasingly, however, students have begun to equate modernity and a liberal mindset with being fearless about wearing jeans and spaghetti tops. The change in mindset has been reduced to a cosmetic 'makeover' at the level of outward appearance.

Notwithstanding these trends, many women's colleges continue to be instruments for women's empowerment. The Women's College at the Aligarh Muslim University is an example. Founded in 1906, first as a school and then as a college, it has been a symbol of the educational aspirations of Muslim women. It has been a pioneer of modern education with nearly 3000 students in both the humanities and science streams.

What I remember about the Women's College when I was a student there in the late '60s may sound incredible in the prevailing conservative state of affairs in the college. In my time, the Women's College was much like other women's colleges in the big cities: most girls fitted easily into the routine of a modern college with debates, drama, sports, NCC and cultural activities that may be unimaginable today, but were quite common then. Then, college plays were a great event and the college auditorium heaved with students on days when plays were staged. Politics, as in national politics, was not an important part of late-night conversations in the hostels. I don't remember any political meetings or discussions in the college organized on any issue of contemporary political interest. Although college elections were fairly vigorously contested, the platforms of the various contestants were personal. Moreover, these elections had nothing to do with the university union elections. Most significant of all was the fact that religion had no visible or public role to play as far as life of the Women's College, or its hostels, was concerned.

Over the years, Women's College has changed from being a modern secular institution to a largely 'Muslim institution' with values and thinking conforming to an Islamic ethos. Even as the college provides opportunities of education to Muslim women from all strata of society, the conservatism manifested in major sartorial shifts as the need to wear a *hijab* or *chador* and more generally to a public display of religion in college life is unmistakable. This change is gradual but very noticeable in the past ten to 15 years, observes Fawzia Mujib, alumnus of the Women's College and Professor of Physics at the Women's College:

> In the '60s and '70s, a few girls would wear a *burqa* in the first year and would invariably give it up in the next year. Such was the liberal and tolerant atmosphere of the time and the feeling of freedom in the college. Now it appears to be the opposite, many girls come under peer pressure to adopt the *hijab* even though they may not have worn it before joining college. The more disturbing trend is the decline of extracurricular activities of any calibre. Then, the Women's College was the site of several plays and cultural and literary activities, now it is frequently the site of *milad* and *majlis*.

From some of my contemporaries who are teaching at the college, I hear that even now there are hardly any discussions on political issues, but lectures on Islam are quite common, and most conversations invariably revolve around the preservation of minority identity or the future of the minorities.

Despite this manifest conservatism, a large number of Muslim girls from Uttar Pradesh and Bihar have gained access to higher education thanks to the Women's College. Women educated in this college have been active professionally, in starting schools, teaching in colleges and universities, and some have had distinguished careers in medicine, engineering, literature and social work.

• • •

Women's colleges in the past two decades of expansion in higher education seem to be thriving with a huge increase in enrolments as more and more women are seeking opportunities of higher education and employment. Obviously, many of these colleges continue to be important instruments for generating 'social capital' and empowerment and promoting positive change in a world that devalues them. Take, for example, a college like Delhi's Lady Sriram (LSR), established in 1956. It is the only all-women's college to be consistently listed among the top ten colleges in India for inculcating an all-round spirit of academic excellence and social responsibility in its students. Several well-known academics, civil servants, social workers, artists, film-makers, authors, educationists and lawyers comprise the alumni of the college. Founded in 1948, Miranda House is also one of the premier women's institutions in Delhi University. With nearly 3,000 students in both science and humanities, it has kept alive a long tradition of liberal education. When it was founded, the college was meant to be a House where Indian women would acquire education befitting to a modern, secular nation. Over the years, these two colleges alone have nurtured thousands of young women who have made a significant contribution to virtually every sphere of public life.

Colleges such as Miranda House have had a distinctive tradition of social activism, which was not very common in women's colleges around the country. As historian Uma Chakravarti observes,

> Our students brought social and political issues for the first time right into the very premises of the college. While an institution like Stephen's produced a small group of young men who went out into the countryside to engender a revolution, our students brought radicalism into the college using that very space for their political activities. Politics was clearly not an excluded domain at Miranda House.'[12]

She notes, in fact, it was the presence of a larger politics of the nation but especially of its alternative strengths that marks the experience of Miranda.[13] Even though several metro colleges did not come under a radical spell, they were not insulated from various movements taking place in other parts of the world. Anyone who was a student in such colleges in the '60s and '70s entered a world that was in the midst of progressive changes with a strong concern for social betterment. Clearly, this was a very different experience from the social reality of today. The intellectual climate of these colleges in the '60s, including the literature and poetry of the time, connected India with world events such as the Vietnamese liberation struggle and radical movements across the globe. By contrast, there is a frightening lack of awareness and disinterest in the distressing developments of our times, such as the American invasion of Iraq, or the continuing occupation of Iraq rarely talked about. The tragic murder of Jessica Lall brought out hundreds of sympathetic students and young people after a popular television campaign. Yet, one is not aware of a similar campaign by LSR students as a college in the recent past to support the lonely struggle of Myanmar's Aung San Suu Kyi (an LSR alumnus).

It is unfair to single out individual colleges. The truth is that not many college students today – male or female – would care to demonstrate their support for the heroic Palestinian struggle for nationhood, to mention one example. Despite the fact that a few do participate now and then in social movements, such as the Narmada Bachao Andolan or the campaign for nuclear disarmament and so on, this is a far cry from the time when hundreds of students actively supported radical causes including the liberation struggles in Vietnam and Latin America and participated in the Naxalite movement – a trend beautifully portrayed in the Sudhir Mishra's film *Hazaaron Khwaishain Aisi*.

One cannot deny that the educational programme in these colleges certainly provides much freedom and many opportunities for personal and educational advancement; the atmosphere in many of them is exciting and stimulating. They have certainly nurtured talent, provided opportunities and supported aspirations to upward mobility. They can take pride in having helped girls grow into mature women with greater social awareness. However, 'freedom from controls' in many of these colleges is increasingly defined in terms of trendy clothing, or the ability to smoke and drink in public. It must be pointed out, however, that this is very much an individual freedom as opposed to the collective freedom of equal opportunities in education and work. The liberalization and privatization of the economy has furthered this trend, giving rise to a more conservative mindset focused on wealth accumulation as a measure of success. For many of these young women, there are hardly any role models outside the glitzy world of films, fashion, media and soap operas. Much of this has to do with the prevalent cult of celebrity-worship and equating successful women with the faces visible in the media. Today the worth of a person or the eminence of college alumni is invariably judged by her visibility or frequency of appearance on Page Three. The result is that while we have brought forth a brave generation of women who have studied at these colleges and impacted virtually every sphere of social and political life, we have also somehow perpetuated a new mentality of success determined almost entirely by market considerations of wealth and income and upward mobility.

• • •

Overall, we have come a long way indeed since the establishment of the first women's college in the pre-independence period. Progress in women's education has been the most remarkable in the history of modern education in India in the past two to three decades. If this momentum continues to build, then in the next decades we can hope to provide access to large numbers of women who are still denied opportunities of college or university education. Despite considerable success, the work that women's colleges pioneered and now share with co-educational institutions is, however, far from complete. Advancing educational opportunities for women across all ethnic, regional, and socio-economic groups, and above all, for women from minority communities, especially Muslim women, continues to be a great unfinished agenda of the twenty-first century.

For the vast majority of Indian women, access to college or university education still remains a distant goal. For many others the more important issue is the development of a social consciousness and critical engagement with public issues that connect them with a world beyond their families and homes. How can we educate Indian citizens to take seriously the reality of lives other than their own and of their families, and who can think of political events accordingly? Citizens who are not simply bothered about success defined by market-determined criteria, but citizens committed to both compassion and justice for the millions who suffer from deprivation and disadvantage and daily preventable problems such as malnutrition and disease or lack of purchasing power? Only when we have done so will we have fulfilled the dreams that lie inside these sacred groves.

•

ENDNOTES:

1. Amartya Sen, 'What's the Point of Women's Education?' Keynote inaugural address at a conference, Women's Education Worldwide, 2004: *Unfinished Agenda*, 2–4 June 2004.
2. For example, there are just sixty active women's colleges in the U.S.
3. Jaya Indiresan, *Education for Women's Empowerment: Gender-positive Initiatives in Pace-Setting Women's Colleges*, Delhi: Konark Publishers Private Limited, 2002.
4. *Ibid.*
5. *India: Country Summary of Higher Education*, 'Higher Education in India, Vision and Action,' Country Paper, UNESCO, 1998, *http://siteresources.worldbank.org/EDUCATION/Resources/278200-1121703274255/1439264-1193249163062/India_CountrySummary.pdf*
6. Louise Knight, Report: 'Educating Asian Women in Women's Colleges and Universities: A World Perspective', *American Journal of Women's Studies*, Vol. 10, No. 4, 2004, pp. 79–86.
7. Vineeta Bal, 'Women Scientists in India: Nowhere Near the Glass Ceiling', *Economic and Political Weekly*, 7 August 2006.
8 *Ibid.*
9. *Ibid.*
10. Joanne Creighton (President of Mount Holyoke College, Mass., U.S.A.), 'Why We Need Women's Colleges', *Boston Globe*, 21 May 2007.
11. Brinda Karat, 'A Personal Remembering: MH 1963–66', in Uma Chakravarti, *et al,* (eds.) *Reliving Miranda*, 1948–98, New Delhi.
12. Uma Chakravarti, 'Parallel Lines: A Personalized History of Miranda House', in op.cit.
13. *Ibid.*

: Zoya Hasan

Capper House, which once belonged to Col. Francis Capper, a military geographer, originally rented, then acquired by the Government in 1915 to house the Madras College for Women (and its Hostel), as Queen Mary's College was then called. The College, founded in 1914, took the name of Queen Mary in 1917 and installed her bust in Capper House. This historic building was demolished in 2001.

Courtesy: T. Baalajee

PHOTO ESSAY:

# Breaching Male Bastions

COMPILED BY: **Malavika Karlekar**

: Malavika Karlekar

### 1. Kadambini Ganguly

When, in 1878, Bengali reformer Dwarakanath Ganguly argued with a somewhat sceptical higher education establishment that Kadambini Basu and Sarala Das should be allowed to sit for the entrance examination to Calcutta University, he undoubtedly had some idea that he was setting up a remarkable precedent: no British university had as yet opened its doors to women. As there were no girls' colleges at that time, Calcutta's Bethune School added special classes, and, in 1882, Kadambini and Chandramukhi Basu became the first women graduates of the University of Calcutta. Kadambini then went on to become one of the two earliest women doctors of the British Indian Empire – the other being Anandibai Joshi who had graduated from Philadelphia in the same year (1886).

In a country where a substantial number of middle-class women observed purdah – and would baulk at being attended to by a male doctor – medicine and nursing were acceptable as well as lucrative occupations for women as fortunate as Kadambini and Anandibai. Interestingly, both had been actively supported – if not goaded – by their determined husbands. Though a medical college teaching Western medicine existed in Bombay, Ananadibai did not attend it. Nor did she have any regular schooling. Her husband was her chief instructor, and in any case, it was not usual for traditional Marathi Brahmin girls to go to school until the last decades of the nineteenth century. Before she sailed for New York in 1883 from Calcutta (where her husband was then employed), Anandibai addressed a full hall at a public meeting and spoke of the lack of women doctors, adding, 'I volunteer to qualify myself as one.' One will never know whether these two strong-willed young women ever met each other. Though Kadambini went on to have a full professional life, Anandibai died of consumption without having a chance of practising in her country.

COURTESY: BETHUNE COLLEGE & SCHOOL CENTENARY VOL. 1849–1949, CALCUTTA

: Malavika Karlekar

## 2. Sarala Debi Chaudhurani

In 1902, of the 177 women students in college, as many as 55 were from Bengal. During 1897-1902, 37 women students – all from Bethune College – graduated from the University of Calcutta as against seven from Madras Presidency and one each from the United Provinces and Bombay. By the 1870s, the camera and the photographic studio had become a part of the discourse of middle-class professionalism. Interestingly, a number of these early pioneers were taken – or went on their own initiative – to photographic studios; higher education had given them the confidence to pose alone, often in cap and gown, commemorating their achievements.

The daughter of Rabindranath Tagore's novelist sister, Swarnakumari Debi, Sarala Debi graduated from the University of Calcutta in 1890 with English Honours – though as she wrote, to be 'just like the boys of the household', she had attended evening classes in Physics as well.

Sarala Debi taught at the Maharani Girls' School in Mysore, wrote in the family magazine, *Bharati*, and in the years before the partition of Bengal (1905) organized an *akhara* (gymnasium) to train young men in physical fitness and the martial arts. In 1905, she married Rambhuj Datta Chaudhuri, a lawyer and Congressman and moved to Lahore. She spent the next 18 years in Punjab participating in anti-British movements and also kept alive her literary interests by bringing out the English edition of the Urdu journal, *Hindustan*. When Gandhi came to Lahore and stayed as a guest of the Chaudhuris, a close friendship developed between Sarala Debi and the Mahatma. She soon became an advocate of non-violence, though after her husband's death, Sarala returned to Bengal and completely withdrew from politics, her interest shifting to religion.

COURTESY: PETER SINAI, BANGALORE

: Malavika Karlekar

### 3. Emmeline da Cunha, 1894

Emmeline da Cunha (later da Costa) was born in Panjim in 1873 and was awarded the L.M.S. degree by Bombay Medical College in 1894. A gold medallist, she was also proficient in Portuguese, French, Italian, English and Konkani besides being a skilled pianist. In the early part of the twentieth century, Emmeline was a medical researcher in the United Kingdom for a brief while; on her return to India, she married Dr. Francis Xavier da Costa and gave up her practice soon after.

COURTESY: ASAD AND HASMINA KARIM KHAN, MUMBAI

: Malavika Karlekar

**4. Janaba Tyeba Begum Sahiba Bilgrami (Mrs. Khedive Jung Bahadur) c. 1898**

When Tyeba Begum took her B.A. examination from the University of Madras in 1894, she became the first Muslim woman to graduate. But, as with Emmeline, things changed soon, and she gave up formal education after her marriage to Dr. Mirza Karim Khan (later known as Nawab Khedive Jung Bahadur), Tyeba Begum continued learning Arabic and Persian. Well acquainted with history and a range of biographies, Tyeba published a collection of Indian folklore in the London-based *Indian Magazine*.

In these three photographs, Emmeline is the only one in formal graduation dress, looking proudly out of the frame. Both Sarala Debi and Tyeba are heavily bejewlled and dressed in elaborate evening wear. It is possible that the photographs were taken on a special occasion, such as a wedding in the family. Or maybe they were especially dressed for the photo shoot! Tyeba is wearing a heavy brocade sari, elaborate necklace with large earrings that were surely supported by a gold or pearl chain that fastened into her hair. A glamourous Sarala poses, with flowing tresses bound loosely with a bejewelled chain, and a *sitahaar* – many-layered pearl strands, each with an enamel pendant. She looks into the middle distance with a certain self-confidence. Her head is tilted slightly upwards, almost as though she does not want to engage with the camera and its handlers. On the other hand, Emmeline and Tyeba look directly at the camera – no shying away for these women – as does Kamala Rathnam. Kamala too, appears to be dressed for the photograph in a gown with mutton-chop sleeves and a belt. Like the others, she looks steadfastly at the camera.

: Malavika Karlekar

**5. Kamala Sattianathan**

At the age of 21, Kamala married widower Samuel Satthianathan, and when she passed her M.A. a year after her son was born, she was dubbed 'double Ma'! In 1901, Kamala started the *'Indian Ladies' Magazine* – the first women's magazine in English that continued till the 1930s. Apart from dealing with women's issues and the social reform movement, it also published Sarojini Naidu's earliest poems. Her Detective Janaki featured a woman investigator and when her husband died leaving her with a six-month-old child, Kamala learned to support herself by becoming tutor to the Rani of Pithapuram in Andhra Pradesh.

COURTESY: VIDYA SHANKAR, CHENNAI

**6. Sister R.S. Subbulakshmi (3rd from left, 2nd row from below) with Miss Lynch and Widow Graduates in 1924.**

By the last decades of the nineteenth century and into the next, male reformers of all religions felt committed to educating women of their communities and worked towards raising funds for institutions of repute. There were a few notable exceptions: widowed at the age of 11, bright young Subbulakshmi's enlightened parents concentrated on her education and in 1911, when she graduated with a B.A. degree from Presidency College, Madras, she was the first Brahmin widow in the city to do so. The following year, encouraged by her father, Subramanya Iyer and Miss Lynch, Inspectress of girls' schools in Coimbatore, Subbulakshmi started a home for young widows in her house. Later, the Widows' Home (known as Ice House) moved to its own premises and many of its residents became teachers. Akka (older sister), as Sister R.S. Subbulakshmi was known, later established the Sarada Ladies Union for the education and support of deserted women and those who remained single but needed help.

In addition, Christian missionaries who, as early as 1821, had started a boarding school for girls in present-day Tirunelveli, trained their eyes on higher education, and Isabella Thoburn College, Lucknow, and Kinnaird College, Lahore, were early examples of their endeavours.

COURTESY: ARATI ROY, NEW DELHI

**7. Isabella Thoburn College, Lucknow**

Known formerly as Lucknow Women's College, the institution began in 1886; it was later re-named after its founder in 1922 when it moved to its present premises – a sprawling 30-acre campus. The college is a significant instance of Methodist missionary enterprise in Asia.

: Malavika Karlekar

COURTESY: ARATI ROY, NEW DELHI

**8. Bina Roy (2nd from left, 1914–94) and Lakshmi Menon (extreme right in bloomers, 1899–1994) at the Teacher's Sports Day at Isabella Thoburn College (L) c.1941**

Bina taught English and later went on to become an educational administrator. Lakshmi was a Congress Party leader who became a minister in the Nehru government. At the time of the sports day shown here, she was an ad hoc teacher at the college.

COURTESY: RAJKUMARI MEHTA, NEW DELHI

**9. Theatricals at Kinnaird College, Lahore, 1931**

Kinnaird College had modest beginnnings as it was started in 1913 by the principal of Kinnaird High school, Lahore, with seven students. In 1933, the college acquired land near Lahore's canal and new buildings were constructed to house the increasing numbers; by 1939 the college had grown into a twenty-acre campus. Its dramatic performances were a must for the city's theatre buffs and this is a scene from *Omar Khayyam*.

COURTESY: OMITA GOYAL, NEW DELHI

**10. Mahatma Gandhi and Kasturba with Tagore**

Non-religious yet liberal ideas for overall education found space for co-education, one of the more unusual and successful experiments being that of Rabindranath Tagore. In 1901, on a bare piece of land amidst tall pampas grass and a rich terracotta soil, Tagore set up a school, and twenty years later, a university (Shantiniketan) and an institution for rural reconstruction (Sriniketan). In this visual, the founder sits with Mahatma Gandhi and Kasturba on the latter's 1938 visit to the campus.

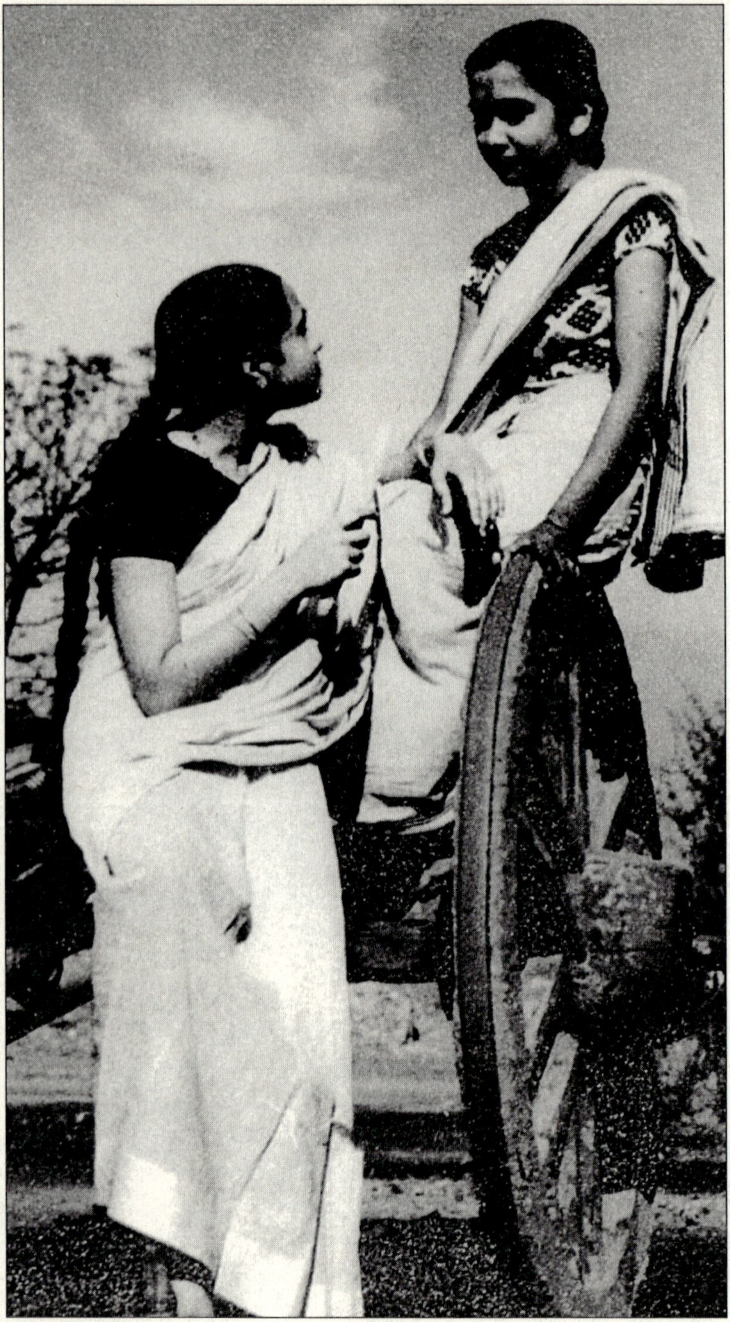

COURTESY: THE LATE GAURA PANT 'SHIVANI', LUCKNOW

: Malavika Karlekar

**11. Gaura Pande (with her back to the camera) poses with a friend**

Photo: Shambhu Shaha, 1939

Well-known for its teaching of fine arts, music and oriental languages – and a belief that 'education should never be dissociated from life' (Tagore), Shantiniketan attracted a number of idealistic and liberal-minded parents from all over the country. Both boys and girls were sent for a holistic education in its enriching semi-rural atmosphere and students included Indira Gandhi (nee Nehru), Satyajit Ray and many others who went on to make a name for themselves. In this 1939 photograph taken by well-known photographer Shambhu Shaha, Gaura (with her back to the camera) poses with a friend. Among the best-known writers of fiction and essays in Hindi in post-Independence India, Gaura – affectionately called Amar Boi (My Book), and Gora by Rabindranath Tagore – started writing in 1955. Her oeuvre was romantic fiction set mostly in her native Kumaon, of the years just before and after Partition, as well as memoirs. She was also known for her essays and travel writing.

COURTESY: THE LATE KAMLA CHOWDHRY, NEW DELHI

**12. Kamla (fourth from left) stands with Mrinalini to her right**

Here are the young Gaura Pande (later Pant, who was to take the pen name Shivani), Kamla Kapur (later Chowdhry) and Mrinalini Swaminathan (later Sarabhai). All three became established figures in their fields – often reflecting back on their Shantiniketan days with affection and regard.

Kamla was actively associated with building national-level institutions such as Indian Institute of Management, Ahmedabad, Institute of Rural Management, Anand, and Centre for Women's Development Studies, New Delhi, and Society for Promotion of Wastelands Development (SPWD). She was Chairperson, Wastelands Development Board, Government of India (1983-87).

Known as the 'high Priestess of Indian dance', Mrinalini has choreographed more than 300 dance dramas and is a pioneer in creative work through classical dance forms and an innovative choreographer. She founded the Darpana Academy of Dance, Drama, Music and Puppetry in Ahmedabad in 1948 and her troupe has travelled extensively.

COURTESY: AALOCHANA, GANGUTAI PATWARDHAN COLLECTION, PUNE

COURTESY: AALOCHANA, GANGUTAI PATWARDHAN COLLECTION, PUNE

: Malavika Karlekar

**13. & 14. Woman's College of the Hingne Stree Shikshan Sanstha (HSSS), Poona**

Going to college not only provided girls access to the world of new ideas and aspirations, physical activity and information and knowledge, but also the ability to interact with others from different worlds. Here, wearing the sari in the Parsi-style, students play basketball and bicycle at the Women's College of the Hingne Stree Shikshan Sanstha (HSSS), Poona. The college was run by the HSSS set up by Annasaheb Karve (better known as Maharshi D.K. Karve) in 1907 for the education of young women. In 1920, with a grant from the Thackerseys it was renamed the SNDT or Shree Nathibai Damodar Thackersey Women's University. This was in 1915, and the photographs form part of the Gangutai Patwardhan collection and was presumably taken when she was a student at the institution; Karve had offered a scholarship to girls who had pledged not to marry till their twelfth year and Gangutai took advantage of this. Later, she became a successful school teacher who believed that sports and personality development were vital for girls.

COURTESY: LILY KUTTY THARAKAN, KOCHI

: Malavika Karlekar

**15. Lily Kutty Anthraper**

Young Lily Kutty Anthraper (later Tharakan) a Syrian Christian learned early to befriend girls from other religions: she said 'It was the policy of the college to mix students caste and community-wise' and this photograph of her with roommates at the Women's College hostel, Trivandrum (now Swati Tirunal Academy), reflect the ideology of the institution. She sits at the bottom right next to Janaki, an Ezhava, while behind (left) is Subhadra Thangachi, a Nair, and next to her is Gomati Ammal, a Brahmin.

# 5: **University Special**

# Gone with the Wind

Thirty years after the historic Sepoy Mutiny of 1857, on 23 September 1887 to be exact, the fourth-oldest university in India, was established in the holy city of Prayag, also known as Allahabad. In 1921, the University of Allahabad became a unitary teaching institution and over the next four decades it slowly rose to become one of the best-known centres of higher learning in the north.

As home town to India's first two prime ministers, Allahabad saw a brief intoxicating period in which eminent scientists, scholars and writers like Meghnad Saha, Prof A.C. Banerji, Firaq Gorakhpuri and Harivansh Rai Bachchan from the university became national icons and opened up intellectual vistas for a whole generation of Midnight's Children. By the late '60s, however, all this had begun to change. Science and higher learning came to be dominated more

By **Mrinal Pande**

*Allahabad University.*

# ACT No. XVIII of 1887.

PASSED BY THE GOVERNOR GENERAL OF INDIA IN COUNCIL.

(*Received the assent of the Governor General on the 23rd September, 1887.*)

An Act to establish a University at Allahabad.

WHEREAS it has been determined to establish a University at Allahabad; It is hereby enacted as follows:—

Title and commencement.

**1.** (*1*) This Act may be called the Allahabad University Act, 1887; and

(*2*) It shall come into force at once.

Establishment and incorporation of University.

**2.** (*1*) A University shall be established at Allahabad, and the Governor General for the time being shall be the Patron of the University.

(*2*) The University shall consist of a Chancellor, a Vice-Chancellor and such number of Fellows as may be determined in manner hereinafter provided.

(*3*) The University shall be a body corporate by the name of the University of Allahabad, having perpetual succession and a common seal, with power to acquire and hold property, moveable or immoveable, to transfer the same, to contract, and to do all other things necessary for or incidental to the purposes of its constitution.

(*4*) The University shall come into existence on such day as the Local Government may, by notification in the official Gazette, appoint in this behalf.

Chancellor.

**3.** The Lieutenant-Governor of the North-Western Provinces for the time being shall be the Chancellor of the University, and the first Chancellor shall be the Honourable Sir Alfred Comyns Lyall, Knight Commander of the Most Honourable Order of the Bath, Knight Commander of the Most Eminent Order of the Indian Empire.

A page from the Act establishing and incorporating a university at Allahabad on 23 September 1887.

Courtesy: The National Archives of India

and more by the political and bureaucratic circles, and the heart went out of things.

During an earlier visit some five years ago, the campus looked derelict to me. There had been a major confrontation between students' groups and after a couple of deaths the university had been closed *sine die*. Then, two years ago, in the year 2005, a long pending demand that the university be re-configured and given the status of a central university, was met. In February of 2008, it threw its gates open for a first-ever meet of its alumni in 121 years.

Thus a second visit.

On the face of it nothing much has changed in Allahahabad. Faintly clownish names of suburbs like Jhoosi and Phaphamau still greet you before the train pulls into Allahabad Junction, and raise light-hearted expectations. The early morning trains still regurgitate their usual load of passengers upon the platform and all of them – babus, netas, the rustic pilgrims with sleepily obedient families in tow and white foreigners trying to look Indian but failing – must trip delicately around dozens of sleeping forms rolled within quilts with stray dogs lying in a huddle near their feet. All hurtle ultimately towards the exit gates where a sleepy *tickut babu*, opening his mouth in an impossibly wide and prolonged yawn, checks a few tickets perfunctorily and waves the rest on.

• • •

The first sight of the university can confuse the visitor. The elegant heritage buildings with the Senate Hall and the departments of English, Economics and the Law Faculty, stand amidst once-lush lawns that now sprout a variety of weeds. Beyond the university walls, the *Katra* area is as dusty, noisy and overcrowded as it always was. A large part of it is now slowly disintegrating and the rubble and stray stones and bricks dislodged from the crumbling tenements result in deadly traffic snarls. The expansion of the university, such as the current widening of roads around the campus, has been rather unplanned and somewhat chaotic. But this is true of urban India, so why blame poor Allahabad alone?

The university lies within the heart of the cantonment city with *katras* dating back to 1801. This 2.6 kms. area has a high population density, with residential and commercial buildings spanning centuries. The edge of the district is owned by private trusts, which run many popular grocery and book shops and eateries that cater to the students. This makes the effort of sealing or removing buildings here like pushing your fist into a wasps' nest. 'Sahib,' says our garrulous driver, 'the union leaders roam about with grenades and guns and knives here. Even the police dares not touch those under their protection.'

Real life has remained on hold for decades in this town. A little architectural charm or a trick of light may sometimes turn other people's poverty to a tourist snapshot, but years of deference to political bullies have wrecked the city. Our hotel with the faux poetic name of 'Kanha Shyam' has smelly corridors, doors with inoperable locks and just one lift operating currently, but it is full of foreigners. These, our driver whispers melodramatically, are Maharishi Mahesh Yogi's disciples. They have come all the way from Amsterdam to immerse their Guru's ashes in the holy city and will leave only after the thirteenth day *Shraddha* ceremony at which they will all get their heads tonsured, like Hindu sons. Perhaps, one should say *unlike* Hindu sons today.

We are received at the university senate hall with genuine warmth and grace. The front rows are filled as usual with wizened but elegant senior citizens, most of them alumni of the university. They patiently riffle through the pages of the special souvenir volume brought out to mark this occasion and make small talk. We all await the honourable minister for human resources development, himself an alumnus, but he has been delayed. Delays are not unusual for the people assembled here. Finally, the honourable minister arrives and the programme begins to move – in common with academic activities the world over – with a certain touching, shuffling and dislocated pomp.

As in a Hindu temple, it is easy to suspend disbelief here. All of us in the hall want the noble premises that had nursed our minds, blessed. We want the long-tormented campus to regain its old peace and the ugly immediate past acknowledged and shriven. Any feeling of anger against hypocrisy and big money masquerading as eminent global citizenry evaporates, because the moving spirit of this particular wandering ceremonial springs from a simple and brief harking back to the ancient personality of the Allahabad University and the hierarchical, half-magical trust of its creators in the essential nobility of the human mind.

• • •

Later, standing in the midst of a chaotic medley of buildings in the women's college, I ask the dean, 'What are you going to do to undo such bad planning over such a large area?'

'Do?' his forehead puckers slightly, 'We'll raze the old building in the middle and replace it with a modern multi-storeyed structure for sure. And,' here his face broke into an enchanting smile, 'we shall plant many gardens. Roses, yes, we shall have an ocean of roses for our girls.'

A lonely man standing in the midst of a wasteland of facts, the dean was perhaps the most apt symbol for this ancient city of slowly dying holy rivers. This is the magic of Allahabad, my alma mater and a city that, as a repository of India's otherness, has somehow sustained the grandest dreams of higher learning for the nation's young minds. Even amid dusty longings and death.

•

This is the Arts Faculty & Law College Building of the Allahabad University, soon after it was completed. It houses the English Department where Firaq Gorakhpuri & Harivansh Rai Bachchan once taught.

Courtesy: The National Archives of India

# The Alumni Remember

In 1987 the University of Allahabad decided to celebrate its centenary in a grand fashion. In addition to lectures and symposia, the university hosted a series of musical concerts and theatrical productions. An effort was made to re-create the ambience of the 1930s and the '40s when the Senate Hall of the university resonated with the music of India's leading performers. A souvenir was also published that year, which carried letters from its alumni. We reproduce a section of the letter written by Arjun Singh, then minister of communications:

> I am very happy to learn that the University of Allahabad will be celebrating its centenary next month...Being one of the premier seats of learning in the country, the university has chiselled (sic) its youth to become leaders of national stature. Pt. Jawahar Lal Nehru, Shri Kailash Nath Katju, Sir Tej Bahadur Sapru, poetess

By **Lalit Joshi**

> Mahadevi Verma, Shri P.N. Haksar and historian of world fame Shri R.P. Tripathi were the products of this esteemed 'RISHIKUL' of modern India.

Another letter written by Govind Narain, former Governor of Karnataka, is full of nostalgic recollections:

> It gives me immense pleasure to learn that my Alma Mater…is celebrating its centenary. The names of great intellectual giants and eminent scientists, who made this University one of the best in India, come easily on the mental horizon. I consider myself fortunate to have come in direct contact with Dr. Megh Nath (sic) Saha, Dr. Nil (sic) Ratan Dhar, Pt. Amar Nath Jha, Dr. Shafat Ahmed Khan, Prof. Beni Prasad, Dr. Ishwari Prasad and so many others.

P.N. Haksar's letter also evokes similar memories. As the Chairman of the Indian Statistical Institute in Kolkata, Haksar wrote:

> …I…would like to pay my respectful homage to all my teachers. Among them were Neel Ratan Dhar, Megh Nath (sic) Saha, Gorakh Prasad…and others. My debt of gratitude to Dr. Amar Nath Jha, the warden of my hostel – Muir Hostel – is immense. All these men of great distinction and tremendous sense of integrity lived up to the standards prescribed for a Guru, who according to the best of our *parampara*, is like *Param Brahma*.

The important thing to note is that in letter after letter published in this volume, almost the same set of teachers are privileged – the majority of them left unlisted. It would be interesting to record the impressions of students who never had the chance of being taught by the privileged few. We also feel that the number of such teachers and students was always very large. A clearer picture of the 'Rishikul' that Arjun Singh mentions could only emerge, while diverse experiences have been recorded and examined. Furthermore, dissenting voices can also be heard within the privileged group.

For example, Aquil Rizvi, a retired professor of Urdu recalls the situation prevailing in the University of Allahabad in 1947:

> That year no one took admission in the postgraduate classes of the Urdu Department. The Urdu students were either leaving for Pakistan or thought that Urdu would have no future in India. The government of Pandit Pant and Sampoornanand had blocked all the paths of Urdu's progress in Uttar Pradesh. As a result the teaching and study of Urdu received a major setback.

The English Department in those days was one of the most prestigious departments in the Arts Faculty. This was solely because it housed some of the finest teachers in India. Like other graduates even Rizvi wanted to join its Master's programme. But he was forced to reconsider his decision:

> The condition of the country had changed so much; the scourge of communalism had spread to such an extent that even if I had obtained a first class in English, I would not have got a job in the English Department. In matters such as these Allahabad University has always discriminated on the basis of religion and continues to do so. Till date no Muslim has been able to get a job in the Science Faculty (Only one Muslim gained entry in the Home Science department after a protracted legal battle but has to suffer every day).... Only Arabic, Persian and Urdu are reserved for Muslims. However, one Muslim has always been appointed in the History Department, the reason being that the original texts of Medieval India are in Persian.

Even though Rizvi is not empirically correct in his observation about the number of Muslims appointed by the university, what is evident from his text is that the notion of a homogenous and unitary past is entirely misplaced. Thus, what constituted *Rishikul* for one alumnus might have been a stifling experience for another. The question that therefore needs to be addressed is 'whose past'?

There are other ways in which the history of the university can be imagined. For example, Akhilesh's story *Chithee,* set in the Allahabad of the 1980s, is a case in point. The story revolves around the lives of five friends – Madan, Pradip, Vinod, Dinanath and Raghuraj, who are students of the university. They are cheerful, brash and intelligent young men, until unemployment forces them to go different ways. They meet for the last time over a couple of drinks. The meeting provides them with an opportunity to reflect about their pasts. In the climactic scene, they start breaking down, one by one. The first one is Madan. 'I have to die many times a day,' he exclaimed. 'As soon as someone asks me about my job I feel like dying.'

It is now Pradip's turn to share his agony. 'You think I am drunk? No, I am in my senses. Unemployment has made me cry many times. Last time on *Rakshabandhan*...I had nothing to offer to my sister. She quietly slipped a hundred rupee note under my pillow...I kept it in my pocket and cried.'

Upon hearing this, Vinod became inconsolable. 'My parents flatter my brother because he is employed but they hate me.'

Finally, it is the turn of Raghuraj, once notorious for chasing girls. 'Let me now share my secret with you. I never ran after girls. I made it all up. Actually, I worked part time in a cloth and medicine shop. The owner paid me two hundred and fifty rupees.... I...I...,' Raghuraj's voice started choking with emotion.

A momentary silence followed. Then all of us started crying. The five friends never met again. Nor did they ever again write *chithees* (letters) to each other.

Most reminiscences about the university generally consist of the voices of men; the voices of women remain unrepresented. One exception, however, is Doodhnath Singh's *Nishkasan*. Set in Allahabad, *Nishkasan* is the tale of a conflict between the superintendent of the university girls hostel and a hapless Dalit inmate. The superintendent (Madam) along with her perfidious husband (Shardul Vikram Singh) often forces inmates to do chores at the superintendent's house. One day, the Dalit girl is summoned to help Madam as the latter has guests in the house. Madam is displeased with the manner in which the girl conducts herself before the guests, so she manipulates the hostel records and charges the girl with unlawful residence. The girl tries to mobilize support among members of her own caste, but fails to turn the tide in her favour. The university holds an inquisition. The girl pleads her innocence. When a member of the committee inquires why charges have been pressed against her if she is innocent, the girl replies that it is because 'she is poor and refuses to compromise with her dignity'. The committee however, finds the girl guilty and she is expelled from the hostel. She tries to find an ally in Lucknow but eventually realizes that even Dalit politics is a game of power. Dejected and defeated, she eventually commits suicide.

Even though a work of fiction, *Nishkasan* points out at the grim possibility of university hostels turning into battlegrounds, where brutal power games will be played out between conflicting interests. Also, how the victim in such cases might easily be young Dalit girls. Further, the book also shows how dominant interests in the university can successfully collude to shield the oppressors. Finally, the book reveals the divergence between the radical agendas of Dalit politics and the vulnerability of ordinary Dalit women.

There is yet another way alumni remember their alma mater – once again not as a sacred space but as a site for conflict and political violence. *Haasil* (2002), directed by Tigmanshu Dhulia, is perhaps one of the boldest political comments on student politics in the university system. Dhulia and his crew sought the permission of the vice chancellor of the University of Allahabad for shooting the film within the campus. The permission was granted. A few days later the student leadership began to object to certain forms of depiction in the film. It declared that student politics in Allahabad was sacrosanct and no one could be allowed to portray it 'negatively'. Dhulia soon began to complain of blackmailing and intimidation. A crisis point was reached when the university administration buckled under pressure and withdrew permission to shoot the film inside the university. Thus, Dhulia and his crew experienced the stark reality of politics that they wanted to partly depict on the silver screen.

The opening scene sets the tone of *Haasil*. A presentation is going on inside the Vizianagaram Hall. A student leader - Gauri Shankar (Ashutosh Rana), followed by his supporters – enters the hall uninvited. One cannot hear the presentation because the voice of the speaker is drowned by a powerful voice over:

'When the institution turns into a battleground and when a premium is placed on violence and politics instead of the acquisition of knowledge, it ceases to produce human beings. In my *des* (Allahabad?), this has been happening for quite some time.'

*Haasil* tries to show how this transformation occurred. Aniruddha (Jimmy Shergill) is the protagonist who plays a university student. He meets Niharika (Hrishita Bhatt) and eventually falls in love with her. Aniruddha learns that some students with strong political connections in Lucknow have been trying to manipulate the university system from time to time. He believes that this has vitiated the academic atmosphere in the campus and needs to be restrained. Gauri Shankar is a leader who manages to register for a new course every two years, so that he can continue to remain in the university. Gauri Shankar's political rival is Ranvijaya Singh (Irfan Khan), who aspires to become a political leader. But Ranvijaya has to first demonstrate his strength in the campus. Unaware of the complexities of university politics, Aniruddha decides to support Ranvijaya. This is resented by Gauri Shankar and leads to a furtherance of the conflict between the two.

It is only during the course of his association with Ranvijaya that Aniruddha comes face to face with the murky world of politics. He blindly places his trust on Ranvijaya who uses him to rally support from what is known as the 'a-political' student community in the university. As the plot thickens, Aniruddh, unmindful of the warnings of his friends, gets sucked into a power game, which is controlled by politicians in Lucknow. The remainder of the film is about how Aniruddha escapes from Ranvijaya's clutches and reunites with Niharika.

As the narrative heads towards closure, the tension is heightened by a series of gory killings. The climactic scenes, shot in the backdrop of the Mahakumbh of 2000, enhance the realism of the narrative. For us the significance of *Haasil* lies not only in its contemporary realism and the rawness with which it treats student politics, but also in the manner in which it challenges the narratives of nostalgia. It would also be interesting to read *Haasil* against the memoirs of a former vice chancellor, Professor R.P. Mishra. Describing the culture of the university in the '80s Mishra writes:

> Students did not go to the University because teachers did not teach and the teachers did not go to the University because the students did not attend classes. Thus a vicious circle was created. And to add to the problem was the interference by the government. The State government had the temerity…to increase the seats in colleges and universities without consulting the vice chancellors.

Mishra's observations on student leadership of the '80s also bring *Haasil* close to the realism that Dhulia was trying to rework on celluloid:

> There was no age limit...even a seventy-year-old person could become a member of the Students Union and contest elections if he were enrolled in any course. And there were courses which no serious student liked to enroll...a fairly good number of politically motivated youths became University students and contested elections...To make a living, quite a few of them became petty contractors forcing the engineering section of the University to parcel out repairs and other jobs to them...They took up popular causes of students like increase in the number of seats in various courses. They organized agitations and indulged in violence.

Mishra's observations notwithstanding, *Haasil* has failed to become a part of public discourse in Allahabad. Nor does the city remember its director, Tigmanshu Dhulia, in the same way as it remembers its civil servants or the political elite.

•

# Encounters in Bihar

I trust the title of these reminiscences is as misleading for the reader as it sounds. In India, and certainly in Bihar, the word 'encounter' connotes killing in cold blood falsely reported by the police as cases of self-defence. 'Encounters' are what sanctimonious human rights activists passionately talk about; they provide our cinema with imaginative film scripts. For the rest of us, however, they are a part of the daily newspaper, of 'a landscape that smiles, suppressive of the zest for the vicissitudes by which men die'.

My recollections are not about 'those' encounters but some bitter-sweet memories of my travels in Bihar 18 years ago on a *sarkari* mission – to formulate and launch a State-wide programme for basic education of women and children. The impulses for the project emanated from an interesting conjuncture in 1989, when India had reached the bottom of its foreign exchange reserves and

By **Amitabh Mukhopadhyay**

all departments of government were asked to garner dollar-rich grants from multilateral donors. With the ascendancy of other backward classes epitomized by the personality of Laloo Yadav, lordly law was severely challenged by a changed political order. A Mandalite government in Delhi was keen to help Laloo with finances. A conference concluded that though primary education was a State subject, social services in Bihar should be viewed as a national concern. A Bihar Education Project had to be formulated and launched as the flagship programme of UNICEF following the Jomtien Resolution on 'Education for All'.

As convener of a group formed to do so, I was acutely aware of the enormity of the task. A mass programme of education devoted to caring for the development of individual personalities – 'child-centred' as the jargon put it – struck me as a contradiction in terms. I was told it had to be 'innovative', so simply fortifying schools and teacher-training would not do. Education for women's equality was critical. Partnership with NGOs, not private capital, was the buzzword those days, and these were to be mobilized for a 'societal' initiative to inundate the countryside with adult literacy, non-formal education centres, *mahila samakhya* groups, *jana shikhsha nilayams*, more schools ....or so went the fable.

The land of the Buddhist *viharas* and Bhojpuri, Maithili, Magahi and Nagpuria had always fascinated me. In panic, instead of putting pencil to paper forthwith, I called up my dear friend Arvind Narain Das, whose book *Changel* had portrayed the aspirations of the *hoi polloi* in Bihar so movingly.

'Surely you know that governments can never educate children, Babulal,' Arvind guffawed. 'But at least try to feed them...the government in Tamilnadu is doing it so well,' was his final bit of advice. As we sat sipping *chai* at a dhaba behind *The Times of India* building where he worked, strains from a chorus in a performance of *Mother Courage* we had watched together in our college days floated through my mind: '...and all you gentlemen who wish to lead us, and teach us to desist from mortal sin, your prior obligation is to feed us; once we've eaten, your preaching can begin...begin...begin!'

Thus fortified, I found myself travelling in Bihar to gather the common weal. The village of Amarpur-Katoria in Bhagalpur, with its large population of unemployed Muslim weavers with traditional skills in using vegetable dyes to make cloth, seemed to be as good a point of departure as any. The ministry had received an application from an NGO arguing that an investment in basic education centres woven around a livelihood-oriented project to revive the dying craft would be a holistic way of rejuvenating education for the weavers.

After a little confusion at Bhagalpur railway station, I spotted the District Adult Education Officer (DAEO) on the platform. He was obviously hot and bothered by the exertions of trying to find me and had tucked a rolled handkerchief between his neck and collar. As soon as he spotted me, his chubby face broke into an obsequious smile, and he bent low over my proffered hand. I returned his '*Pranaam*, sir' with a *pranaam* of my own and warmly shook his hand. Visibly reassured by this display of federalist spirit, he grinned genially.

He would hear nothing of my insistence to roll my overnighter along and briskly snapped rhetorical-abuse at the two 'casual labour' who had accompanied him. '*Burbak-baa? Sa'eb kaa Dehli se basta tohre *** sukhane laihe?*' (Are you stupid? Do you imagine this gentleman has lugged his suitcase all the way from Delhi to dry your *** with?) So, with this strange retinue in tow, I was ceremoniously led to the town of Bhagalpur.

Our World War II model jeep meandered through wide city streets flanked by occasional palm-adorned bungalows until we drew up at the large portico of the ungated Circuit House. An ample veranda loomed behind its pillared grandeur. I was taken to a cavernous room with mosquito nets folded up on the beds. The gush of water as soon as I touched the tap in the attached toilet reassured me. I lowered myself into a cane easy-chair and looked up thankfully at the ceiling fan cranking away: thank god I would have running water and electricity. The DAEO pulled up another chair and barked at the lurking 'casuals' to fetch a peg table from another room.

'Have you drawn up any schedule for the day?' I asked. He hadn't, and said quite constructively that after I had got 'fresh' and had some *chai-jalpaan* we could do whatever I was interested in. The Bengali in me instantly liked this flexible and potty-first kind of approach.

I felt in even better humour after I'd tucked in an orientalist breakfast of dwarf bananas, pounded rice flakes, creamy *dahi* and jaggery followed by generously-buttered burnt toast and boiled eggs, and rounded off by *mithai* with coffee at a dining table whose ancestor was surely a billiards table. Stepping out on to the veranda, I announced my readiness for my tour. The DAEO regretted that it wasn't immediately possible because the jeep had gone to the workshop for repairs. How long would that take? He wasn't sure, but hopefully, in another two hours? Meanwhile, would Sir rest awhile in his room? Since that would take us closer to lunchtime, so perhaps, only if Sir permitted it of course, he himself could go home briefly and return? Well, all right, I shrugged, and retired to my room to introspect on my impatience.

Post lunch, I finished the last part of Mahasweta Devi's *Jangal ke Davedar*. The story of the father of Jharkhand, Birsa Munda, who dropped out of a Christian missionary school to pursue his struggles to feed his mother rice, what the *dikhus* (outsiders to the Chotanagpur forests) ate, not the customary coarse grains, was particularly moving. Then I searched all along the veranda for the DAEO but there was still no sign of him.

At about 4 pm he arrived and explained he'd personally checked at the garage on his way back. The repairs would take longer, possibly till noon the next day. 'Can't your director get me another jeep?' I asked, unable to hide my frustration any longer. The director certainly would try to, but unfortunately, it was a Sunday. 'What about the Collector?' I asked. Of course...definitely *he* could if he wanted to... he was known for commandeering project vehicles across departments at will.

It struck me it wouldn't be a bad idea to call on the Collector anyhow. I waved aside his protests about it being a day of rest and we trudged off to the Collector's residence, mercifully close by. The freshly laid red gravel in the driveway announced us crunchily to the several gardeners pruning the shrubs at the stately residence. They looked up, shears in hand, like birds disturbed. We were ushered into the Collector's study and a young man in pyjamas and kurta slid into the chair behind the secretariat table. I explained my mission and, in order not to sound mystical, unwittingly added that I might visit some Adult Education (AE) centres on the way to Amarpur-Katoria. He looked enthusiastic about the idea of Bihar Education Project (BEP) and offered to travel along with me the next day. 'That's not a problem at all,' he said about the vehicle under repairs and graciously instructed his personal assistant to make one available straightaway, which would remain at my service throughout my tour. Then he turned to the DAEO and asked which AE centres would fall on our way.

The DAEO shifted uneasily in his chair. As Sir was fully aware, there were, in fact, no AE centres on the way. A glint appeared in the Collector's eyes. He grinned at me and said, 'In fact, there are no AE centres in the entire district,' and turned his face to the DAEO. 'Am I right?' he asked. The DAEO squirmed a bit but smilingly accepted the fact. What could he say? Sir knew everything. 'Why don't you set up one AE centre – as a sort of, you know, showpiece – and we can visit that tomorrow?' offered the Collector.

Here's the soft State at its improvisational best, I thought to myself. The DAEO, however, frowned this time and said flatly that it wasn't really possible to do that. He explained: 'As Sir is aware, and the matter was also discussed several times at the district level monthly coordination meetings chaired by Sir, the AE primers had not been received from Patna and, as Sir must have personally noted on his tours, the village folk were so uncooperative about providing any space to conduct classes or turning up at all that ....' He tapered off. 'Besides,' he went on, 'what is the point in trying to mislead Sir who anyway knows all?'

'Well then, he can see some schools on the way?' the Collector asked, a little crestfallen by now. The DAEO acknowledged the superior intelligence of the Collector but was constrained to point out that schools were not part of his jurisdiction. After assuaging the embarrassment of the Collector about the obdurate DAEO and thanking him profusely for the jeep, I drove back to the Circuit House.

Early next morning I set off for Amarpur-Katoria. The DAEO had reported with the Project Officer (PO) of AE for the development block and reassured me that the PO knew the area well. I wondered why the PO should know the area of a non-existent project, but kept my counsel. Perhaps he hailed from the area? In that case he might be able to fill me in with a lot about the block, I mused. As it turned out, he wasn't from that block and didn't know the roads either; it was the driver whose village was located at the far end of the block who was quite knowledgeable. He knew all about the NGO that had supported the activities of the weavers at Amarpur-Katoria for several years though he hadn't seen the elderly ladies who used to visit the village for some months now. He ventured it might a good idea for me to pick up a sari for my wife, or maybe a bedsheet or two. I corrected him by explaining the nature of my mission. He modified his suggestion instantly: the cloth they produced was, in fact, rather over priced and only the odd piece might be worth it. I couldn't tell whether he was exchanging glances with the DAEO but I did find it odd that he should be looking at his rear-view mirror ever so often on an empty road.

We turned off a dirt road after about an hour of negotiating causeways and drove past orchards, dried-up ponds and uninteresting paddy fields to Amarpur, which sported a bus-stop and a couple of shanty shops. Amarpur-Katoria itself was located, a bit removed, on a mound. A few young men gazed at us quizzically. Two of them came up to the jeep once it stopped, and peered inside to ask where we were headed. The DAEO announced me in flattering tones as a mighty officer from Delhi and I must admit as I alighted from the jeep, I felt a sense of importance come over me. Other young men who were watching from a distance joined us. All four of us, driver included, each in his own way, explained why we'd come. Guided by their guesses about whether it was bedsheets we were after or desired generally to talk to them about unemployment, we were led to the courtyard of the *khaprail*-roofed hut where one of them lived.

We were seated on *charpais* with a swarm of young men, boys and little girls as an interested audience. I wanted to smoke but felt it might be too vulgar to light up an extravagant-looking filter-king cigarette in that glare of publicity. The children simply smiled at each other conspiratorially when I asked if they attended reading-writing classes at the *madrassa*. The young men thought the hand-woven cloth never sold well and wanted to know if the government could set up a cloth mill in the vicinity for them to work for. Presently, an elderly, grey-bearded man in a *lungi-kurta* with a white cap joined us. He was a little more concerned about the dying art of weaving vegetable-dyed yarn and volunteered to show us the looms.

These were located in burrows through which we reached huge underground spaces fitted out with massive hardwood handlooms. He said even the ordinary Bhagalpuri *lungis* they used to produce in the good old days were no longer popular. New designs and an assured market for high-value hand-woven cloth located in Calcutta or Bombay was all they needed for the shuttles to start working again. Since I could neither promise a factory nor any marketing outfits, it was quite clear no livelihood-based education project was feasible. We walked around the lanes of Amarpur-Katoria desultorily and then headed back to Bhagalpur.

As we entered Bhagalpur city, the DAEO asked if I wanted to meet some eminent educationists. It was nearing four in the evening and since there was nothing else to do I agreed and we drove towards the university. I looked appreciatively at the impressive expanse of the campus. The car drew up at the gate of a bungalow and we walked into the driveway where a Doordarshan (DD) camera crew and a host of short-statured jeans-clad local journalists mobbed me instantly. Did I support the striking teachers or the vice chancellor of Bhagalpur University? Was New Delhi convinced an intervention was necessary? Could I please make a short statement? The DD crew politely said they were prepared to wait for an interview till I'd finished my parley with Professor Jha. I reeled under the impact of this unexpected reception.

To say I did not know Professor Jha from Adam would not have passed muster and to say I knew nothing about the strike would have made me seem a complete ass. So I donned the role of an 'emissary' and nodded to my right and left in a tight-lipped-know-all manner and walked into the small garden. There, clad in a white pyjama and a brown dressing gown with his hands clasped behind his head, the eminently long figure of the educationist, Professor Jha was sprawled on a *takht*. The DAEO whispered in my ears that he was the pro-vice chancellor who was masterminding the strike from his home. Not quite the reclining Vishnu, but somewhere there, I thought to myself as I took in the picture.

'It has entered its hundred-th day today,' beamed the Professor, continuing to gaze into middle distance. I parked myself on a secretariat chair that was closest to the *takht* and explained the inchoate idea of BEP I had fabricated in my mind. I dressed it up as best I could with allusions to Bihar's pristine glories – Nalanda, the confluence of religious discourses at Rajgir, the Vidyapeeths and *maktabs* of Purnea and Bhojpuri *kathas* – and did not forget to mention the money the Centre wanted to pour in. He listened intently without interrupting even once and then let out one long sigh. '*Jab higher hi nahin hoga, tab lower kayse hoga?*' he said in a philosophical tone. Then he got up and went into the house. The troupe of journalists also rushed inside. I was informed by the DAEO that his press briefing was about to start and the quality of recording by DD and All India Radio (AIR) would naturally be much better inside. Summarily dismissed, for a while I pondered whether our ministry at New Delhi understood the crucial role of universities in producing good graduates to serve as teachers for programmes like BEP, or would persist with 'pedagogies of the oppressed' *sans* their ideological core. Then I went out to the jeep and was soon back at the Circuit house.

Next afternoon, we were at the railway platform once again: it was time for my return. The DAEO had come to see me off. My coach was next to the guard's, at the tail end of the train. Having settled in after the casuals had secured my overnighter to the legs of the berth with a brass-plated chain and lock, I stood on the platform, looking out through the haze of my cigarette smoke beyond the parallel tracks on to the other side of our platform, waiting for the train to depart. Three separate groups of young men were crossing the tracks with large idols of Saraswati (goddess of learning) hoisted on their shoulders. As I gazed at them, the DAEO who had correctly read my chain of thoughts trailing off to the importance Saraswati puja occupies in the calendar of festivals in Bengal. As the guard blew his shrill whistle and I stepped on to the footboard of the barely moving train, he shouted: '*Bihar mein Saraswati ki bahut pratishtha hai*, Sir!' (The people of Bihar really know how to worship learning). His parting shot fell like a tight slap across my face. Don't judge a people or province by the performance of its government's undertakings, it reminded me.

• • •

Back at Delhi, I found Arvind had sounded T. Vijayendra, a self-styled *jajabor* (bedouin, or nomad), and another old Bihar hand. He agreed to join the ministry as a consultant and proved to be a terrific ready-reckoner. The pair of us happily trotted around the length and breadth of Bihar for a good six months.

The first thing Vijju was keen to show me was the original *sulabh shauchalayas* at Patna. 'It is Bihar's most remarkable contribution to development', he said, with his inimitable chuckle. Apparently, the elite living in colonies near the historic Gandhi Maidan needed rickshaws to take their children to school and so the rickshaw-pullers used to sleep the nights in the neighbourhood. Naturally, they defecated wherever they could at the crack of dawn and the mounting stench bothered the elite. This is what led to Bindeshwar Pathak's famous invention of sulabh shauchalay.[1] Vijju's appreciation of the premises adorned with flower pots and the smell of incense was catching as he proudly pointed out the street lights circling Gandhi Maidan, all lit by the gas produced from the latrines.

Across the bridge over the Ganga from Patna, at Vaishali, we visited a public library run since 1923 by Jagannath Sah, the venerable Gandhian and by then the only living founder member of the Hindi Hitaiyshi Sabha. It was a privilege to see the dimunitive figure come alive as he spoke on the subject of public libraries. He was barely 16 when Gandhi visited his school and asked him to join the national movement. In reply to his query about what he would have to do, Gandhi had asked him to buy 15 acres of land, till the soil to generate funds and set up a public library. That was what he did till date. He walked us through the interconnected rooms of his two-storey-high library building, instructing us on the relative merits of an open-shelf and closed-shelf stacking of books and periodicals. He was particularly proud of the music room and the variety of musical instruments, each neatly tied up in cloth. The imposing halls of the building and the tour seemed like a scene out of Satyajit Ray's *Jalsaghar*.

He showed us all the letters he had addressed to various ministers about the importance of a National Library Act to support the thousands of public libraries started in villages and towns by eminent educationists at different points of time. 'We took everything from the British in Indian administration, except the idea of public libraries as a means of social reform,' he said ruefully. 'Even communists in Russia paid greater attention to public education than the so-called social democrats at New Delhi. In 1917, the year of the Bolshevik Revolution, Lenin spent more time at London crafting the national library bill than on other matters! In India we relegated libraries as a subject to be dealt with by state governments without any resources.'

It was fascinating to go through the close documentation maintained by the library regarding the reading interests, not merely of those who visited the library at Vaishali, but all the children in 150 villages around Vaishali that had benefited from the outreach schemes of his library. Under the 'Bell-Bicycle Scheme', the volunteers of free India would carry story books for children to the villages and ring the bicycle bell to announce themselves. They covered 50 kms. every day. Each child reader had a ledger leaf devoted to recording the progression in his interests – from the preference for ghost-stories and folk tales to reading on football, science, astronomy, biographies, health, you name it – and the idea was to ensure the children were free readers rather than captives of any propaganda machinery like political parties or proselytizers belonging to different religions or denominations that usually undertake to educate people. The excitable old man lamented his failing health and inability to work on his fields to support the library any longer.

I jumped at the opportunity for government to take over the library at Vaishali as the hub of the continuing education component of BEP. The wise old Gandhian, however, declined my offer. When I persisted with my request, he said: 'Government does not understand valuation and paying for the true worth of work. See how you treat primary school teachers, *aanganvadi*-workers and *dais*. Why do you invariably pay them less than office clerks at the ministries?'

I bowed my head in shame.

Vijju and I scoured the countryside for three months, trying to correlate the phenomenon of widespread teacher-absenteeism in government schools on the one hand with the popularity of private tutors teaching huddled children in cramped spaces, on the other. Our travels revealed that there was clearly a groundswell of a demand for education of children, certainly among the poorest households. The obsession of the central government with a strategy of encirclement of schools through government-run programmes, such as adult literacy and non-formal education centres to generate an 'environment' for learning, was skirting the issue of robust administrative measures to actually run schools and libraries – with quality graduates and proper pay for school teachers/librarians.

Clearly, socialism in Laloo's Bihar had categorically rejected the 'socialistic' rhetoric and was praying for a deliverance from the bureaucracy of education.

•

ENDNOTE:

1. See UNDP's Human Development Report, 2006.

# A Sacred Grove*

As one writer after another sent in their essays, one read with deepening sorrow of what is happening today in campuses across the country. Somewhere in the race to proliferate our university network, we have evidently lost sight of the reason why universities were set up in the first place. It seems very much as if developing an information network is now considered more important than developing faculties of the mind. The dreary desert sand of dead knowledge has buried the clear stream of reason.

Yet there was a time, long before the Age of Enlightenment arrived in the Western world, when India was considered the true sanctuary of knowledge and wisdom. From dim memories of school history lessons one can recall the names of certain Indian universities that were considered the Ivy League institutions of their time. So we reached out to a friend, Raji Ramanan, who helped to gather from a variety of sources, fragments of the writings of Xuanzang (602–644 AD)

* Compiled by Raji Ramanan

and I-Ching (635–713 AD), two intrepid Chinese scholars who have left behind fascinating accounts of ancient Indian universities, particularly those at Nalanda and Vikramashila.

However difficult it may be to believe this today but, once upon a time, Bihar had the world's most famous university: Nalanda, situated in the region occupied by present-day Patna. Its dreaming spires are described by Xuanzang thus:

> ...The whole establishment is surrounded by a brick wall, which encloses the entire convent from without. One gate opens into the great college, from which are separated eight other halls, standing in the middle .... The richly adorned towers, and the fairy-like turrets, like pointed hill tops are congregated together. The observatories seem to be lost in the vapours..., and the upper rooms tower above the clouds....

Education, it appears, had little to do in securing professions for the students who came to universities such as Nalanda: they pursued knowledge for its own sake. Dedicated to this noble pursuit, the average 'university' student in ancient India spent eight to 12 years at a monastery (Vihara) or a Gurukul. He served his master as a servant or a loving son, clad in a dhoti and an *uttariya* (an upper garment) if a Hindu, and a robe, made from rags collected from dust heaps and dyed yellow, if a Buddhist. After he had stripped himself of all vanity and pledged to practise chastity, the student offered himself to a teacher.

It must also be remembered that although higher education was then largely free, in the sense that no academic fees was charged of students, it was not freely given to all. This enabled universities such as Nalanda to develop a pedagogical system largely devoted to widening the spiritual horizon. Such exclusive attention to inculcating moral values may appear politically inappropriate and even dangerous today, yet the absence of a value-based education, whatever that may mean to various people, is becoming increasingly a matter of concern.

The educational history of this period reveals little other than a quest for the means to acquire 'higher knowledge'. For the Buddhist student, this meant an attempt to realize a state of Nirvana while to the non-Buddhist student, such a pursuit was a means to reach the Unknown. Naturally, students needed teachers to help them in their quest and this mutual relationship is best articulated by the Buddha: 'The preceptor, O Bhikkhus', he says, 'ought to consider the pupil as a son; the pupil ought to consider the preceptor as a father.' Incidentally, the word for 'preceptor' in Pali and one often used in the Vinaya texts is *Upajjhaya* (Sanskrit, *Upadhyaya*).

The following passage from I-Ching tells us how completely the student gave himself up to the teacher for the acquisition of knowledge, which could never be dreamt of in Europe in the Middle Ages, to say nothing of modern India:

> He goes to his teacher at the first watch and at the last watch in the night. First the teacher bids him to sit down comfortably. Selecting some passages from the *Tripitakas*, he gives a lesson in a way that suits circumstances, and does not leave any fact or theory unexplained. He inspects his pupil's moral conduct, and warns him of defects and transgressions. Whenever he finds his pupil at fault, he makes him seek remedies and repent. The pupil rubs the teacher's body, folds his clothes, or sometimes sweeps the apartment and the yard. Then, having examined water to see whether there are insects in it, he gives it to the teacher. Thus, if there is anything to be done, he does all on behalf of his teacher.

I-Ching also writes:

> Thus instructed by their teachers and instructing others they (students) pass two or three years, generally in the Nalanda monastery in Central India or in the country of Valabhi in Western India. There eminent and accomplished men assemble in crowds, discuss possible and impossible doctrines and, after being assured of the excellence of their opinions by wise men, become far-famed for their wisdom.

A strict system regulated the entry of students into a university, so that only the truly deserving candidates were allowed in. It is said that Plato's Academy, another legendary ancient 'university', declared that anyone who did not know geometry should not enter its gates. To return to India, the 'entrance exams' to a university such as Nalanda were conducted by learned pundits called Dwaracharyas (gate-keepers). Vikramasila had six gates, guarded by as many eminent pundits who presided over the 'entrance exams'. Among these, Ratnavajra, Acarya Jetari and Ratnakirti were the most distinguished 'examiners'. Aspirants to the university had to show their skill in refuting doctrines, and many argumentative Indians went away, rejected after humiliating defeats at these learned debates. In addition to the 'entrance examiners', the teaching staff at Vikramasila consisted of 108 professors. Like the senate or the academic council of our modern universities, there was a board of eminent professors, whose main function was to supervise and issue instructions to the various professors. This was one of the reasons, Xuanzang tells us, that such universities performed the important function 'of enabling the students to form each other, of learning the greatest art of living, in helping to form an intelligent society'.

Nalanda, though primarily known for its Buddhist studies, welcomed students of other faiths as well. Also, unlike universities such as Taksasila – famous for their specialization in medicine and other sciences – Nalanda imparted knowledge in a variety of arts and sciences, philosophies and religions. Buddhism was the primary focus of academic attention, but Vedantic studies were not entirely neglected. Thus, a place was founded for *Cikitsavidya* (the science of medicine) in the curriculum. Nalanda also gave students an opportunity to change their subject of study while still remaining at the same place.

Xuanzang says, for instance, that a student was expected to have studied deeply both old and new books before being granted admission at Nalanda. By 'old and new books', Xuanzang evidently means works such as the Vedas, the Upanisads, works of different systems – Samkhya, Vaisesika, Nyaya and all the works of Mahayana and Hinayana Buddhism.

Although students did not take up all the subjects a university offered, there were some subjects that were 'compulsory', as we now understand the term. The subject next to theology and philosophy in importance was logic. Though it was not compulsory, exigencies of those times, when debates and discussion were very frequent, made it almost compulsory for students. We also learn from Xuanzang that the method of conducting examinations followed at Nalanda was most innovative. An examination consisted of 'any process of inquiry' and the examiners, we are told, were no other than the learned Gate

Keepers, who entered into a discussion with the candidates. The chances of success depended upon the students' ability to please and satisfy the examiners after a tough round of debates and discussions.

From the records of Xuanzang it would appear that, in a majority of cases, the method of teaching followed in the university was what we now know as the tutorial. As he puts it: 'The old and the young mutually help one another'. Translated into today's language, this would mean that the 'old' teacher helped the 'young' student in his studies. Xuanzang himself was taught the Yoga sastra by Silabhadra and other works by Jayasena among other 'old' teachers. Next to this tutorial method was discussion, and the student absorbed a large part of his knowledge by listening to the discussions carried on from morning till night. Both Xuanzang and I-Ching seem to have been deeply impressed by this part of Nalanda's activities.

There were some subjects, however, mainly pertaining to the religious side of Buddhism and not to the philosophical, in which we can, with some propriety, say that lectures were delivered. Hwui Li is quite clear on this point. He writes: '...within the Temple they arrange every day about 100 pulpits for preaching, and the students attend these discourse without fail, even for a minute.'

Not all who came to Nalanda sought transcendental knowledge. Some students came to Buddhist centres of learning for, what we would now probably term, refresher courses. I-Ching tells us that those who had received a degree in famous universities like Nalanda and Valabhi and declared eminent debaters by wise men received grants of land; while others were advanced to a high rank and as a further reward, their names were written on lofty gates (the equivalent, one supposes, of the Roll of Honour in a modern university).

Reading these accounts today, with the din of the creamy layer and noisy parliamentary debates on quotas and reservations ringing in one's ears, one wonders where this Utopian academic system went. The answer is that, like so many iconic institutions of the past (the Library of Alexandria among them), Nalanda was sacked and destroyed in the late twelfth century when the Khiljis overran Bihar and Bengal. Its vast store of manuscripts and texts was torched, but a small fragment of these was retrieved by Buddhist monks and spirited away to Tibet. For centuries, they were guarded by the monks in Tibetan monasteries. Then, in a flight reminiscent of the exodus from Nalanda all those centuries ago, they were carried back to India by the entourage of monks who accompanied the Dalai Lama when he was forced to flee Tibet in 1959.

This treasure, the Dalai Lama is fond reminding us, belongs to India. The Tibetan monks were its guardians for close to 700 years, perhaps now it is our turn to protect and build on this heritage.

•

# Contributors

**RAMACHANDRA GUHA** has taught at the universities of Oslo, Stanford and Yale, and at the Indian Institute of Science. After a peripatetic academic career Guha is now a full-time writer, based in Bangalore. Guha's books cover a wide range of themes: and his entire career, he says, seems in retrospect to have been an extended (and painful) preparation for the writing of his most recent book, *India After Gandhi*.

**A.P.J. ABDUL KALAM** was India's eleventh President, and one of India's most distinguished scientists with the unique honour of receiving honorary doctorates from thirty universities and institutions. Kalam's focus is on transforming India into a developed nation by 2020. He has been awarded the Padma Bhushan (1981) and Padma Vibhushan (1990) and the country's highest civilian award, Bharat Ratna, in 1997.

**BIBEK DEBROY** is Research Professor at the Centre for Policy Research, Professor at the International Management Institute, and Contributing Editor to the *Indian Express* group. An economist, he has earlier worked in universities, research institutes, industry and for the government.

**SAM PITRODA** has spent four decades between the three continents of North America, Asia and Europe in the world of telecommunications, helping bridge the global communications divide. In the 1980s, Pitroda helped transform India's telecommunication and information technology infrastructure. Pitroda was the first Chairman of the Telecom Commission in India, and is currently Chairman of the National Knowledge Commission.

**MOHAMMAD SHAHEER** taught at the School of Planning and Architecture, New Delhi from 1976 to 2003. A landscape architecture consultant for about thirty years, he serves on national level government committees concerned with environment, conservation and city planning.

**SATISH DESHPANDE** teaches sociology at Delhi University. Apart from the history and politics of the social sciences, he also works on caste and class inequalities and policy design for social justice. His most recent (co-edited) work is *Anthropology in the East: Founders of Indian Sociology and Social Anthropology* (Permanent Black, 2007).

**P.V. INDIRESAN** taught for forty years at various IITs, and was Director, IIT Madras for five years. Indiresan was President, Indian National Academy of Engineering. He is the recipient of many awards such the lifetime achievement award from the Indian Institute of Science, and the Padma Bhushan.

**SHOBHIT MAHAJAN** teaches physics at the University of Delhi. He is the author of several books on popular science and writes on issues of science and technology in several newspapers and magazines.

**SUMAN SAHAI** is the Director of Gene Campaign, a research and advocacy organization working on food and livelihood security, farmers' and community rights. Sahai is a member of several national policy forums on international trade, biodiversity and environment, biotechnology and bioethics, intellectual property rights, and research and education.

**RANJIT ROY CHAUDHURY** is a leading medical educationist in the country. He has served as the Professor of Pharmacology and Dean at the Post-graduate Institute of Medical Education and Research, Chandigarh, where he established the D.M. Course in Clinical Pharmacology in 1979. After a distinguished career at the World Heath Organization he returned to India in 1991 and has headed a number of organizations and committees in India.

**AMITABH MATTOO** is Vice Chancellor of the University of Jammu. He has been Professor of International Studies at JNU and Chairperson of the Centre of the International Politics, Organization and Disarmament. He has been Visiting Professor at the University of

Notre Dame and Stanford University. Professor Mattoo was recently awarded the Padmashri for his contribution to education.

**B.K. JOSHI** is a former Vice Chancellor of Kumaon University, Nainital, and a former Director of the Giri Institute of Development Studies, Lucknow. He has also been a Member of the Second State Finance Commission, Uttarakhand and Chairman, Eleventh Plan Formulation Committee. At present he is Honorary Director at the Doon Library and Research Centre.

**DEVESH KAPUR** is an alumnus of the Institute of Technology of BHU and is currently Director of University of Pennsylvania's Centre for Advanced Study of India after having taught at Harvard for several years. The author of several books, his forthcoming publication is *Democracy, Death and Diamonds: The Impact of Migration from India on India*.

**PRATAP BHANU MEHTA** is an Indian political scientist, constitutional expert, columnist and commentator. Currently, he heads the Centre for Policy Research, New Delhi. His most recent publications are *The Burden of Democracy* and *Public Institutions in India: Performance and Design*.

**HARSH V. PANT** teaches at King's College, London, in the Department of Defence Studies. He is also an Associate with the King's Centre for Science and Security, where he joined after completing his doctorate at the University of Notre Dame (USA). He holds a BA (Hons.) from the University of Delhi and MA and M. Phil degrees from JNU in New Delhi.

**MEGHNAD DESAI** is Professor Emeritus of Economics at the London School of Economics and a member of the House of Lords. He was recently awarded the Padma Bhushan.

**A.K. DAMODARAN** joined the Indian Foreign Service and retired as Ambassador to Italy after having served in China, Sweden and the Soviet Union. He taught in JNU for two years after retirement, returning to government service for another six years. His publications include *Jawaharlal Nehru: Communicator and Democratic Leader* and *Beyond Autonomy: the Roots of Indian Foreign Policy*.

**NARAYANI GUPTA** retired as Professor of History at Jamia Millia Islamia and is at present a consultant with INTACH and a member of the Delhi Urban Arts Commission. She has written extensively on urban history and on the conservation of historic architecture.

**IRA PANDE** worked as a university teacher for 15 years, and then as an editor at *Seminar, Biblio*, Dorling Kindersley and Roli Books. She is currently Chief Editor, IIC Publications.

**SHASHI THAROOR** is the prize-winning author of ten books, both fiction and non-fiction, and a widely published critic, commentator and columnist. In 2007, he concluded a 29-year old career with the United Nations, culminating as the Under-Secretary-General for Communications and Public Information. He was awarded the Pravasi Bharatiya Samman, India's highest honour for overseas Indians.

**KUMKUM BHATTACHARYA** is Professor in the Department of Social Work, Visva-Bharati and Director, V.B. Publishing Department. Her research interests lie in the area of culture-personality studies and minority communities. She is currently engaged in publication of the Tagore corpus and related titles in English and other Indian languages.

**ZOYA HASAN** is Professor at the Jawaharlal Nehru University and Member of the National Commission for Minorities. Her most recent books include *Quest for Power: Oppositional Movements and Post-Congress Politics in Uttar Pradesh* and *Unequal Citizens: A Study of Muslim Women in India* (co-authored). Her forthcoming book is titled *Politics of Inclusion: Caste, Minority and Representation in India*.

**MALAVIKA KARLEKAR** is Editor of the *Indian Journal of Gender Studies* and Curator of 'Re-presenting Indian Women, A Visual Documentary, 1875–1947' at the Centre for Women's Development Studies, New Delhi. She has been a university teacher and is now an author, editor, archivist, researcher as well as an artist and gardener.

**MRINAL PANDE**, editor and writer, is currently Chief Editor of *Hindustan, Kadambini* and *Nandan*. She is the author of two novels, three collections of short stories, four stage plays and three collections of essays, all in Hindi. She has published four novels in English, the most recent being *My Own Witness*.

**LALIT JOSHI** teaches history at the University of Allahabad. His areas of academic research include cultural globalization and the history of cinema. He has published extensively, both in Hindi and English, in reputed national and international journals and anthologies. His manual on Hindi cinema, *Housefull*, is now in its second edition.

**AMITABH MUKHOPADHYAY** is a member of the Indian Audit and Accounts Service and works at present with the Parliamentary Committees on Finance. Mukhopadhyay has an abiding interest in campaigns for the right to information and social audit for the deepening of democracy in India.

•